TO
REJOICE
AS
WOMEN

Other volumes in the Women's Conference Series:

TO

REJOICE

AS

WOMEN

TALKS FROM THE 1994
WOMEN'S CONFERENCE

EDITED BY
SUSETTE FLETCHER GREEN
AND DAWN HALL ANDERSON

DESERET BOOK COMPANY
SALT LAKE CITY, UTAH

Cover painting: *Handcart Pioneers,* Minerva K. Teichert, 1930, oil on canvas, 68" x 51", courtesy Museum of Church History and Art, Salt Lake City, Utah.

Library of Congress Cataloging-in-Publication Data

Women's Conference (1994 : Brigham Young University)
    To rejoice as women : talks from the 1994 Women's Conference / edited by Susette Fletcher Green and Dawn Hall Anderson.
        p.   cm.
    Includes bibliographical references and index.
    ISBN 0-87579-894-2 (hbk.)
    1. Mormon women—Congresses. 2. Church of Jesus Christ of Latter-day Saints—Congresses. I. Green, Susette Fletcher.
II. Anderson, Dawn Hall. III. Title.
BX8641.W73   1994
289.3'32'082—dc20   95-5177
                                                     CIP

Printed in the United States of America

10 9   8   7   6   5   4   3   2   1

CONTENTS

CONSIDERING COVENANTS

INTERNATIONAL FRIENDSHIP

CHALLENGES WITH CHILDREN

PREFACE

This book is the ninth in the series from the annual Women's Conference sponsored jointly by Brigham Young University and the Relief Society of The Church of Jesus Christ of Latter-day Saints. The essays and poems in this volume were delivered at the 1994 conference.

We thank all those who made this volume possible. Jeanne Inouye chaired the conference and with her able committee of BYU faculty members and Relief Society representatives spent countless hours planning and coordinating the sessions. She also helped select manuscripts for publication in this volume.

We thank Marilyn Damron White for inputting the manuscript onto computer, preparing it for publication, taking care of correspondence, and offering valuable suggestions. Suzanne Brady of Deseret Book has offered superb support, advice, and assistance in facilitating the transformation of manuscript into book.

Very few of our authors are professional writers, and we particularly thank them for risking to tell their stories and to share their successes and failures, their insights and expertise with the larger community of Latter-day Saint women.

COVENANTS, COME WHAT MAY

ELAINE L. JACK

As the Lord's covenant people in the last days, we have much to celebrate: the restored gospel, opportunities to serve and be served, blessings of the priesthood, the Spirit that speaks to us individually, and a Father in Heaven who loves us all. Covenants bring down all those blessings from heaven. To rejoice in our covenants is to understand their importance in our eternal progression. Covenants are the essence of our mortal experience, the measure of our devotion and diligence. Kept, honored, renewed, and held sacred, covenants bind us to God.

"Wherefore, lift up thy heart and rejoice, and cleave unto the covenants which thou hast made" (D&C 25:13). The Lord covenants with us: "I, the Lord, am bound when ye do what I say; but when ye do not what I say, ye have no promise" (D&C 82:10). He is bound to bless us and reward us. No earthly promise compares with his assurance of love and blessing.

The very word *covenant* may seem exacting and hard. It may seem removed from pressing tasks at hand, if we think of our covenants primarily as historical events, such as our baptism, or as the title of our latter-day scriptures, the Doctrine and Covenants. What does it mean to be a covenant people with the Lord? Why is it important in our individual lives? Is honoring

Elaine L. Jack grew up in Cardston, Alberta, Canada. She and her husband, Joseph E. Jack, are the parents of four sons and have thirteen grandchildren. Sister Jack serves as general president of the Relief Society of The Church of Jesus Christ of Latter-day Saints.

our covenants just one more item in a long list of things we should be doing? And how can we give our covenants priority when we are having trouble some mornings just putting on our shoes?

Our covenants embrace the full experience of righteous living. They speak of keeping the commandments, having the Spirit with us, remembering the Savior, valuing a temple marriage, putting our families first, and serving one another. No one else can fulfill our covenants for us, and no one else can experience the joy that lights our souls when we do our part. Covenants are active, two-way commitments that bring the Savior into our very lives and change us. We treat each other with charity. We create homes centered on gospel teachings. We work hard at being good parents, the greatest calling in the kingdom of God. And we pray. During my four years as general president of the Relief Society, nothing has meant more to me than when someone says, "Sister Jack, we are praying for you."

Imagine for just a minute that Jesus Christ is right next door, that you can walk in and talk with him at will. My little grandson David has spent some time with me lately because there is a new baby at his home. He comes into the kitchen and asks me a thousand questions, needs help with something, shows me things, or wants to make plans for our next activity. So it is with us and the Savior. Picture yourself sitting near him and going over the things he has asked you to do. The two of you shape a covenant, and then you are off to do what you have promised.

Covenant making is that simple, and Christ can be that close. He establishes the ground rules and the great rewards that follow. No earthly organization or institution can take away our opportunity to be one with God.

Others, letting God's Spirit work in them, help us keep our covenants. I was once fretting about my fourteen-year-old son, who was being consistently disagreeable. "What am I going to do with that boy?" I asked. From my wise friend Doral came this counsel, "Just love him." That's what I needed to hear. And it's what I vowed to do. It was the only thing I did all year that he didn't disagree with. I know that the Lord prompted Doral to lead me that day.

That experience reminds me of the words of a dear song, "Lead me, guide me, walk beside me / Help me find the way."[1] The Lord works miracles in our lives but not by fixing things. He didn't change my son, but he helped me to have a new attitude. The change wasn't worthy of a write-up in the *Church News*—though can't you see the headline: "Mother of Four Boys Shows Love to Teenage Son"? Then again, that might be worthy of a big story. Being there for our families is the daily living of our covenants. As I loved this precious son, I loved the Lord and drew near to him.

Our covenants are beautifully detailed in the Book of Mormon account of the baptisms at the waters of Mormon. Alma teaches us that when we go into the waters of baptism, we covenant to come into the fold of Christ and be numbered with his people. We covenant to take upon ourselves the name of Christ and be saints in very deed; to bear one another's burdens, that they may be light; to mourn with those who mourn; to comfort those who need comfort. We covenant to stand as witnesses of God at all times and in all things and in all places, even until death. Then, in summary, Alma says, "If this be the desire of your hearts, . . . ye have entered into a covenant with him, that ye will serve him and keep his commandments, that he may pour out his Spirit more abundantly upon you" (Mosiah 18:8–10). Now, that is cause to rejoice!

Our joy increases when we attend the temple, covenant to follow the Savior, and focus on our eternal progression. Living our temple covenants increases our strength and effectiveness. The dedicatory prayer for the Kirtland Temple says: "And that all people who shall enter upon the threshold of the Lord's house may feel thy power. . . . And we ask thee, Holy Father, that thy servants may go forth from this house armed with thy power" (D&C 109:13, 22).

The temple is indeed a source of strength. I grew up watching my mother press her cotton temple dress before attending the Alberta Temple nearby. Our remote Canadian enclave of Mormons had no paved streets, but the temple made our whole community seem noble and grand. As a child I spent many hours on the temple grounds. My mother's parents, who lived just next door to us, had joined the Church in Scotland when they were courting; my grandmother's family immediately disowned her. She and my grandfather were alone and in love, yet they waited to be married until they could get to "Zion" and be sealed in the Endowment House in Salt Lake City. They knew, better than I knew when I was married in the temple in Cardston, that those covenants would change the course of their lives. Grandfather Anderson worked as a stone mason on the temple construction and later as the custodian, a devoted temple worker, and a patriarch. His life bore testimony of a clear spiritual understanding: "I came into the world to do the will of my Father" (3 Nephi 27:13). His spiritual strength came from the sacrifices he and Grandmother had made to live their covenants.

There is power in those eternal commitments. As we honor our commitments, the ways of the world grow less and less appealing. Each week we renew our covenants by partaking of the sacrament. That reminder gives us the opportunity to recommit, to reflect, and to look forward.

Sisters have told me of their desire to strengthen their understanding of the Lord's sacrifice. A woman in England related a spiritual experience that made Christ's atonement real to her. "I was feeling sorry for myself," she said. "I'd been struggling for nine years on my own, with children. I looked at a picture of the Savior and felt his eyes come to life. They seemed to look into my very soul, and at the same time these words came to my mind: 'I am here. I've always been by your

4

side, taking the pain you feel as well. I drank the bitter cup for you. I'll always be here with you, every step of the way.'"

Christ's suffering in his final hours and on the cross are difficult to comprehend. He could have withdrawn, but he was able to look ahead with commitment. His love for his disciples contrasts sharply with the behavior of his detractors: his forgiveness, kindness, humility, and quiet majesty stand against a background of jeers, hollow triumphs, and cold-hearted hatred. Those final hours culminated a ministry marked by exceptional experiences: feeding the five thousand, raising Lazarus, quiet moments with close family and friends, a bitter march dragging his cross through the streets of Jerusalem. I think of those hours when my commitment lags; he was asked to do more than I will ever understand.

To "always remember him" means to think not only of his crucifixion but of his life. As I take the sacrament, I like to ponder the scriptures that reveal a gentle but forceful leader healing the sick, a dear friend rescuing his faltering disciple from the sea, a listener and teacher to the woman at the well, a compassionate leader who blessed children one by one, and a Savior who gently spoke "Mary" to the woman in the garden and heard her answer, "Rabboni." These scriptural accounts help me to "remember Jesus." To always remember him is to remember his example and his love. Our sacramental worship can be a renewal of covenants with our Savior in a sacred setting designed to draw us to him.

Keeping our covenants is a process. We start where we are—imperfect but trying to do better, converted but needing to learn and apply principles. The process, however, is not easy. Children falter; friends move or fall away. We mend our marriages like we used to mend socks. Sickness, death, and other experiences can devastate us if we do not trust the Lord and remember his encouragement: "Press forward with a steadfastness in Christ, having a perfect brightness of hope" (2 Nephi 31:20).

5

Though the way is hard, the journey is worthwhile. After the struggle come promised blessings—not always manna from heaven but covenant blessings. Always they are what we need, though sometimes they are not what we want. I've learned a lesson about that, too. When what I want is what the Savior bestows, then I know I am making progress.

A stake Relief Society president told me of an experience she had visiting a ward. During the lesson, a sister commented that her life hadn't turned out as she had expected. Several other sisters expressed the same feeling. After some discussion, they agreed that they had learned to follow the commandments—"come what may." We all will have times of "come what may." But following the commandments can turn "come what may" into "come unto Christ."

Our covenant relationship sets us apart from the world. Eliza R. Snow, general president of the Relief Society more than one hundred years ago, knew the power of covenants when she said, "We stand in a different position . . . ; we have made covenants with God; we understand his order."[2] To be a woman of covenant in these latter days is a sacred and holy responsibility. I rejoice, sisters, that we can discern what really matters in this life. Covenants matter.

Our covenants go two ways: we do our part, and the Lord does his. I have told sisters all over the Church to turn to the Lord when they need help; if we remember him, he will be there. Women tell me of their struggles and speak of the enormous challenges they face. One divorced mother of three said, "I work forty-five to fifty hours a week, and then I pray like the dickens my child support check will be in the mail." When you do all that you can, the Lord will make up the difference.

With a deep feeling of responsibility, last spring I prepared to speak at general conference. Speaking in that setting is both a great blessing and a tremendous challenge. I prayerfully considered what to say and then worked through my ideas and phrasing, draft after draft. I remembered once seeing a ninth draft for a conference talk from one of the general authorities and thought I might pass his mark. I prayed for guidance, and my husband, Joe, gave me a blessing.

Waiting for my turn to speak that Saturday morning, I wondered: "I have done all that I can. . . . Do I really believe the counsel I have given to Relief Society leaders? Do I believe that he will make up the difference?"

Then I started to worry not only about the content of my talk but the time as well. The meeting was running behind. Suddenly a calm assurance from the Lord came over me, and I knew he was with me. I climbed the stairs to the podium, rejoicing inside with a testimony of his promise: "I will go before your face. I will be on your right hand and on your left, and my Spirit shall be in your hearts, and mine angels round about you, to bear you up" (D&C 84:88).

I marvel at how the Lord made a meager number of fishes and loaves sufficient to feed five thousand. But then, aren't we all latter-day fishes and loaves? The Lord works with each of us and makes our contributions and sacrifices sufficient. He is mindful of what we are doing. He assures us: "I know thy works, and charity, and service, and faith, and thy patience, and thy works; and the last to be more than the first" (Revelation 2:19).

The sustaining power of our covenants makes a huge difference in a world that is skipping beats in all directions. The Lord's work supports us, but we must be prayerful and careful to distinguish between the Lord's work and busy work. That is not a new challenge for women. When Emmeline B. Wells was called as general president of Relief Society in 1910, she faced sweeping national movements for change. She felt outside pressure to step up Relief Society involvement in many social issues, to redefine and reshape the organization, to refocus the attention of the Relief Society on community causes. Emmeline stood firm, advocating that sisters in the Church hold fast to their sacred covenants. Recognizing that many organizations do good in the world, Emmeline also understood that Relief Society had a much broader responsibility—to save souls, not just for now, but for all eternity. Through Emmeline's leadership Relief Society maintained a sense of separate identity, uniqueness, and sacred mission to be understood only within the context of the restoration of all things.[3]

We see similar pressures today. Sometimes Relief Society sisters try to do it all—the world's way. That is not what the Lord has in mind. Our Relief Society today is the Lord's organization for women, prepared for the next century and the one that will follow as well. The Lord gives direction, and we follow. As President Spencer W. Kimball said, the work of the Church will progress as "the women of the Church are seen as distinct and different—in happy ways—from the women of the world."[4]

The Relief Society is working hard to expand literacy. Stories pour in from all over the world describing how lives have changed as Relief Society sisters have increased personal and family scripture study, set up summer book groups for children, helped Scouts gather books for homeless shelters, and volunteered in community literacy efforts. Some of our efforts are close to home. A friend of mine had a Native American student living with her family for six years. She grew close to this young man and loved him as if he were her own. As she has done with her children, she taught him to keep a journal so that he could see the Lord's hand in his life. Even though, years later, this young man no longer keeps his covenants, when he visits my friend he asks to see his journal. Together the two remember some of his spiritual experiences. She is grateful for that resource, those feelings on the page that he recorded and perhaps will feel again.

Each soul is valuable to our Father in Heaven. The Church has no borders, no restrictions by culture, race, or language. But illiteracy is a barrier. Members must be able to read to understand the scriptures as well as the messages of latter-day prophets.

A patriarch told of his stake president's challenge to read the Book of Mormon in a month. His wife bought a missionary copy to carry around with her and immediately began making notes in the margin as she read. His experience, however, was different. He had graduated from high school reading on only a fourth grade level. He could read the words, but his progress was painfully slow. Years earlier he had taken the challenge to read the Book of Mormon within a year and after four months was only to Alma. Reading the whole book in thirty-one days seemed impossible. Nevertheless, he sat down on March first and opened the book to 1 Nephi. He thought of Nephi returning for the plates and building a boat in the wilderness. Both had seemed impossible tasks. But, like Nephi, he began, remembering his covenant with the Lord to do all he was asked. The first day he read thirty-one pages and the next day just as many, and so it went. He finished the Book of Mormon in less than three weeks. He was blessed by the Lord to read quickly, and the skill has stayed with him, long after the challenge was fulfilled.

Our literacy efforts also help unlock the wonders of good books. In Doctrine and Covenants 88:118 we are told, "Seek ye out of the best books words of wisdom; seek learning, even by study and also by faith." The thirteenth article of faith is a good reminder for us, "If there is anything virtuous, lovely, or of good report or praiseworthy, we seek after these things."

The beauty of the world, the majesty of good literature, fine art, and music can soften the jangle of daily living. I often think of the hymn "Where Can I Turn for Peace?" when I feel in turmoil. This hymn, written by Emma Lou Thayne and put to music by Joleen Meredith, expresses a rich understanding of the Lord's covenants.

> Where can I turn for peace?
> Where is my solace
> When other sources cease to make me whole?
> When with a wounded heart, anger, or malice,

I draw myself apart,
Searching my soul?

. . . .

He answers privately,
Reaches my reaching
In my Gethsemane, Savior and Friend.
Gentle the peace he finds for my beseeching.
Constant he is and kind,
Love without end.[5]

Living the commandments and standing as witnesses of God has been the challenge of the Lord's covenant people through the ages. When they are righteous, they have his spirit with them; when they turn from their covenants, they stumble. The book of Numbers tells of Moses leading the Israelites in the wilderness. "I am not able to bear all this people alone," he cries to the Lord, for they did not keep their covenants (Numbers 11:14). Their belief faltered, their strength left them, and they were easy prey to the ways of the world. Hence the first time they stood at the borders of the promised land, they were afraid of what they might encounter. "The people be strong . . . and the cities are walled, and very great," they said (13:28). "We saw . . . giants," said the scouts (v. 33). And the people believed and cried, "Would God that we had died in the land of Egypt" (14:2). A few of them stood stalwart. Caleb said, "Let us go up at once, and possess it; for we are well able to overcome it" (13:30). Joshua, who eventually led the people to the promised land in Moses' stead, declared: "The Lord is with us: fear them not" (14:9). But the Israelites had distanced themselves from their covenants, and they wandered in the wilderness another thirty-eight years.

How many of us are up against giants? A mother I know of described the trials of her life. She had stopped attending church, stopped praying, and had given up on religion. One night she dreamt that she stood before Jesus on the Day of

Judgment. She was resigned to accept a lesser kingdom for herself until she was told to say farewell for eternity to her children. "I begged, I pleaded, I promised to change," she said. "But Jesus was not going to be swayed by my rantings and pleadings. I knew in my heart he was right. I was bound by my baptism the same as he was bound by covenants. I awoke with the most physical, heartbreaking pain. . . . I was at church the next week and have never missed since." Standing as a witness of God against the powerful adversary is hard, but worth it. To see someone come back is cause for rejoicing!

Covenants are not invisible. They reach out from what we say, do, and create to touch others. Keeping our covenants, come what may, brings blessings from the Lord. These blessings may come as a gentleness of spirit, a light in our eyes, and a peace in our souls that speaks dramatically of the goodness of God. As women of covenant, we are trying to be saints. May we rejoice in the covenants we have made with the Lord and in the promises he has made to us.

NOTES

1. Naomi Ward Randall, "I Am a Child of God," *Children's Songbook of The Church of Jesus Christ of Latter-day Saints* (Salt Lake City: The Church of Jesus Christ of Latter-day Saints, 1989), 3; or *Hymns of The Church of Jesus Christ of Latter-day Saints* (Salt Lake City: The Church of Jesus Christ of Latter-day Saints, 1985), no. 301.

2. Eliza R. Snow, *Millennial Star* 33 (12 September 1871): 578.

3. See "Emmeline B. Wells, Holding Fast the Covenant, 1910–1921," in *Women of Covenant: The Story of Relief Society,* Jill Mulvay Derr, Janath Russell Cannon, and Maureen Ursenbach Beecher (Salt Lake City: Deseret Book Co., 1992), 180–223.

4. Spencer W. Kimball, "The Role of Righteous Women," *Ensign,* Nov. 1979, 104.

5. *Hymns,* no. 129.

THE REJOICING WOMEN
IN THE ART OF
MINERVA TEICHERT

MARIAN EASTWOOD WARDLE

Handcart Pioneers, painted in 1930 and reproduced on the cover of this volume, is one of many images of faithful, religious women in the art of Minerva Kohlhepp Teichert (1888–1976). These images strike a responsive chord among Latter-day Saint women of today. We resonate to the joy and spirituality embodied in her powerful female figures, focal points of her canvases. Her depictions of pioneer and scriptural women ennoble the work done by those women and celebrate the faith that sustained them. Through her paintings—in her choice of subject and composition, her loose, impressionistic brush, and her use of light and color—Teichert creates a vision of righteous womanhood that encourages us and lifts our souls.

Minerva Teichert was a contemporary of the artist Georgia O'Keeffe (1887–1986), and she and O'Keeffe have several points in common. Both were reared in rural communities. Both studied at the Art Institute of Chicago under John Vanderpoel (1857–1911). Neither ever studied in Europe. But

Marian Eastwood Wardle is an instructor in art history at Brigham Young University and a doctoral student in art history at the University of Maryland–College Park. She and her husband, Lynn D. Wardle, have two sons. She is a granddaughter of Minerva Teichert.

there the similarities end; both their lives and their art were very different. O'Keeffe sometimes lived alone and sometimes with the photographer Alfred Stieglitz (1864–1946), whom she eventually married. Whether living in tall buildings in New York City with Stieglitz, or later in the artists' colony of Taos, New Mexico, she devoted herself to her art amidst other artists.[1] She is best known for her abstracted and very linear floral images. Teichert, on the other hand, became a ranch wife and the mother of five children, isolated from other artists in the small town of Cokeville, Wyoming. She is best known for her large, public murals executed with a loose, painterly brush. She painted at least sixty murals for public buildings during the 1930s alone.[2]

It may seem strange that an artist in a small cattle town painted so many public murals, but Teichert's mural production was the natural result of her training and her convictions. When Minerva Teichert, Idaho horsewoman and farm girl, entered the Art Institute of Chicago in 1909, she wanted to be a watercolorist. The influence of turn-of-the-century mural painters, however, led her to change her ambitions. Muralists who lectured at the Art Institute, such as Edwin H. Blashfield (1848–1936), stressed the importance of mural decoration in public buildings to educate people and increase their awareness of beauty. They decorated state capitols and courthouses across America with large-scale paintings celebrating history and progress so "that he who runs may read."[3] Teichert embraced this concept of educating those too hurried to read, and even those unable to read, and she came to regard murals as the highest form of art.

Turn-of-the-century American muralists were trained under French masters in the beaux-arts tradition of mural painting. They emphasized figure drawing, using human figures in their murals as allegorical symbols for such concepts as hope, freedom, and industry. Edwin H. Blashfield's 1897 mural in the dome of the main reading room of the Jefferson Building of the

*The Development of Civilization, Edwin H. Blashfield, 1897, Dome,
Main Reading Room, Thomas Jefferson Building,
Library of Congress, Washington, D.C.*

Library of Congress is a good example of the beaux-arts tradition. The twelve seated figures demonstrate the sound draftsmanship and knowledge of the human figure that were important to the academic artists as the chief instrument of artistic expression. Of utmost importance to Blashfield was the concept of mural art as a public educator.[4] The message he wanted to teach in his dome mural was the story of developing civilization, with America as the culmination of that development.[5]

Teichert had many messages and stories to tell— stories of the settlement of the American West, of her own pioneer heritage, and stories depicting her religious convictions. She came to see mural art as a vehicle through which she could publicly teach those important messages. She was further encouraged by her teacher Robert Henri (1865–1929) during her art studies in New York. Stylistically, Henri influenced

Teichert to depart from the sculpturesque and linear form of the beaux-arts mural tradition and to develop a looser brush. At the same time, however, he heightened her determination to paint murals by encouraging her to paint her Mormon story.

When Teichert returned home to Pocatello, Idaho, in 1916, she let it be known everywhere that she wanted to paint murals. By then, however, the beaux-arts movement was waning, and she had few opportunities to satisfy her muralist ambitions until the 1930s, when another American mural movement surfaced, spurred by government patronage. Under Franklin D. Roosevelt's New Deal, government art projects of the Work Projects Administration hired artists to paint murals for large cities and small towns all across America.[6] From coast to coast, government-sponsored murals decorated post offices, schools, libraries, and courthouses. These murals came to be lumped together under the label "WPA art."[7]

When the mural movement of the 1930s began, Teichert was a Wyoming ranch wife with five children and no studio but her living room. But her desire to paint murals was so strong that she painted on large canvases tacked to her living room wall, inverting a pair of binoculars to see the paintings as if from a distance. Working under those circumstances, she placed sixty or more murals in public buildings in Wyoming and Utah during the 1930s. At least six of them were government commissions for the state of Wyoming.[8] These WPA murals include her 1936 *Jim Bridger's Yellowstone* and *Stage Coach Robbery,* painted for the Rock Springs, Wyoming, high school.[9] (They belong to a large body of Teichert paintings that do not include women and therefore are not discussed in this paper.) More important for Teichert's mural production than her government commissions, however, was the new demand created for mural art in public buildings in general. She was able to place many murals in public buildings in Idaho, Wyoming, and Utah.

Government officials sought a mural style that could be easily understood by the public. They did not favor abstract art,

The Fertile Land Remembers, *Louise Ronnebeck, 1938, oil on canvas,*
United States Post Office, Casper, Wyoming.

and they also steered away from academic allegories in the beaux-arts tradition. They favored the stylistic midground of regionalist Thomas Hart Benton (1889–1975), a noted muralist whose murals of American scenes with angular figures and bold colors influenced both the style and the subject matter of WPA murals.[10]

Louise Ronnebeck's 1938 *The Fertile Land Remembers,* now in the United States Post Office in Casper, Wyoming, falls into that midground between academic allegory and abstract art. This work illustrates two other aspects typical of WPA murals as well. It portrays local history, the most common subject matter for WPA murals,[11] and it displays what Barbara Melosh has recently called the "comradely ideal"—"a recurring configuration show[ing] men and women side by side, working together or fighting for a common goal."[12]

The comradely ideal in 1930s depictions of the frontier provides a meaningful contrast to Minerva Teichert's images of pioneer women, which do not employ that convention. Ronnebeck's mural portrays local history, or the passage of time, by means of a sky-bound covered wagon above the oil fields of modern Wyoming passing through cloudlike images of earlier inhabitants of the plains: Indians and buffalo. A pioneer family forms the focal point of the painting, the woman and the man taking equal space, side by side, as they participate in their joint endeavor. Subtle gestures, however, portray the man as the stronger figure. As the mother protects her child with her encircling arms, so the father places a protective arm around the mother's shoulders.

This comradely ideal of the frontier, slightly privileging the male position, was a common element of the New Deal vocabulary. Yet a preliminary sketch for a historical mural in the post office building in Washington, D.C., now the Federal Building, departs from the tradition of the comradely ideal. Ward Lockwood's 1937 sketch for *Opening the West* depicts a pioneer woman wielding an ax at the center of the composition. In the final mural, however, Lockwood moved the woman off center and paired her with an escort. The figures still convey purpose and action, but the woman is now softened and contained pictorially against the male figure's protective body.[13]

Lockwood's mural also provides an interesting comparison with Minerva Teichert's pioneer mural of 1930, one of several Teichert murals entitled *Handcart Pioneers* (see the jacket of this volume). What has happened to the comradely ideal? Again we see a pioneer family, the man and woman together pushing their handcart into the Salt Lake Valley. After their long

Opening the West, *Ward Lockwood, 1937, oil on canvas, Post Office Department Building, Washington, D.C.*

trek, a joint enterprise, they have finally arrived at their destination. But in Teichert's mural the woman claims the focus of our attention and occupies the dominant position. The man and the boy continue their trek with their backs toward us, but the woman faces the viewer and with her gesture invites our participation in her moment of celebration. Unlike Lockwood's pioneer woman, she is not sheltered by the body of a man, and even more important, she is rejoicing, whereas Lockwood's woman is persevering.

Is this difference in portrayal due merely to one artist's being a man and the other a woman? Though the artist's gender may have some bearing, it is not the sole factor, as a juxtaposition of Louise Ronnebeck's *The Fertile Land Remembers* with Teichert's *Handcart Pioneers* illustrates. Though Ronnebeck is a woman, her pioneer couple share equal space and garner equal attention, and the man assumes the slightly dominant position of protector. Even more significant, however, is the portrayal of the status of the two women. Both are shown as equal partners, but Ronnebeck portrays the woman as somewhat dependent on her husband, whereas Teichert portrays her pioneer as a woman of spiritual strength. This is not to say that Teichert's mural denies interdependence between the woman and the man, but that interdependence is not what she emphasizes. She emphasizes the spiritual strength of the woman who has completed a long and courageous journey.

This difference in the status of Teichert's women also appears when comparing Ronnebeck's work with another Teichert pioneer mural painted in 1918, long before the New Deal art projects. In this mural, which now hangs in a stake center in Pocatello, Idaho, Teichert paints the story of Mary Fielding Smith, widow of Hyrum Smith, who made the trek to the Salt Lake Valley without a man.

Many stories have been told of the strength of this spiritual woman as she made her trek west, the most well known being that of her faith in requesting the anointing and healing of a

Not Alone, *Minerva K. Teichert, 1918, oil on canvas, courtesy Museum of Church History and Art, Salt Lake City, Utah.*

dying ox.[13] "The Priesthood brethren poured oil on the head of the ox and with their hands upon it rebuked the power of the destroyer and commanded the ox to get up and be well. Immediately the animal with a grunt and a snort rose from the yoke and within a few minutes began pulling as though nothing had ever happened."[14] Teichert portrays Mary Fielding Smith with her arm on the shoulder of her son, the young Joseph F. Smith, and as the title of the work states, she is *Not Alone*. The hosts of heaven in the spiritual realm of the painting accompany this strong woman of faith. Of course, the wild horses and Indians of Ronnebeck's mural also represent a more spiritual realm. Ronnebeck's spiritual figures, however, evoke the land's history, whereas Teichert's represent the spiritual strength of the woman protagonist and her access to divine protection and help.

Wash Day on the Plains, *Minerva K. Teichert, 1938, oil on canvas, Teichert Family Collection. Used by permission.*

Barbara Melosh notes in her study of New Deal art that pioneer women are almost always confined within the narrative of the comradely ideal. According to Melosh, "female figures rarely appear alone or in the company of other women; there is no female counterpart to the conventions of the solitary farmer or manly camaraderie of shared labor."[15] As we look at Minerva Teichert's 1938 painting *Wash Day on the Plains* from the same era, however, we see another departure from the comradely ideal. Here she lauds the work of women; their mundane contribution to the colonizing of the West, that of clean clothes, seems almost heroic. The women themselves are monumentalized. They appear strong, independent, and engaged in significant labor. Teichert also portrays in this work the womanly camaraderie of shared labor. *Wash Day on the Plains* celebrates the virtue, the necessity, and the pleasure of pioneer women's shared physical labor. Men and women work in separate spheres: a man in the background fixes a wagon wheel and another in the foreground stokes the fire while the women wash clothes. Both spheres are valued, but the important contribution of women in the westward expansion is what this image lauds. The women are not even depicted in the context of family as they cheerfully interact, nor can we tell if they are married or single, mothers or childless. That does not matter.

What matters is their strength and their contribution to the important work in progress.

Minerva Teichert's perception of the Latter-day Saint woman's role, shaped by her own pioneer ancestors, colored her portrayal of pioneer women. Her grandmother, Minerva Wade, for whom she was named, was driven out of Nauvoo with her family. She and her mother were left alone at Council Bluffs, Iowa, when her father and her brother departed with the Mormon Battalion. While they were gone, her mother died; on her own, a teenage girl, she buried her mother. Later, she married into polygamy, the third of ten wives, and bore eight children. After a very difficult marriage, she left her husband. Family legend has it that during this stressful time, she built a stone house for her family with her own hands. A hard worker, she also rendered countless hours of service as a much-needed and sought-after midwife in the North Ogden area. Although she suffered considerable hardship and adversity, she remained true to her covenants. Teichert lived with her grandmother on several occasions and knew her intimately.

Teichert's mother, Ella Hickman Kohlhepp, was the mother of eleven children, four of whom died in childhood. An energetic worker like her mother before her, she supported her large family while her husband served a mission in Switzerland and Germany. Later she supported the family and her husband, too, when he became an invalid. A woman who combined faith and works, she often called upon the Spirit to help her. On one occasion about 1912, when she was traveling with her daughter's family, who were moving from Idaho to Arizona, her faith accomplished a minor miracle. They had reached the Colorado River with their wagon only to find the river too high to cross. Some people were camped on the opposite bank, also waiting for the water level to drop so they could cross. Sister Kohlhepp shouted the crucial question, How long had they been waiting? They replied, "Two weeks." Ella Kohlhepp knew the family didn't have enough food—for them or their animals—to spend much time waiting. So, she stood on the bank and commanded the river in the name of the Lord to go down. And it did. Her grandson, sitting on the back of their wagon with his feet dangling, said the water never touched his feet as they crossed.[16]

Following in the footsteps of her grandmother and her mother, Minerva Teichert herself was a hardworking and very spiritual woman. She produced perhaps more paintings of Latter-day Saint subject matter than any other artist, and at the same time she also raised her own chickens, grew a large and productive garden, cooked on a wood-burning stove, made her own soap, churned her own butter, helped with the ranch work on occasion, reared five children, and completed a staggering amount of genealogical research. One of my grandmother's traits that I remember most clearly is that there was no task too menial for her, no chore she felt was beneath her. She even found time to help me, one of thirty-five grandchildren. In my journal is this reminiscence of a summer my sisters and I stayed with her in Cokeville: "The summer I spent in Cokeville when I was eleven, Jeanette and I were in the summer program at Primary. The older girls had to be in a funny fashion show. I was assigned to wear a 'garden hat,' to be covered with vegetables. Grandma helped me sew vegetables from her garden all over her big, black chicken hat. A big head of lettuce perched right on top and carrots hung down from the brim into my eyes. It was hilarious and stole the show." Teichert extended her kindness to neighbors as well, often sharing milk from the family dairy with those in need. She also enabled many young people, from other towns as well as Cokeville, to attend college by donating paintings to Brigham Young University in exchange for "scholarships."

Through her many kindnesses to family and friends, my grandmother invested herself in relationships with her husband, children, neighbors, and grandchildren, and especially with her Heavenly Father. Her scripture study was perpetual.

She loved Isaiah and Hosea, Joel and Daniel, and quoted from them often. She made every painting a matter of prayer, and I remember thinking she was a visionary woman when she recounted her dreams. Whether she intended to give women the dominant role in her paintings, her own conception of Latter-day Saint women allowed her no alternative. Her heritage and her own life led her naturally to monumentalize their hard work and spirituality.

The meaning in her paintings of pioneer women does not end here. We as viewers also contribute to their meaning, for how we perceive the role of Latter-day Saint women colors our interpretation of her works. The world today would have us believe that much labor is trivial and not worthwhile, particularly the labor involved in housework and child care. Many of us, however, still see these endeavors as dignified, worthwhile, of eternal significance, and worthy of being celebrated. We resonate to the dignity such tasks are afforded in Minerva Teichert's murals of pioneer women. We also recognize that, like Mary Fielding Smith, many of us are in some measure alone, whether unmarried, widowed, divorced, in difficult marriages, or with husbands who spend countless hours in church service. We are alone, and yet also like Mary Fielding Smith, we are *not* alone. We rely on faith and our own spiritual strength to see our way and sometimes simply to survive. As we resonate to the spiritual strength of Teichert's pioneer women, we participate in the production of their meaning.

Women who are not Latter-day Saints also respond to the spirituality created by the formal qualities of Teichert's art. One woman assembling paintings for a national exhibition of women's art, which will include two of Teichert's murals, responded to stylistic elements in the paintings, describing them as "ethereal."[17] A number of stylistic devices contribute to the spiritual quality of Teichert's pioneer women. One is the idealizing of her images, as in *Handcart Pioneers,* 1930 (jacket of this volume). Teichert here combines a classical pyramidal composition

23

and monumental female figure, inspired by beaux-arts ideals, with the loose brushwork of a more impressionistic style. She also unites the real with the ideal: although the handcart pioneers are a realist subject drawn from history, the figure of the woman is idealized, bearing no signs of the physical exertion of her long trek. She is lovely, young and strong, and beautifully dressed—almost as if Teichert has painted not the physical woman but her exultant spirit after she has endured through faith and hard work.

Teichert painted another rendition of *Handcart Pioneers* in 1939. In this image we see the loose impressionistic brush that Teichert employed, another formal device that imparts a certain ethereal quality and spirituality to her works. Though the man in the second handcart painting is straining to push the cart up the rocky terrain, our eye is first drawn to the woman, because of the garment she wears. This garment, a paisley shawl, is a favorite Teichert motif, a bright spot of color that focuses attention on the woman. Real pioneer women immigrating from Paisley, Scotland, carried these bright shawls with

Handcart Pioneers, *Minerva K. Teichert, 1939, oil on canvas, 59" x 46", courtesy Museum of Church History and Art, Salt Lake City, Utah.*

them, but they were saved for best, not worn on the trek. Minerva Teichert herself owned one. She consistently incorporated the paisley shawl into her images of pioneer women, where it functions as another idealizing agent.

The bearing of the women in the two handcart pioneer paintings reveals yet another convention Teichert employs to celebrate the achievements of pioneer women. Their erect postures and upheld heads draw our attention and emphasize their spiritual strength and independence.

Another Teichert mural, *Get Ye Up into the High Mountains,* 1949, is very noticeably idealized. Well-dressed pioneers play musical instruments and bear gifts while they trek through rugged mountains. This work is an allegory, a picture that portrays one thing and means another. Of course the pioneers did not wear lovely clothing and play musical instruments as they struggled up mountain passes. Rather, the mural is an allegory of their triumphs and achievements to the glory of God. The

Get Ye Up into the High Mountains, *Minerva K. Teichert, 1949, oil on canvas, private collection. Used by permission.*

25

achievements of the women are particularly lauded through the formal device of color. The men are painted for the most part with a monochromatic palette, but the women wear spectacular color combinations of green and purple and in one case a blue dress with a bright paisley shawl. Many of the formal elements Teichert employs to evoke spiritual ideality and celebration can be seen in this mural: loose brushwork, music, erect figures with upheld heads, the paisley shawl, and vibrant color.

Another rendering of *Handcart Pioneers* has hung for many years at the front of the chapel in Cokeville, Wyoming. Once again an idealized woman forms the major focal point. Her entire family has been blessed on their way because of her physical and spiritual strength. Evident again is the erect carriage of the figure and the bright color of the paisley shawl, which cause viewers to join in rejoicing over her achievement and to identify with her conquest of adversity. This painting, which the women of Cokeville view every Sunday, year after year, has undoubtedly contributed to their perception of the role of a faithful LDS woman.

A well-known Teichert mural, *The Coming of the Gulls,* 1935, employs another formal device to focus on faithful womanhood: drama.[18] In this work, several pioneers kneel to thank the Lord for saving their crops from hoards of crickets by sending seagulls to devour them. Once again the focus is a faithful woman, her figure positioned forward and centered in the picture, but her dramatic pose is what immediately draws our attention. The combination of the painterly brush and the drama of the woman's stance and upturned eyes gives us the impression that this woman of faith is directly communing with a higher realm. We join her in rejoicing that her prayers have been answered.

Comparisons with Minerva Teichert's scriptural subject matter are harder to find in WPA murals, but some of her contemporaries did paint scriptural themes. A noted painter of Book of Mormon themes is Arnold Friberg (b. 1913), whose paintings are still reproduced in popular editions of the Book of Mormon. His paintings contrast strikingly with Teichert's.

Friberg does not illustrate the few examples where women figure prominently in Book of Mormon accounts, but Teichert does. Witness her *Morianton's Servant,* a story related in two verses in Alma 50:30–31. Morianton beat his maidservant, and she fled to the camp of Moroni, where she disclosed Morianton's military strategy. Teichert uses light, color, and drama to make this young woman's courageous deed the focal point of the painting. In another mural, the daughters of Ishmael are portrayed leaving their comfortable home in Jerusalem to go into the wilderness to do the will of the Lord in becoming the wives of Lehi's sons (1 Nephi 7:1–5). Teichert makes her focal point the dancing young women with their tambourines as she celebrates their righteous sacrifice through

Morianton's Servant, *Minerva K. Teichert, c. 1950, oil on panel, 36" x 48",* © *courtesy Museum of Art, Brigham Young University. All rights reserved.*

Lehi Departs Jerusalem, *Minerva K. Teichert, sketch, c. 1941, oil on paper, 11" x 16", private collection. Used by permission.*

the use of color, music, and dance. Her intriguing title for this painting is *The Love Story*.[19]

Both Friberg and Teichert paint the journey of Lehi's family to the land of promise, though Teichert depicts the early part of the journey with the family leaving Jerusalem, and Friberg depicts the end of the ocean voyage (1 Nephi 2:2–4; 18:7).[20] Friberg portrays Lehi and Sariah in a manner reminiscent of Melosh's comradely ideal. They form the focal point of the painting together, with Sariah leaning against Lehi, her protector. In contrast, Teichert's Sariah sits upright, competent and capable on her own camel. The upright heads of Lehi and Sariah frame the center of the canvas, each endowed with spiritual strength in their joint venture. Sariah is not diminished as she follows her priesthood leader in righteousness.

Both artists also depict Alma baptizing in the waters of Mormon (Mosiah 18:5–16).[21] Compositionally, the paintings are similar, crowds of people framing the pool of water, the crowds parting to reveal Alma baptizing in the center. Stylistically, however, they are quite different. Friberg's work is very tight and linear, whereas Teichert employs her usual loose, painterly brush, evocative of the Spirit. Another notable difference is in the peripheral scene on the left of each painting: in Friberg's, a man helps a woman from the waters of baptism; in Teichert's, a woman helps a child.

Another example of Teichert's Book of Mormon murals is *Escape from the Land of Nephi* (Mosiah 22:10–11). At this moment of escape, the guards now drunk with wine, women play an important role. In the oil sketch for Teichert's mural, a woman with a child in her arms and a finger to her lips reminds her older child behind her that silence is imperative. This crucial task is not recorded in the Book of Mormon account. Minerva Teichert's murals offer us the refreshing opportunity to read the Book of Mormon through the eyes of a woman of faith.

Teichert also painted biblical scenes involving women. One is *Queen Esther,* as she approaches King Ahasuerus in behalf of her people (Esther 5:1–2). Aware as we now are of Teichert's artistic vocabulary, the idealized figure with its

Escape from the Land of Nephi, *Minerva K. Teichert, sketch, c. 1941, oil on paper, 11" x 16", private collection. Used by permission.*

dignified carriage and the loose brush with which Esther is depicted leave no doubt that the Spirit accompanied Esther in her courageous task.[22]

One of my favorites is Teichert's *Christ in the Home of Mary and Martha,* based on the account of Christ's visit to the home of the sisters of Lazarus, whom Christ raised from the dead. Martha, preoccupied with preparing food and caring for Christ's physical comfort, questioned her sister's lack of concern for these matters when Mary chose instead to sit and be taught at the Master's feet (Luke 10:38–42). In this work I find portrayed the Mary-Martha dilemma in my own nature.

Minerva Teichert felt the impulses of both Mary and Martha in her life. As a ranch wife and mother, she was often occupied with the practical concerns of cooking, cleaning, gardening, and tending children. On the other hand, she yearned to spend more time in reading, scripture study, and the creative outlets of writing and painting. This dilemma, shared by many of us, is powerfully embodied in her mural. There can be no doubt

Christ in the Home of Mary and Martha, *1941, oil on canvas, 36" x 48",*
© *courtesy Museum of Art, Brigham Young University. All rights reserved.*

which sister's nature appealed most to Teichert, for though Christ is the light source, Mary occupies the center of the composition and is bathed in the light of Christ's presence. Moreover, following the line formed by Christ's hand and finger, we are led to focus on the figure of Mary, who is clad in a bright garment inspired by a paisley shawl. At the same time, Martha's task is portrayed as dignified and important. The loose brushwork and erect bearing of her figure indicate that she is a woman of great faith herself. Teichert's mural celebrates a combination of faith and works, the right blending of which we all seek through the guidance of the Spirit, so that we too can be women endowed with power from on high.

As Latter-day Saint women ourselves, we relate to Teichert's women. We see our own efforts at overcoming adversity through spiritual strength lauded, and our souls are lifted. Through her use of such formal elements as light, color, brushwork, composition, and choice of subject, Minerva Teichert celebrates faith and works. By ennobling the work of pioneer and scriptural women and visually depicting the faith that sustained them, Teichert's paintings enrich our perception of the role of the faithful Latter-day Saint woman. Her paintings encourage us to rejoice in our covenant roles as women of Zion.

NOTES

1. One of many recent biographies of O'Keeffe is Laurie Lisle, *Portrait of an Artist: A Biography of Georgia O'Keeffe* (Albuquerque: University of New Mexico Press, 1986).

2. For a list of Teichert's 1930s murals, see Marian Eastwood Wardle, "Minerva Teichert's Murals: The Motivation for Her Large-Scale Production," master's thesis (Brigham Young University, 1988), appendix. For biographical sketches of Teichert, see Richard and Susan Oman, "A Passion for Painting: Minerva Kohlhepp Teichert," *Ensign,* Dec. 1976, 52–58; Laurie Teichert Eastwood and Robert O. Davis, *Rich in Story, Great in Faith: The Art of Minerva Kohlhepp Teichert* (Salt Lake City: Museum of Church History and Art, 1988); Marian Ashby Johnson, "Minerva's Calling," *Dialogue: A Journal of Mormon Thought* 21 (Spring 1988): 127–43; Jan Underwood Pinborough, "With a Bold Brush: Minerva Kohlhepp Teichert," *Ensign,* Apr. 1989, 34–41;

Wardle, "Minerva Teichert's Murals," 8–20; Nancy Webb, "Minerva Kohlhepp Teichert," *Southwest Art* (November 1989): 90–94, 171–74.

3. Edwin Howland Blashfield, *Mural Painting in America: The Scammon Lectures* (New York: Charles Scribner's Sons, 1913), 175–76.

4. Ibid., 8.

5. Herbert Small, *The Library of Congress: Its Architecture and Decoration,* ed. Henry Hope Reed (New York: W. W. Norton, 1982), 105–10.

6. In 1934, the Public Works of Art Project (PWAP) was established. This program, which hired more than thirty-seven hundred artists, lasted only seven months. Only four hundred of the fifteen thousand paintings and sculptures produced under PWAP were murals, but they were the works that caught the public eye, and people soon believed that government-sponsored art was mural art. After the demise of PWAP, the government continued to hire artists through the Federal Art Project and the Treasury Section on Painting and Sculpture until 1939, when the WPA art units were abolished. James Scales Watrous, "Mural Painting in the United States: A History of Its Style and Techniques," Ph.D. dissertation (University of Wisconsin, 1939), 114. Karal Ann Marling, *Wall-to-Wall America: A Cultural History of Post-Office Murals in the Great Depression* (Minneapolis: University of Minnesota Press, 1982), 43–49.

7. For a study of government-sponsored murals of the 1930s, see Marlene Park and Gerald E. Markowitz, *Democratic Vistas: Post Offices and Public Art in the New Deal* (Philadelphia: Temple University Press, 1984).

8. Wardle, "Minerva Teichert's Murals," appendix.

9. These two murals, along with two others painted by Teichert for the high school in Rock Springs, *Bridger meets Jedediah Smith at the Tetons* and *Pony Express,* are now in the Community Fine Arts Center, Rock Springs, Wyoming.

10. Marling, 10, 13.

11. Ibid., 20.

12. Barbara Melosh, *Engendering Culture: Manhood and Womanhood in New Deal Public Art and Theater* (Washington, D.C.: Smithsonian Institution Press, 1991), 4.

13. Ibid., 47.

14. Ivan J. Barrett, *Mary—Heroine—Martyr [Mary Fielding Smith],* Mormon History Series (n. p.: RIC Publishing, 1984), 97.

15. Melosh, *Engendering Culture,* 61.

16. I am grateful to my mother, Laurie Teichert Eastwood, for sharing stories about my grandmother and her ancestors with me.

17. Patricia Trenton, interview by Laurie Teichert Eastwood, 16 Feb. 1994.

18. Minerva K. Teichert, *The Miracle of the Gulls,* 1935, Museum of Art, Brigham Young University, is reproduced on the cover of Davis and Eastwood, *Rich in Story, Great in Faith* and in Pinborough, "With a Bold Brush" and Johnson, "Minerva's Calling." It has also been reproduced as a poster by the Museum of Church History and Art.

19. Minerva K. Teichert, *The Love Story,* Museum of Art, Brigham Young University, Provo, Utah.

20. Arnold Friberg, *Lehi and His People Arrive in the Promised Land,* is reproduced in many editions of the Book of Mormon.

21. Minerva K. Teichert, *Baptism,* Museum of Art, Brigham Young University, Provo, Utah; Arnold Friberg's *Alma Baptizes in the Waters of Mormon* is reproduced in many editions of the Book of Mormon.

22. Minerva K. Teichert, *Queen Esther,* 1939, private collection, appears on the cover of *Relief Society Courses of Study* (Salt Lake City: The Church of Jesus Christ of Latter-day Saints, 1986).

TO REJOICE AS WOMEN: GROWING AND COPING IN A COMPLEX WORLD

VIRGINIA H. PEARCE

While pondering the theme I have been asked to discuss, I thought about the things that cause me to rejoice—sunsets, early-morning walks with good friends, and chocolate. Then I thought a little deeper: about happy occasions; family successes; good, honest relationships with other people; worthwhile work; righteousness.

I asked myself, What is there that I absolutely could not do without and still rejoice? What do I absolutely need if I am to have an attitude of rejoicing? As I made a new list, I realized that the most fundamental causes for rejoicing have nothing to do with gender but everything to do with us as children of God, working out our second estate with other children of God. The foundation principles of the gospel apply to every gender, race, and individual human circumstance imaginable. If it were not so, our Father in Heaven's plan could not operate successfully.

To understand those foundation principles, we must go back to the beginning, to that great Council in Heaven in

---

Virginia H. Pearce and her husband, James R. Pearce, are the parents of five daughters and one son. Sister Pearce has served on the Primary General Board and as first counselor in the Young Women General Presidency. She received her bachelor's degree in history and English and her master's degree in social work from the University of Utah.

which those principles were explained to us. I remember a scripture in Job: "The morning stars sang together, and all the sons of God shouted for joy" (Job 38:7). What happened there that made us all shout for joy? Could it have been the prospect of getting a body? Didn't we know how much trouble bodies can be? If I had had a clear picture of the shape of my own, there is no way I would have shouted for joy. Even long, lithe, lovely bodies ache and hurt and cause trouble. No, I don't think we shouted for joy at the prospect of a body.

What, then, created such excitement? Probably many things, but one of the fundamentally happy things about this life is that it is based, absolutely and finally, upon personal agency—a chance to make our own choices, take responsibility for ourselves, control our own destiny. Now that is a real cause for rejoicing! President David O. McKay said about agency: "Man's greatest endowment in mortal life is the power of choice—the divine gift of free agency. No true character was ever developed without a sense of soul freedom. . . . Next to the bestowal of life itself, the right to direct that life is God's greatest gift."[1]

No thought so enlivens me. Conversely, no despair is quite so overwhelming as when I have momentarily thought no choices were available and I am nothing more than a victim of the actions of others.

"The Eldest Son said: 'Here am I'; and then he added, 'Send me.' But the second one, which was 'Lucifer, Son of the Morning,' said, 'Lord, here am I, send me, I will redeem every son and daughter of Adam and Eve that lives on the earth, or that ever goes on the earth.' 'But,' says the Father, 'that will not answer at all. I give each and every individual his agency; all must use that in order to gain exaltation in my kingdom; inasmuch as they have the power of choice they must exercise that power. They are my children; the attributes which you see in me are in my children and they must use their agency.'"[2]

What does this agency mean to us now, day to day? First, we do not have the luxury of blaming others for our own

35

actions or weaknesses. Blaming, a natural defense mechanism, is hard to give up. The way we are is our mother's fault or our husband's fault, or society is to blame. As immature human beings we want to assign blame. Adam and Eve's initial immaturity is evident in their story. When confronted with their choice of eating the forbidden fruit, Adam first blames Eve—it was "the woman thou gavest me" (Moses 4:18). Then Eve says, "The serpent beguiled me" (v. 19). They sound like children who are adept at passing the buck! As Adam and Eve come to grips with their choice, however, their language changes from blaming to accepting personal responsibility. Adam says: "For because of *my* transgression my eyes are opened." And Eve: "Were it not for *our* transgression we never should have had seed, and never should have known good and evil, and the joy of our redemption, and the eternal life which God giveth unto all the obedient" (Moses 5:10–11; emphasis added).

My friend Ruth Wright related the following conversation to me: "One day my sister and I were commiserating on the phone about our messy kitchens. We really didn't know how to clean kitchens because we always worked for our father when we were young and thus never learned how to clean and do all the domestic things that we wanted to do when we became homemakers. We missed out. We were really blaming our mother: Why didn't she teach us this and why didn't she teach us that? Suddenly we realized that Mom didn't teach us because we were never home to be taught, but now that we were grown, adult women, we could learn ourselves. Once we came to this amazing realization, we forgave Mother immediately. We needed to be responsible for our own decisions. That realization was a turning point for both of us; we started looking at ourselves. Every time we were tempted to assign fault, we knew that we could do something about the experiences we hadn't had." Lucky for Ruth that she lives in the same ward as housecleaning wizard Daryl Hoole. When a door closes, a window opens!

We've all seen ourselves as victims of someone else's behavior. Changing our thinking to focus on the given circumstances and our responsibility for current choices can be liberating. Mary Ann felt that her agency had been taken from her when she was repeatedly sexually molested as a child. At age twenty-two, she had to have a hysterectomy; her choice to have a child was also taken from her. For a time she anguished, Why had the Lord abandoned her when all she wanted was a family? Why hadn't her parents protected her? All her whys didn't change her circumstances. When she was about twenty-four, she began to realize that she needed to pick herself up from where she had been dropped and make choices that would affect her life for good. The first choice she made was to join the Church. "I have subsequently made ten choices to adopt special children," she says. "I have the most beautiful children imaginable. And I know now why I went through the experiences I did. I've taken children who have been abused, and I can truly say to them, 'I understand what you have gone through because I, too, have been through it.' My life is now a blessing, and I thank my Heavenly Father for each and every day." Choices that Mary Ann hadn't made caused her to see herself as helpless for a time. Thoughts of lost choices and a limited ability to direct her life filled her with despair. Focusing on who was to blame, she remained in a cycle of despair. When she finally said, "Not all my choices have been taken away; I can still make others," her life began to change.

President Brigham Young said: "There is not an individual upon the earth but what has within himself ability to save or to destroy himself."[3] No one can keep us from coming to the Savior. That does not mean that we will move through this life without pain, but no matter what our circumstances, we do have the power to move toward him ourselves. We always have the right to accept the Savior and his atonement, which

37

restores to us a wholeness that our mistakes or the mistakes of others have temporarily destroyed.

If we truly understand and rejoice in agency, then we cannot get stuck blaming others. We also are not allowed the luxury of blaming ourselves for the actions or choices of others. Women are really good at this type of blaming. We readily absorb the responsibility for every substandard thing our children do, from earning poor grades to refusing to cut their hair to choosing evil over good. We just lower our heads and raise our hands immediately: Guilty as charged. We also heroically think that it is our job—our ultimate and total responsibility—to get those we love back to the Savior, no matter the methods. Think about that in terms of the Council in Heaven. Whose plan does that sound like?

Let me give an example of how we blame ourselves entirely for the choices that others have made. Years ago a woman who was recently divorced moved into the ward I was in at the time. I sat by her the first week in Sunday School, and we learned we had a lot in common. It became obvious to me that she was suffering, that her divorce had been a terrible, bitter blow to her faith and her sense of self-worth. Her children were also having difficulty. I made some efforts—not monumental, but some efforts—to invite them over. My children liked them, and we included them sometimes in our activities. I really grew to love her. Though we continue to share good times together, she rarely attends church anymore. Sometimes I think of all the times I didn't invite her to dinner. Some days I take the entire responsibility for her inactivity, blaming myself and my procrastinating habits for her choices. Then I have to think that through again. I do wish I had done more. And I want to do more. But if I understand agency, I also have to understand that part of the responsibility is hers. In fact, the ultimate responsibility is hers. My responsibility is to be available, supportive, and open to the promptings of the Spirit.

In the context of personal agency, what is our responsibility for others? We can create loving, accepting environments, we can pray, hope, encourage, mourn with one another, rejoice together, teach, share one another's burdens. We have covenanted to do those things as the seed of Abraham, as part of the Lord's covenant people. I believe we took a responsibility upon ourselves in the premortal existence to help the Savior with his work. We promised to help create environments and do things that would help our brothers and sisters return to him. Elder John A. Widtsoe said: "We agreed, right then and there [in the premortal existence], to be not only saviors for ourselves but measurably, saviors for the whole human family. We went into a partnership with the Lord. The working out of the plan became then not merely the Father's work, and the Savior's work, but also our work. The least of us, the humblest, in partnership with the Almighty in achieving the purpose of the eternal plan of salvation. That places us in a very responsible attitude towards the human race."[4]

What is the Lord's responsibility? Do you think he feels guilty when one of us makes poor choices and doesn't return to our Heavenly Father? I don't think he feels guilt; I think he feels terrible sorrow. He does everything he can, to the laying down of his life and suffering for every one of our poor choices, but he never accepts responsibility for them.

When we join him in that partnership, we need to model that same kind of behavior. When we do those things joyfully and willingly, knowing that the important choice always rests with the individual, we become like the Savior. He creates an environment (the earth, eternal principles, and law) and support (the Holy Spirit), knowing that we will have to make the important choices for ourselves.

When we make the choice to join the Savior in his work, we assume personal responsibility for our destiny; when we become other-centered, losing ourselves in the service of others, in their needs and in their well-being, we gain our own exaltation. It is the gospel paradox. Thus, "He that loseth his

39

life . . . shall find it" (Matthew 10:39), not "She that assumeth all responsibility for everyone's life shall find eternal life." She who forgets herself, moving with love into the lives of others— feeling sorrow when they make poor choices, but not guilt— becomes a partner with the Savior.

President J. Reuben Clark Jr. said, "There is no growth on this earth, intellectually or otherwise, save by the exercise of our free agency, by our choosing our own course and growing in it."[5] So exercising agency brings growth, and we all want to "grow up."

I love Alice T. Clark's definition of humility in the *Encyclopedia of Mormonism:* "[To] joyfully, voluntarily, and quietly submit one's whole life to God's will."[6] That is what I want to do with my great gift of agency—to joyfully, voluntarily, and quietly submit my whole life to God's will. In other words, I want to use the gift of agency to give my life back to him.

NOTES

1. David O. McKay, *Gospel Ideals: Selections from the Discourses of David O. McKay* (Salt Lake City: Deseret News Press, 1953), 299.

2. Brigham Young, *The Discourses of Brigham Young,* sel. John A. Widtsoe (Salt Lake City: Deseret Book Co., 1954), 54.

3. Ibid., 67.

4. John A. Widtsoe, "The Worth of Souls," *Utah Genealogical and Historical Magazine* 25 (October 1934): 189.

5. J. Reuben Clark Jr., "A Simple Faith," in *Our Leaders Speak,* sel. Soren F. Cox (Salt Lake City: Deseret Book, 1957), 55.

6. Alice T. Clark, "Humility," in *Encyclopedia of Mormonism,* ed. Daniel H. Ludlow, 4 vols. (New York: Macmillan Publishing Co., 1992), 2:663.

THE SPIRIT SAID UNTO ME: LOOK!

EMILY MADSEN REYNOLDS

Thinking about the Holy Ghost and the question of making right decisions takes me back more than twenty years to a time in my late teens when I was a student at Brigham Young University. Reared in the Church, I had a solid grounding in the gospel, and as I began to emerge as an adult, blessed by the tutelage of fine religion teachers such as Arthur Henry King and Robert K. Thomas, a lot of things came together at once, and my knowledge of the gospel took on new dimensions.

It was an exciting time, and in the midst of that excitement I had what I thought was a brilliant insight. I wondered why it had taken me so long to see it—or why other people weren't already onto it. It was so simple. All I had to do was learn all of the commandments and from then on I could make right choices all the time. Clearly there were some commandments I was not yet obeying, but even allowing time for them to be added to my repertoire at some reasonable rate, I didn't see why I couldn't be perfect within a year, or eighteen months at the very most. If every decision I made was in harmony with the commandments of God, everything would be taken care of. I couldn't help thinking how terrific it would be if I could be perfect before I met the man I was going to marry.

It will come as no surprise to you, I'm sure, that my plan

Emily Madsen Reynolds and her husband, Mark Reynolds, are the parents of seven children. She holds a master's degree in psychology and is a part-time faculty member at Brigham Young University.

didn't work. A number of things were wrong with it, but I'd like to focus on just two.

The first concerns my preoccupation with making choices. I began to understand then, though years would pass before I had the language to articulate it, that conscious, explicit decisions are only part of the story of our lives. To be sure, they are an important part, often marking turning points. As in Robert Frost's "The Road Not Taken," many decisions we make, though seemingly small, make "all the difference." So it is no wonder that we frequently seek the guidance and confirmation of the Spirit when we face conscious decisions. But at least as important are the myriad of decisions that we make without conscious consideration, without careful reasoning or any weighing of alternatives. Those decisions simply flow out of what we believe, what we are trying to do, what we take events to mean—in sum, out of our perspective on the world. Much of this perspective develops without any explicit awareness, and it may never occur to us to inquire of the Lord whether we *should* see things the way we do.

My favorite metaphor for how this works was given to me as I watched a friend who loves baseball. He has played it all his life. Baseball is for him the one true sport. One afternoon I saw him in practice with a team of Little Leaguers he was coaching. As he talked to one player, another player tossed him the ball. There was an arresting grace in the way his hand went out for the ball as he went on talking, never missing a beat in the conversation, not even looking at the ball as far as I could tell. He didn't have to stop to consider whether or how to catch it. Its flight was so familiar to him that his response came without effort, almost without awareness.

I believe that most of our responses are, if not so graceful or so fitting, at least as unconsidered as that hand going out for the ball. We spend most of our days in familiar, comfortable territory, caught up entirely with the continuing ebb and flow of daily living, responding without having the time to deliberate and consider. It is only the exceptional decisions that we stop to think about. So, making sure that my conscious decisions were right was never going to be enough.

The other problem with my plan was that it required me to be sufficiently independent of the people around me to stand apart from them and the context we shared and make all my right decisions on a timetable of my own devising. I was even expecting to be independent not only of others but also of God. It was as though all I needed was what he'd already said, bundled up as a set of static principles to be carried off to some private corner of the universe, where I would set about becoming perfect without ever listening to him again. My plan ignored completely our continuing relationship.

Fortunately, though it spelled disaster for my idealistic plan, no such independence is possible. We are born into a web of relationships, eternal and earthly, and nearly all of our decisions, both the conscious, explicit ones and the unconsidered, implicit ones, are *about* relationships, even when they seem to be about something else. The ones that have little relational significance (which socks to wear, whether to have the soup or the salad) seem relatively insignificant. The only reason that we feel decisions are important—the only reason that going one way or another makes a difference—is that it makes a difference in the continuing flow of our relationships to each other and of our relationship to God. Because all truly important decisions involve relationships, then, becoming perfect on my own wasn't going to happen.

My plan for perfection died a quiet and natural death in less than a week. But it had been born of a deeply felt desire to somehow find my way home to heaven—and that desire remains, although lately I find that I care much less about making myself perfect and much more about engaging in relationships that are sustainable for eternity. When the prophet tells us, as he has, that we must prepare to redeem Zion, something in me—in many of us, I think—responds, "Yes—oh, please, yes!" I want to understand how to be pure in heart and of one heart with my brothers and sisters.

At this point a series of scriptural phrases tumble in on me. The first is God explaining to Samuel, "Man looketh on the outward appearance, but the Lord looketh on the heart" (1 Samuel 16:7). Apparently, however, this discrepancy between us and the Lord is remediable because John tells us, "Beloved, now are we the sons of God, and it doth not yet appear what we shall be: but we know that, when he shall appear, we shall be like him; for we shall see him as he is" (1 John 3:2). So then the question is, How? How do we learn to see each other as the Lord sees us and to see him as he is? Moroni tells us, "And by the power of the Holy Ghost ye may know the truth of all things" (Moroni 10:5). I love that word *all*. It includes knowing the truth of our relations to each other and to God. The Holy Ghost will teach us that truth. And that leads to the phrase from Nephi that I borrowed for my title, because it describes for me how this process often works: "And it came to pass that the Spirit said unto me: Look! And I looked" (1 Nephi 11:8).

To be honest, I think that fairly often the Spirit says "Look!" and we don't look, which brings another scriptural phrase to mind, the recurring one about the Spirit "striv[ing] with man" (Genesis 6:3; 1 Nephi 7:14; D&C 1:33; Moses 8:17). I always think the word *striving* gives a sense of what hard work it must be for the Spirit most days. But sometimes we do look, and when we look under the influence of the Holy Ghost, our perspective shifts, and we respond differently, often without even having to think about it. The Holy Ghost draws us together with his revelations, erasing with mercy the boundaries we sometimes draw, teaching us how to be members one of another, bringing to our remembrance the atonement of Jesus Christ, healing the wounds that divide us.

I know that can happen because I have experienced it, if only in glimmers compared to what I sense is possible. Just the same, I've had some experiences that have helped me to glimpse the possibilities.

As a newlywed, I was called to teach the Blazers in Primary. We lived in a part of town that was in general less affluent than the rest of the town. A significant number of the members on our ward records did not attend church, but their children often attended Primary on Wednesday afternoons with their schoolmates. All of that was explained to me by the Primary president. She told me a little about the family situations of several of the boys who would be in my class. Two or three had unhappy stories of broken families, alcoholism, being repeatedly pulled out of the home at the insistence of social workers and then returned home for a while when things were going better. "And by the way," she added, "James Brown is learning disabled. He can't read, and, of course, he won't be able to memorize the Articles of Faith. He can't really even understand them." We were walking through the upper hall of the meetinghouse to the Primary closet, and I could take you to the spot where I was standing when the Spirit whispered with quiet insistence, "Do not believe what they say about James Brown." While the Primary president encouraged me just to let him be in the class and not make an issue of his difficulties, I puzzled over this prompting.

As I slowly walked the three or four blocks to my apartment, I thought about this little boy I hadn't even met yet. I was nineteen years old; my upbringing had been comfortable and in some ways even sheltered. I had almost no experience with poverty or alcoholism. I had always loved school and done well. I didn't have much to bring to an understanding of this child. But it turned out that I had all I needed: "Do not believe what they say about James Brown."

For some purposes it would make a better story if I could report a tidy and purposeful set of steps I took to make a difference to James, but I can't. I remember happening onto a snowball fight after Primary one day in which he was getting the worst of things. I mopped him up a bit, took him home, and met his mother and the twins and the cat, though I'm afraid I made my escape as soon as I decently could. I also remember being emboldened by that first whisper of the Spirit to encourage him to try to read and memorize. I didn't know anything about teaching reading, but I did what made sense to me, and if it seemed to make sense to him, then I did it some more. When, during the lesson on the sacrament, it became clear that James and a couple of the other boys didn't know what the sacrament was because they'd never been to church on Sunday, I arranged to pick them up for sacrament meeting the next week. What I did doesn't amount to much. The only thing that really counted was that I trusted the Spirit and didn't believe what they said about James Brown.

By springtime, James Brown read just fine in Primary, though he still didn't read at school. He went slowly at first but more strongly as the year progressed. And he memorized the Articles of Faith. I will never forget the shine in his eyes when he finished off number ten, *paradisiacal* and all. And he knew what all of it meant. The Spirit had told me the truth. James wasn't learning disabled at all.

With twenty years more of life to bring to my understanding of that child, I wish I had done a great deal more. I wish I hadn't been afraid to go into his home and offer friendship to his mother. Reading in Primary probably didn't free him much because I didn't have the sense to talk to his mother or his schoolteacher about it, to find out what was really behind his not reading at school. I loved him, but I could have loved him better.

James must be all grown up by now. We moved at the end of the school year, and I lost touch with him soon after. I picture him sometimes, almost always wearing a shirt that was many sizes too big and often not very clean. James Brown did not look much like the bright and happy child that God knew he could be, and I didn't look much like a person who could love a child who looked like James Brown; but with a single truthful sentence, the Spirit linked us, made us friends, and taught us both to do things we didn't know we could do.

The second story is about a young mother, my mother, whose children happened not to have been born yet. One night she had a dream. My father's journal records, "Ann dreamed that she had a baby. A beautiful daughter. She showed me at dinnertime Wednesday a picture in the paper that reminded her of it. Later on, near bedtime, as she spoke of the spirit, the 'personality,' she said it was so wonderful to have her, to be close to her, and to nurse her. There were tears in her eyes." From that dream, my mother knew my name, but more than that, she knew me and remembered that before coming to earth we had been best friends.

A little over a year later, I was born. As a child, I was, of course, told about the dream. I cannot remember a time when I didn't know about it. It defined my relationship with my mother from the very beginning. Later on, however, there came a time when my mother and I didn't look very much like best friends. The details of all that may not matter very much in this context. It's an old story. When it comes to mothers and daughters, the adversary fights in many ways to prevent what will bless us most. In our case, as in many others, there was pain and there was resentment. And in spite of a real desire in both of us to change, that pain and resentment often seemed only to be renewed by much of our time together.

People who knew us both seemed to become resigned to the situation. At times I was almost resigned to it myself, but the Holy Ghost kept bringing something to my remembrance: that dream. My participation in the dream had been before my mortal birth and so I had no mortal memory of it, but over the years as the Spirit periodically bore witness to me of its truthfulness, the dream became more and more vivid in my mind, and I knew that it was a truer picture of my relation to my mother than any I could form from our present experience. My

47

mother seemed to remember it, too, though it must have been wistfully. She bought a postcard once, a picture of two girls walking together in a field of flowers, and sent it to me. I knew before she told me that it reminded her of the dream because it reminded me of the dream, too. Still, things between us were not much like that.

I didn't realize how much strength I was drawing from that dream or what an important part of my perspective it was until I was talking to a friend one day about some hopeful signs in my relationship with my mother. He knew us both well, and as we talked it became apparent that he felt a real concern that my expectations not become unrealistic, that I not get hurt. He was happy to hear that I thought things might be starting to get better but, he said, "Now, Emily, you may have to face the fact that some problems just don't get solved in this life. This relationship may never really change." My answer, though its passion and immediacy surprised me, was as effortless as the hand going out for the ball: "Oh, no. You don't understand. When Mom and I get this all worked out, we're going to be friends in a way most people never dream of being friends." And I felt the witness of the Spirit all over again that it was true.

That conversation took place seven or eight years ago. There has been a considerable amount of repenting and forgiving between us since then and, of course, the promptings of the Spirit have aided us all along the way. And we're not through. Our relationship still holds the promise of growth and learning for both of us, as it should. But it is a wonderful moment—and it happens more and more often these days—when we are talking earnestly about important things and one or the other of us stops and says, "This is just like the dream."

The third story is more difficult to share. It is hard to tell, not because I'm a private person (I'm not), but because it seems hard to hear. It gets genuinely grim in the middle. But I will tell you at the beginning that this story, too, has a happy ending, and perhaps that will help.

Some years ago, there were two or three years during which I was in almost constant emotional crisis. The troubles that I have described with my mother were, at that time, only one aspect of an unrelenting pain that frequently threatened to engulf me. My own mothering became increasingly difficult, my marriage was strained to the breaking point by trying circumstances that required a unity of response at which we never seemed to arrive, and worst of all, I was beginning to realize that I didn't really have any idea who God was. I had somehow developed the idea of him as the great blessing dispenser in the sky. You put your obedience in the slot and, voilà, out came the blessing. But it wasn't happening that way.

I was doing all the right things I knew. I was having a family, serving as Primary president, supporting my husband as the Young Men's president, working in the PTA, ultimately becoming its president and liaison to the school board, planting a garden, baking bread, and the list goes on. It is an incredible list to me now because when I think back to how I felt, to the way every single act seemed an impossible hurdle, I don't know how I did anything at all. I was in so much pain that sometimes I didn't know how I kept breathing. I knew exactly what blessings I needed, I was sure. I worked for them, I prayed for them, I begged for them. And they simply weren't coming. When I was utterly desperate, I sometimes asked my husband, Mark, for a priesthood blessing. Over and over the Lord promised that I could get through this without breaking and, more than that, that this experience would prepare me to serve him and my fellow Saints.

One day, I was sitting in a rocking chair in the corner of our living room nursing my infant son. I don't remember what I was thinking and feeling, but I was soon in a downward spiral that had become increasingly familiar. The next thing I can remember is being curled up in a ball in the corner behind the chair, my baby still in my arms, though I was not aware of that at first. As I came to, I began pleading with the Lord, though not at all humbly, to let me go, to revoke all his promises to me, to let me just crack up completely. I sensed some possibility of escape there, and I was quite willing to spend the rest of my life in a rubber room if I just didn't have to do this any more. Then, thinking of all the assurances that these experiences were preparing me to serve my brothers and sisters, I said a thing that seems terrible, even blasphemous, to me now: "I don't care if I can save the whole human race by enduring this for five more minutes. I can't! Let me go!"

I think it is pretty clear that at that moment I was not worthy of the companionship of the Holy Ghost in the ways we usually talk about. I would hesitate to call my raging at God prayer. I was not asking for help in making the decision. I had made my decision, though at the time I would have said it had been made for me by circumstance, and I knew it went contrary to his will. But the Spirit came to comfort me just the same, and it seems to me in retrospect that all the love in the universe was contained in two quiet words, "Get up."

Please note it was *in retrospect* that this seemed loving to me. At the time the beauty of all that escaped me completely. I couldn't believe what I had heard. I was so angry. I said, "Didn't you hear me? I'm not getting up any more. I've gotten up and gotten up and I can't do it again." Again it came. "Get up, Emily. It's all right. Get up."

At that moment my son began to wriggle. I think he had fallen asleep at my breast as he often did, and perhaps he awoke because he was so tightly wedged between my legs and my chest; but I have sometimes wondered if the Spirit didn't wake him up to help make his point. At any rate, the feel of that sweet, healthy little body helped to pull me back from the brink, and I got up.

The happy ending to this story didn't come right then, or the next day, or even very soon. In truth, there are very real ways in which it's still coming. The important part of the story for me is that at a time when my decisions were flowing out of a view of myself and my relationship to God that was just plain wrong, the Spirit intervened to begin the work of teaching me, line upon line, "the truth of all things" (Moroni 10:5). He showed me that I was not the helpless, hopeless heap in the corner of a living room in a corner of Wyoming that I thought I was. I was still, though I didn't fully understand it, a daughter of God and, though I understood this even less, he loved me. We still had things to do and, if I would let him teach me what they were, we would do them.

These three experiences, and others like them, have increased my appreciation of a passage from C. S. Lewis's essay, "The Weight of Glory": "The load, or weight, or burden of my neighbor's glory should be laid on my back, a load so heavy that only humility can carry it, and the backs of the proud will be broken. It is a serious thing to live in a society of possible gods and goddesses, to remember that the dullest and most uninteresting person you can talk to may one day be a creature which, if you saw it now, you would be strongly tempted to worship, or else a horror and a corruption such as you now meet, if at all, only in a nightmare. All day long we are, in some degree, helping each other to one or other of these destinations. It is in the light of these overwhelming pos-sibilities, it is with the awe and circumspection proper to them, that we should conduct all our dealings with one another, all friendships, all loves, all play, all politics. There are no *ordi-nary* people. You have never talked to a mere mortal."[1]

Living in a mortal world where my neighbor's glory is sometimes difficult to see, I thank God for the gift of the Holy Ghost. It is with joy and gratitude that I testify that although the "Spirit shall not *always* strive with man," it will strive for a very long time. When we are burdened and in pain and our own potential glory seems lost, when our marriages are difficult and troubled, when our children struggle, are disobedient and way-ward, when the sisters we are called to visiting teach are outside of our comfort zone, when our neighbor needs us, and

51

even when there is just someone in our world whom we haven't yet noticed we should love, the Spirit will say to us, "Look!"

May we choose to look.

NOTE

1. C. S. Lewis, "The Weight of Glory," *The Weight of Glory and Other Addresses* (1949; rpt. New York: Macmillan, 1980), 18–19.

IF YOU'RE A DRUMMER

SUSAN KAMEI LEUNG

One gospel concept I especially love is that the Lord created us each to be an individual. He sent each of us to earth to serve a unique set of missions in our own excellent, often different, ways. We serve him best by being the best of whomever he made us individually to be.

The Christmas song "The Little Drummer Boy" captures this simple but profoundly important concept. The little drummer boy wanted to give something special to the baby Jesus, but he was poor and could not afford the fine gold, frankincense, or myrrh that others had brought. Instead, he looked into his soul and found there his present—his music. When the time came to approach the stable, the little drummer boy didn't try to be what he wasn't. He didn't suddenly take up the violin or the trumpet. He realized that his ability to play the drum was his divine gift, and so he decided, "I'll play my best for him, pah-rum-pah-pum-pum." His gift of himself as a drummer boy, presented with all his heart, was a present more valuable than fine gold to the Christ child, who lovingly accepted his gift.

But to tell the truth, it has taken me some time and courage to understand that it is okay to be the little drummer boy while everyone else is playing the harp. When I first investigated the

Susan Kamei Leung has practiced corporate and real estate law and teaches in the graduate program of real estate development at the University of Southern California. She and her husband, W. Bing Leung, have one daughter. As stake historian, she wrote *How Firm a Foundation: The Story of the Pasadena Stake,* published in 1994.

Church, and for many years after my baptism, I was overwhelmed with the feeling that I didn't fit in. First I was the lonely convert who chose the "Families Are Forever" church over her own family. Then I was the wife of a nonmember, without priesthood blessings in my home. For several years, my husband and I endured Mother's Day programs and endless questions of "Aren't you having children? What are you waiting for?"

Perhaps you can relate to some of these feelings. It takes an eternal perspective to recognize that we each have a different role to play in this life, but it needn't take an eternity before we can enjoy and even take pride in our respective roles, even if they are not the same as others' roles, and especially if they are not what we thought our roles would be. Whatever our situations in life, the beauty of the gospel is that we can find acceptance and support from our Latter-day Saint brothers and sisters and certainly at all times from the Lord. Let me explain.

My decision at age twenty to join the Church did not come about because I had seen a vision or had heard angelic voices. Rather, my testimony evolved over an extended period of time, created by a layering of good examples and good feelings. I had to be sure of my feelings, because while I investigated the Church as a high-school and then college student, my parents very clearly disapproved. Born in southern California but raised in two very traditional Japanese homes, my parents feel no spiritual affinity to the Buddhism practiced by my grandparents, but neither do they consider themselves to be Christian or religious in any sense. They also have their own unfortunate misperceptions about the Church and its members, formed long before my interest in Mormonism.

They said up front that they did not want me involved with this "cult" and warned me that they would stop at nothing to keep me from joining. When I told them of my desire to be baptized, they said they would cut me off from the family. As far as they were concerned, I would no longer exist. I knew that my grandfathers had been cut off by their families when they left Japan about eighty years ago to find their fortunes in America. In fact, the names of those who emigrated from Japan were removed from the family registers with the government, so truly it is as if they never existed. Knowing this bit of family history and having seen similar events in other Japanese families, I knew full well my parents meant what they said.

In spite of their warnings, I reached the point during my senior year in college when I could no longer ignore the promptings of the Holy Ghost and was baptized. To say that my parents were livid is an understatement. Almost immediately they handled their anger by treating me as if I were a ghost, acting as if I were invisible. I think they felt that if they acknowledged me, they thereby acknowledged my new church membership. This continued, in varying degrees, for years. More than sixteen years later, talking about that painful and lonely time is still very difficult for me.

Please understand that my parents are wonderful people. My home, growing up, had been a happy one. I instantly understood the role of home and visiting teachers when I first heard about them because my parents are the quintessential home and visiting teachers. I have seen my mom single-handedly act like an entire Relief Society when someone was ill or in need. But my good, loving parents pressured me in the most powerful way they could to keep me from what they sincerely considered to be a big mistake. Once I disobeyed them, they felt they had to follow through on their threats or they would lose face. Even though I did what I thought was right by joining the Church, I know I have caused them great pain and that they will not understand my decision in this life.

My patriarchal blessing has always been a great comfort to me in my loneliness. It says in part, "You come from a race of people steeped in tradition, and find it . . . very difficult for the older members to understand the new things found in the lives of their children. This has been a difficult and trying experience

Completely typical example

55

for you in your family." I remember thinking at that point in the blessing, "That's putting it mildly!"

But I will always remember feeling the Lord speaking these next words through the patriarch, who did not know me very well. What he said has kept me going all these years: "But you are the key through which Heavenly Father is going to bless your family. They have been choice people, and Heavenly Father is very much aware of their need to have the gospel come into their lives. . . . So remain strong, faithful, and prayerful, that Heavenly Father's blessings can continue to pour down upon your entire family through you. In time, all of them will be able to give thanks to Heavenly Father for the great courage and strength that you have exhibited in breaking tradition and accepting the gospel that their lives may be enriched."

Over time, I have come to truly relate to Adam and Eve. Being the one in my family to leave a happy home (indeed, the Garden of Eden of homes) and break away for the fulness of the gospel has its share of lumps, but I have also come to realize that I play an unparalleled role in my family's eternal line. I feel honored that of all the individuals throughout eternity in my family line, Heavenly Father would give *me* the chance to bring my family into the house of Israel. Therefore, I have set about through family history and temple work to fulfill in some measure the destiny the Lord set forth for me as our family's gospel pioneer.

Once in ballet class, the ballet mistress said, "Use the opposition of forces to make the line beautiful." Temple work has turned the opposition of forces among my earthly family into a priority for making my eternal family line beautiful. Because of some sweet and sacred experiences in his holy house, I know that some of my ancestors indeed were waiting for their work to be done and have readily accepted the ordinances done on their behalf. Focusing on the eternal perspective has helped me deal with the temporal one. Remembering I have a role as the blessed, honored gospel pioneer has helped me deal with the sacrifices of pioneering.

Three factors have helped thaw my relationship with my parents over the years: my marriage to a then-nonmember, a life-threatening incident, and, at long last, a granddaughter. Blessings and lessons most decidedly do not always come the way one dreams they will.

My parents, who had begun to warm toward me when I began dating Bing, feared exclusion from their only daughter's wedding, were it to be in a temple. So they were delighted to hear Bing and I planned to marry in the Catholic church, his family's religion. They heartily approved of Bing from the beginning of our courtship: another Asian-American, a Stanford friend of my brother's, a dental student at Georgetown where I was a law student. That he was not a member of the Church was icing on the cake. My mother told Bing she expected him "to get me out of this Mormon nonsense."

I knew the risk I was taking, but I never made his joining the Church a condition of our relationship or love. I had heard of that working for others, but I did not ever feel that approach would be right for us. What I did feel, however, was that we were right for each other. From our second date, we resolved not to let our religious differences get in the way, and we looked for ways to focus on the many beliefs we had in common.

As newlyweds we worked out a Sunday schedule so that I could attend mass with Bing and he could attend sacrament meeting with me. In time, friendships, acts of service, and gospel teachings touched him, though not to the point of his feeling the need to join the Church. But ten years ago, we were all shaken out of our status quo when I started having terrible and inexplicable headaches. I ended up in the hospital with serious and worsening neurological damage caused by an injury to my brain, the consequence of a seemingly inconsequential fall on an escalator several months earlier one morning on my way to work.

At the time I was admitted to the hospital, I was partially paralyzed and couldn't stand or dress myself. My vision, hearing, and senses of smell and taste were impaired and failing fast. The pain was excruciating. The doctors finally determined that a large subdural hematoma was causing the swelling inside my cranium, and my nervous system was shutting down. The doctors told me I needed surgery to save my life. What they didn't tell me, and didn't need to tell me, was that I could die during surgery, and if I survived, I might not have the same quality of life I had enjoyed up to that point. My parents and brothers rushed to my hospital bedside from across the country, bygones at least for the moment bygones.

That night, I lay contemplating that I might be reporting to Heavenly Father on my twenty-seven-year-old life within the next twelve hours. My mind reviewed my life in slow motion. I will always remember that my only regret was that I had not had more time on earth. I found myself surprisingly satisfied with what I had done and felt that the Lord would be satisfied, too, with all my imperfections yet to be perfected and my missions yet to be fulfilled. I felt comforted, assured he would acknowledge that in some areas I had tried hard and achieved something, in others I had tried hard without achieving much of anything, and in others I hadn't tried hard enough, but that all of it was okay.

The next morning, I told Bing not to worry, that I knew our love was eternal, and spared him the reminder that our marriage was not. We had been married only about eighteen months. As the nurses nudged him out of my room to prepare me for surgery, Bing left without saying good-bye because, as he later told me, he could not bear the thought that he might not see me alive again.

Afterwards, in the first days of my recovery when I could do nothing except lie flat on my back in a dark room, I thought about why the Lord was letting me continue here on earth. For many months, the best I could do to fulfill the Lord's plans for me was not to practice law or to play the piano but to learn to walk again. About a year after the surgery, Bing gave me a gift certificate for ballet lessons as part of a physical therapy program to help me regain my coordination. I continue the ballet lessons to this day, no longer needed as physical therapy but because I have come to enjoy and treasure them as a token of my husband's thoughtfulness.

In the months and even years that followed, I had to work hard at recovering and learning to be patient with the rest of my life. Some consequences of that injury have been very hard to take, especially the impediment to my having children. But I have since realized that the Lord has plans for me. I believe that if I consecrate my life to the Lord, pursuing what he wants me to pursue and being what he wants me to be, that I will feel his peace and receive his blessings. My ultimate spiritual challenge is to live each day of the rest of my life in such a way that when my time does come to report to Heavenly Father, I will have the same feeling of acceptance and peace that I had that night in the hospital.

I would not have asked for these trials, but neither could I have imagined or hoped for the blessings that have followed. During my medical ordeal, Bing saw the power of priesthood blessings and wanted to exercise that power on my behalf himself. After almost losing me, he wanted our marriage to be sealed for time and all eternity. Within a few years of my surgery, Bing was baptized, when the time was right for him. He joined, willing to do whatever it took to worthily hold the Lord's priesthood. I am very proud of the gentle, capable leader he has become and grateful for his unflagging dedication to serving the Lord.

Now that we have a child (a miracle itself—but that's another story), our relationship with my parents has evolved into one of "don't ask, don't tell." For instance, my mother no

59

longer calls Sunday afternoons demanding to know where we have been all day, so she doesn't have to hear the answer that we were at church. She is now eager to have us come over—especially Kemi—so we can be together. To the saying, "Time heals what reason cannot," I would add that "grandchildren also help."

My family is geographically spread out, and our get-togethers are invariably on Sundays. On those relatively infrequent occasions, Bing and I extricate ourselves from our Sunday responsibilities because we feel it is important to be with my family. A bishop once told me that because we are commanded to be in sacrament meeting every Sunday, he thought our choice was wrong; if my family wasn't going to be in church with me, then I should be in church without them. He may have been right, but I feel I can't be a member missionary or an example to family I don't spend time with. Each of us is entitled to personal revelation and direct assurances from the Lord that we are making the choices he would have us make. We pray to choose the right course of action, and we must then trust in our relationship with Heavenly Father if our path takes us against the grain. That friend and bishop later acknowledged that not all decisions can be made strictly by the book.

Emotionally, though, this pull-and-tug is still trying, because our Church activity is an all-encompassing part of our lives. We want to share special Church-related events with my parents, such as our daughter's blessing. We see road show performances and seminary graduations on the not-so-distant horizon. We want them to be excited with us and for us, but that golden moment hasn't come yet. So the separation and emptiness continue to some degree.

Meanwhile, a loving circle of eternal friends has been like family along the way, sharing our joys and our sorrows. My dear friend Wendy Garey knew what it was like preparing to go to the temple for the first time alone. Among the many discreet yet practical ways she helped us when we didn't even know what help we needed was to volunteer to go with us to that counter at Beehive Clothing for the first time. Bing remembers how wonderful it was to have ward members at his baptism to welcome him into fellowship, so he attends as many baptisms in our ward as he can to extend that hand of friendship to new members.

Not all of us will have to face the challenges of gospel pioneering, health limitations, or part-member families. Not all of us are going to be Relief Society presidents (and you may say, "Thank heaven!"), or den mothers, or even mothers. We all will have different obstacles to overcome, different decisions to make, different callings to fulfill. I firmly believe that whatever our gifts to the stable may be—from arranging flowers to arranging funerals, from presiding in the boardroom to presiding in the rumpus room—that whatever we offer with righteous intent and pursue with divine guidance is worthy and acceptable to the Lord.

My feelings at first that I didn't fit into the Church without Church-member parents, a temple marriage, or children were in large part a function of my not realizing that there is no perfect mold to fit into. I now try to remember that others have their own disappointments and unfulfilled expectations as real as mine, that heartaches make us more empathetic to the struggles of others, and that what counts is that we serve the Lord as we are, with what we have, from where we are.

Please do not let yourself feel that what you can do isn't important or worthy enough. A sister once said to me, "Oh, I could never do all the wonderful things you do." Yet this wonderful sister has been a valued athletic director; I couldn't throw a softball to save my life. Someone else recently said to me that my calling as an assistant in the nursery was not a real calling, and certainly not as important as some of my other callings, such as writing and producing a book on the history of our Pasadena stake. What do you think the nursery-age children, or their parents, or our Primary president, or the Lord himself would say to that? I don't think our callings, our talents, our gifts of consecration have comparative value to the Lord. So if you're a drummer, drum away.

Let us not be intimidated by our life circumstances from striving for a life consecrated to fulfilling our divine nature in the best way we can. Let us be patient with those whom we love. Let us be patient with ourselves, for I believe the Lord will accept us, as he accepted that little drummer boy in the stable, with a smile and outstretched arms.

DAILY ACTS OF CONSECRATION

ROSEMARY CURTIS NEIDER

Are daily acts of consecration opportunities to do kind deeds? Recently I agreed to take out the garbage for my neighbors while they were out of town. My household was in such an uproar that week that I completely forgot about the garbage. My unfortunate but loyal husband removed the seats from our van and carried their two oversized containers to an innocent-looking dumpster. That was an act of sanitation, not consecration.

Later that week, I planned to take a little birthday something to my brother. Enroute I was not only hit by another car but, while waiting for the police, was plastered with wet, slushy snow tossed through my open window by an obliging snowplow. Thoroughly soaked, I finally spoke to a police officer, totally unaware that my two-year-old was busily decorating our velour car seats with a blue marking pen. That was an act of frustration.

Then there was the homemade chicken soup incident. My cousin, who lives quite a distance from me, was ill, and I wanted to help. Shortly before pulling up to her home with a delicious soup, I hit a bump, and the sudden jolt decorated the ceiling and windows of my car with peas, noodles, and bits of chicken. My treasured china tureen shattered. I had no money

Rosemary Curtis Neider received her bachelor's degree from Brigham Young University and has taught sixth grade. A homemaker, she and her husband, Michael A. Neider, are the parents of eight children. She serves as education counselor in her ward Relief Society.

with me, and small, hungry children were waiting to be fed. I could only hand my cousin's husband, who was visibly disappointed, the loaf of bread. That was an act of humiliation.

My life often reminds me of my favorite childhood movie, *Tarzan,* with Johnny Weismuller. Remember? Time after time visitors to the jungle were pursuing something precious—ivory tusks, jewels, rare rubies. The angry natives captured and tortured the intruders, sometimes tying their arms and legs to wild animals to stretch them in four different directions, catapulting them across a ravine, or throwing them into an alligator-infested river. Too often my life feels just like that. I am the prisoner whose outstretched arms and legs are tied to bamboo trees, who waits with a headache for the background drums to reach their frenzied peak so the natives can split me apart.

We are all in a jungle of sorts, pursuing what we think is precious: raising a family, loving a husband, making a living, fulfilling a Church calling. Daily acts of consecration may seem like the furthest thing from our agenda. Consecration usually comes in the form of inconveniences: alligators, restless natives, elephant stampedes. I am beginning to see that we refer to acts of consecration as being daily mostly because on the day they were needed, they were given.

I was blessed to learn about gentle acts of consecration from my parents. When I was thirteen, I was delivering political tracts for a relative running for office in our community. At one home, a woman read the flyer and began to make bitter, heated, unkind comments about my extended family. Tears streamed down my face as I made my way home, anxious to tell my mother. She wouldn't let this woman get away with such offensive, insulting behavior. When I told my sad tale, Mom suggested that we make cookies for the woman. I really couldn't believe what I was hearing; maybe Mom hadn't understood. But an hour later, I sat in the car with a plate of cookies. "Just say you're sorry you upset her and wish her a good day," Mom encouraged, dropping me off at the woman's doorstep.

Consecration is returning cookies for unkindness.

A young woman I know struggled so with her home life that she ran away and eventually moved in with a friend of mine. At age sixteen, she had rarely been treated or spoken to kindly. Hoping for a fresh start, she changed high schools. I helped her check out of her old school. Most teachers marked F on her checkout slip and looked at her as if she were a hopeless case. I could feel their disdain as they tallied up her absences. No one asked why she was leaving or where she was headed. Her last stop was the library, where she needed a signature verifying she had no fines. Here a kindly older woman with a beautiful smile looked at her checkout slip, signed in the appropriate place, and then turned to this troubled young woman. "This isn't you," she said. She put her arms around the girl and hugged her warmly, "I know you'll do well in your next school. This isn't you."

Consecration is valuing another.

My mother died when she was in her early forties. She left seven children, ranging in age from a five-year-old to a newly-wed (me). I remember well the rainy November evening of her funeral. On a long, built-in seat against the window in our family room, my father lined up brown paper grocery sacks and filled them one by one with plants and the lovely food we had received from caring neighbors and friends. I couldn't imagine what he was doing. In the dark and cold, he carried the sacks out to our station wagon. I'll never forget his explanation: "This is more than we can possibly use. Your mother would want this food taken to those who are less fortunate."

Some would be surprised that he was aware of anyone less fortunate than we were that night. But we were surrounded by rich feelings of the Spirit, which flooded our home with love and a sense of well-being. To my heart, it made perfect sense for my father to remember the needs of others in his time of need.

Consecration is absolute gratitude.

Shortly before my mother died, the doctors counseled my father to call the family in to see her one last time. It was late on a Saturday night. My father, who was the stake president, had just completed the Saturday evening adult session of stake conference. He hadn't wanted to attend, but my mother insisted that he deliver his talk on the Book of Mormon, which they had prepared together in the previous weeks. We rounded up teenagers from dates, rousted little ones from bed, and drove to the hospital. As we entered her room, Mother, who had had difficulty breathing and had been quite uncomfortable, was now beautiful and serene as she sat up in her bed, smiled at each of us, and extended her arms to us.

I don't know what she said to each child. I recall only what she said to me as I took my turn to be close to her and feel her touch. She reminded me of her confidence in me and love and then asked me to stay in touch with two girls I had known since childhood. They weren't particularly close friends, and I hadn't thought about them for some time. I was a newlywed, completely absorbed in the events of my own life. But she expressed concern for their welfare. Her final words intrigued me, and as the years have gone by, I see that Mother showed me consecration as an attitude of concern for others.

The sacred, ongoing acts of caring for others on our journey through the jungle lead us to real wealth. None of these stories is a "daily" story. Mothers die only once, thank heaven, and cookies are not often required as part of a campaign. We get only so many chances to change schools or make compassionate gestures to people who might be hurting as much or more than we are. I don't think Tarzan had to save people every day. Some days he just hung around the tree house with Jane and drank coconut milk. But when the need arose, he was there.

Usually acts of consecration come in the form of inconveniences and bad timing, leading us to confuse them with frustration, humiliation, and even sanitation. Consecration is our willingness to give of ourselves and of our resources in daily acts of kindness. How do we do that when we ourselves are overwhelmed?

It helps to be where we should be when we should be there. We need to keep doing what the Savior would have us do because that is the time he will best be able to strengthen us.

I once attended sacrament meeting when I was really discouraged. I had had sick children for weeks and was exhausted. My husband and I were dealing with problems I couldn't discuss with anyone. One of the tortures I experience is acting as if everything is fine when inside I am crying out for help. Not all problems can appropriately be shared.

Two men gave talks at that sacrament service, and as I listened, I was bathed with a feeling that all would be well. Understanding, peace, and strength filled me. I looked around the room; it seemed to be just another meeting to everyone else. But I knew that inspiring message from a loving Heavenly Father was specially delivered to me through these servants.

Shortly before Easter this year I realized that my visiting teaching wasn't done. I was tempted to make phone visits . . . again. A message from President Gordon B. Hinckley in the *Ensign* prompted me to make one last effort. He said the symbol of our religion should be found in the lives of our members. As I sat in the home of an eighty-seven-year-old woman who had only limited experience with gospel living, I was impressed to read to her about the Nephites touching the hands and feet of the resurrected Savior. We read on about the little children being brought to him and of the angels ministering to them. She concentrated longer than I had ever expected, and she kept saying, "Here, now, put a piece of paper in that page so I can find it again later. Oh, put one there, too."

What can I say? I felt the Spirit strongly in her home, and my complex, hurried schedule didn't matter anymore. I felt gratitude and an increase of strength for many days afterward.

Spiritual satisfaction comes almost daily if we put our lives in accordance with his will.

In the kitchen of my childhood home, a plaque on the wall read: "To do carefully and constantly and kindly many little things is not a little thing." While some people have been out in the world doing great things, I have been home doing many little things that hardly seem worth mentioning and yet have been very challenging to me. We had two more babies while in our forties and have known three years with barely a full night's rest. My husband has been a bishop or stake president for much of our marriage and has therefore been gone a great deal. His consecration is also my consecration. He could not do what he does without my doing what I do at home, even though I may feel frustrated and isolated at times.

I love the scripture in which Joshua speaks to the tribes of Israel as they face a most difficult task: "Sanctify yourselves: for to morrow the Lord will do wonders among you" (Joshua 3:5). Giving the benefit of the doubt, listening, problem solving, instilling belief, praising, returning goodness for unkindness— these take conscious effort. They are a "wonder," and I am very much a student in learning to do them.

Though little things rarely sound great and sometimes seem of little value, consecration is doing the little things carefully and constantly and kindly. For instance, over the last twenty-three years of our married life, my husband, Mike, has generally come through the door of our home cheerfully calling out, "How can I help?"

How *can* we help? If we have an attitude of consecration and prayer in our hearts, the Lord will use each of us to work a mighty wonder.

CHOICES AND

THE HOLY GHOST

SHIRLEY W. THOMAS

In a letter dated 5 December 1839, the Prophet Joseph Smith and Church historian Elias Higbee wrote to the high council in Nauvoo from Washington City, as it was then called, to report on their visit with the president of the United States, Martin Van Buren. They were seeking redress for wrongs suffered by the saints in Missouri. In part the letter read: "In the most honorable cause that ever graced the pages of human existence . . . we have taken up our cross. . . . Arrived . . . 28th November, and spent the most of that day in looking [for] . . . as cheap boarding as can be had in this city."[1] Reading that they had to spend time looking for the cheapest boarding in town makes me feel tender about them but not sorry for them. They were on the Lord's errand and filled with his Spirit; that's not a piteous state.

The letter continued: "On Friday morning, 29th, we proceeded to the house of the President . . . a very large and splendid palace . . . decorated with all the fineries and elegancies of this world. We went to the door and requested to see the President, when we were immediately introduced into an

Shirley W. Thomas has served as a counselor in the Relief Society General Presidency and as a member of the Relief Society General Board. She and her husband, Robert K. Thomas, formerly academic vice-president at Brigham Young University, are the parents of three children.

upper apartment, where we met the President." They next described the meeting, in which they showed remarkable poise at President Van Buren's prompt rebuff: "'What can I do? I can do nothing for you.'" They wrote, "We were not to be intimidated; and demanded a hearing [before the Congress], and constitutional rights."[2] The confidence of those two, lacking as they did training or experience in matters of politics or state, witnesses how decisive one can be when accompanied with the power of the Spirit.

Then, in a long postscript to the letter, Joseph Smith recorded an interesting statement about the Holy Ghost. Answering President Van Buren's question of how the Latter-day Saint religion differed from other churches of the day, Joseph said, "We differed in mode of baptism, and the gift of the Holy Ghost by the laying on of hands. We considered that all other considerations were contained in the gift of the Holy Ghost."[3] That is an unusual expression of breadth in the role of the Holy Ghost. Joseph understood that the Holy Ghost plays a crucial part in bringing to our finite world of decision making the infinite verities of truth and love. "Yea, by the unspeakable gift of the Holy Ghost," says the scripture, "God shall give unto you knowledge by his Holy Spirit" (D&C 121:26).

The Holy Ghost is also a means for the Father to stay close to us. As the Spirit touches our lives, the truth he conveys bears witness of the Father's love. Making the right decisions matters. God wants us to succeed. He wants us to return to him. And the Holy Ghost is our great ally. He sheds the light of truth on decisions we face, until right choices become clear.

We get an idea of the importance of this truth to us and how determined the Almighty is that we have it in his emphatic and reassuring statement to a discouraged Joseph Smith in Liberty Jail: "As well might man stretch forth his puny arm to stop the Missouri river in its decreed course, or to turn it up stream, as to hinder the Almighty from pouring down knowledge from heaven upon the heads of the Latter-day Saints" (D&C 121:33).

Elder Marion G. Romney counseled the women of the Relief Society: "Learn to recognize and follow the guidance of the Holy Spirit. Without such guidance, even a knowledge of the word of God is unfruitful. . . . Properly cultivated and developed, this gift is of inestimable value. . . . [It] will enlighten our minds, quicken our understandings, and increase our intelligence."[4]

I needed all these—light, understanding, and intelligence—when at age fifteen I was deciding whether to be baptized into the Church. I lacked the advantage of attending Primary to learn about the Holy Ghost and choosing the right. Also, because my association with the Church was through friendshipping efforts of members and at that time not every stake seemed to have missionaries, I missed receiving missionary discussions and did not have an acquaintance with the Book of Mormon, either. But I did, finally, have the permission of both my parents to become a member of the Church if I chose to. I wanted to know if the Church was true, but I did not hear a resounding *yes*. I received no impression or answer that I could call certain, but I had a good feeling about going to the church, a sense of being at home. I believed what I was learning there and liked the way I felt when I was with the members. I wanted to be one with them. So I chose to be baptized, and I didn't ever wonder again about the Church being true. I knew that it was. I have since learned that the Holy Ghost's quiet persuasion was what led me to baptism and witnessed to me the truth of the gospel.

I find important meaning in the scripture, "Rejoice, and cleave unto the covenants which thou hast made" (D&C 25:13). In the covenant of baptism, for example, we commit to following Christ, to being called by his name, and we are given a wondrous source of eternal truth, the Holy Ghost. In such covenants we can sense the heart of our Father in Heaven. He wants for his children all he can give, and so he grants them individual agency, despite the jeopardy that poses for them. Then, to bring about their safe passage through earth life, he establishes covenants. He wants us to return, and covenants, by defining the way of holiness and our commitment to it, form a protection against the power of evil.

I learned through the experience of coming to baptism that the Holy Ghost often manifests truth through good feelings. That may be the most common way—the response we usually call the feeling of peace, of accord. Moroni 7:16 states: "I show unto you the way to judge; for every thing which inviteth to do good, and to persuade to believe in Christ, is sent forth by the power and gift of Christ; wherefore ye may know with a perfect knowledge it is of God." The inviteth-to-do-good feeling is a useful guide.

After I had been a member of the Church nearly four years, I had a much different experience in making an important decision. At this time, I was a sophomore at Brigham Young University, sitting at my desk in Amanda Knight Hall writing a letter to a young lieutenant in the Air Force. I was telling him that I had approval from my parents to stay a day or two in California with my aunt en route home from school that spring. He was posted at nearby Santa Ana Air Base. He was a very nice Latter-day Saint young man whom I had met and dated the year before while I was home for Christmas. We had since been corresponding, a typical wartime friendship. As I was writing this letter, I received a message from the Spirit—in words. Often messages come to us in what we call strong feelings, but this message came in distinct, clearly defined words: "He is not the right one for you."

I had not known that could happen, and if I had, I certainly would not have expected it to happen to me. I dropped my pen, stopped writing, and never wrote to him again. (It would have been nice to have written something, but I didn't.) I was amazed. It was many years before I felt I could tell anyone about the experience. It was so personal, so singular, and so sacred. I have since heard of similar expressions of the Spirit, but it was new to me that day.

Although in the two instances I have shared with you the Holy Ghost manifested the truth differently, the truths in each case were equally valid. The decision made because of the quiet persuasion of a peaceful feeling following personal inquiry, weighing, "study[ing] it out in [my] mind" was as right as the one made because the Spirit intervened in what I was planning with a compelling, unmistakable direction that could not be misunderstood (D&C 9:8). Both reflected my need at the time; both were of eternal consequence. One decision was as right as the other. What's important is that we identify the Spirit, however it is manifest, and not only recognize it but act upon it. The marvel is that we can and do have the Spirit come to us. It is amazing to me that a member of the eternal Godhead can actually be a companion to me and to you. I don't even worry about the metaphysics of it. I have had experience enough to know that it is true, and as the hymn says, "I scarce can take it in."[5]

This same feeling of joyous surprise was shared with me by a dear sister many years ago after a sacrament meeting in the Hyde Park chapel in London. Her experience had to do with prayer. Deciding what to ask in our prayers is one of the important choices we have. Reading of the Nephite disciples of Jesus being given the words to pray suggests to us how the Holy Ghost has guided others (3 Nephi 19:24). That is sometimes called praying in the Spirit (D&C 46:28, 30).

That Sunday in London was in June 1978, the weekend of the announcement of the revelation on the priesthood. I happened to be in England on a Relief Society assignment. The lovely sister I spoke with was the mother of two boys of Aaronic Priesthood age. The family was of African heritage. At the sacrament meeting, just finished, these two newly ordained priesthood holders had passed the sacrament for the first time. The tearful mother was receiving expressions of love from the also-tearful ward members. They shared her joy. Those two young men had faithfully attended priesthood meetings, hoping for the day they could fully participate. I knew how faithfully because one of our sons, participating in the BYU Semester Abroad in London the year before, had taught the teachers quorum in the ward. He had written from London to tell us about his class that each week consisted of three boys, two of whom were the sons of this woman. He had told us particularly of his admiration for the dedication and devotion of those two young men.

As the people in the foyer dispersed, the mother of the boys told the small group remaining that only a few days before, as she was praying, she had received the extraordinary invitation by the Spirit that she might ask whatever she would like. With her eyes brimming, she told us how overwhelmed she had been by the experience. She had always tried to feel the direction of the Spirit in her prayers and had never felt it appropriate to ask for the priesthood for her sons, even though that had always been what she really wanted. Now, after this experience was followed so soon by the announcement from Church headquarters, she realized that while the revelation was for the entire Church, the Lord acknowledged her individual hopes and addressed them personally. The Holy Ghost had invited her to pray for whatever she would like, knowing that this most important desire could now be realized.

Although people have remarkable experiences with the Spirit, most daily decisions we make are guided by peaceful feelings or by promptings—the quiet workings of the Holy Ghost—still and small. Many decisions must be made quickly, and for me, it is in these, with the continual fine-tuning of my will to the Lord's that these require, that I most often sense the companionship of the Holy Ghost. I have learned to recognize the disruptive feeling that comes if I offend the Spirit; I know quickly that something is wrong. As for the more unusual manifestations, they are just that, unusual, and though we cherish them, it may not be given us to ask for or even anticipate them. President Spencer W. Kimball counseled that "expecting the spectacular, one may not be fully alerted to the constant flow of revealed communication."[6] Knowing the communication is constant prompts us to keep close to the Spirit, ready to receive. Elder Marion G. Romney said to the sisters, "Seek [the Holy Ghost] by faith and by prayer, by study, and by righteous living. Learn what the scriptures say about it, including, particularly, the teachings of the Prophet Joseph Smith."[7]

In the scriptures we learn of the breadth of the role of the Holy Ghost. Besides bringing wisdom, understanding, a sound mind, boldness, power, revelation, testimony, and healing, the Holy Ghost sanctifies (3 Nephi 27:20). When we are filled with the Spirit, we have no more disposition to choose anything contrary to the Lord's will; we purify our souls and yield our hearts unto God. That is not always easy.

Three years ago, one of our sons called to tell us they had just learned their oldest child, Sean, a handsome fourteen-year-old teacher in the Aaronic Priesthood, honor student, and Eagle Scout, had a brain tumor. I tried to finish vacuuming the floor I had been cleaning, but I kept stopping to plead with the Lord. My prayer went something like, "Surely, this can't be! There must be a mistake. Isn't there some other way? I know about thy Son, but that was such an important part of the plan, and there would seem to be nothing gained by this." After a long time there came the promised feeling of calm and a strong sense that it would be all right. I thought, Yes, Sean will be all right. I began to believe that it would just be a matter of time until he would be well again and shooting baskets on the driveway.

After the surgery and learning that the growth was actually larger than the image seemed to show and one grade more malignant than the doctors had at first believed, we had to realign our hopes. But maybe, I thought, they had been able to remove it all, and maybe the radiation would assure no tumor cell growth. For three years we watched and prayed. When each MRI (magnetic resonance imaging) gave a clear reading, we learned to hope that his would be one of the exceptional cases. I kept remembering the feeling I'd had.

Then in January the MRI was not clear. The tumor had returned. This time surgery was not possible, for the growth was too random. *Terminal* can be a terrifying word, but our son related this worst-case news, acknowledged our grief, and with an understanding born of faith and tried in pain, said, "Yes, it is hard," and then the words, "*but it's all right.*"

What he and his wife had come to know, and what we all must, is that finally—and it may be in some of the most difficult of choices, the dearest of desires—our decision-making becomes acceptance. We come closer to Christ and, yielding our hearts, want only what is God's will. We may still hope for a "ram in the thicket"—I do—yet we know that, by choice, we must give our hearts to God. I have learned that in even trying to do this, we can feel peace, and in the love conveyed by the Holy Spirit, we can "cleave unto the covenants which [we have] made" and "lift up [our] heart[s]" (D&C 25:13). As Joseph Smith wrote that day in the city of Washington, all other considerations are caught up in this unspeakable gift, which testifies to us of the truth of God's love.

NOTES

1. Joseph Smith, *History of The Church of Jesus Christ of Latter-day Saints,* 2d ed. rev., ed. B. H. Roberts, 7 vols. (Salt Lake City: Deseret Book Co., 1960), 4:40.

2. Ibid.

3. Ibid., 4:42.

4. Marion G. Romney, "The Guidance of the Holy Spirit," *Relief Society Magazine,* Feb. 1965, 90–91.

5. *Hymns of The Church of Jesus Christ of Latter-day Saints* (Salt Lake City: The Church of Jesus Christ of Latter-day Saints, 1985), no. 86.

6. Spencer W. Kimball, *The Teachings of Spencer W. Kimball,* ed. Edward L. Kimball (Salt Lake City: Bookcraft, 1982), 457.

7. Romney, "Guidance of the Holy Spirit," 91.

GOOD SEASONS AND HOT PEPPER
IN A STRING BEAN CASSEROLE

SHERLENE HALL BARTHOLOMEW

My mother, Ida-Rose Langford Hall, married at twenty and mothered seven children, of whom I am the eldest. She was my heroine while I was growing up—at least until my teen years, when I discovered I knew more than she ever could about the truly important things. But at least until then, I was impressed that my mother, even without a college degree, could do just about anything.

Mom took a few college courses before she stopped to bear children and help my father get his Ph.D., but she is basically a self-educated woman. When she wanted to research Scandinavian genealogy, she took a class, learned how, and showed Sherlock Holmes the door. When she decided to refinish furniture, she read a book, and soon an entire wall of cabinets with a set-in, matching piano emerged in the caressed polish of her artistry.

Mother sewed tailored, lined coats and elegant prom dresses for five daughters, tied Scout knots of the most secure kind with two sons and a few dozen Blazer boys, ran a creative and successful business enterprise when we children were

---

Sherlene Hall Bartholomew has taught English in the public schools and composition at Brigham Young University and the University of Utah. She served a mission in Germany and stake missions in Illinois, New York, and New Jersey. She and her husband, Dan R. Bartholomew, have two children. Sister Bartholomew teaches family history in her Orem ward and at BYU.

grown, published a book on family history, tended exquisite orchids and roses, was a community and church leader, and never lacked for interesting and helpful projects.

She and my father enjoy a solid, supportive marriage. Undoubtedly through the years they had trials, but I overlooked them. As I grew and watched them, I thought each year of their lives seemed better and more prosperous. My parents were an inspiring example of the American and also the Latter-day Saint dream come true. I resolved to follow their pattern.

I participated with solemn commitment in all those MIA rose-tying ceremonies, fully believing that as long as I lived a clean life and followed the commandments, my life would be as fragrant and unbruised as one of those perfect, white roses. I felt certain that by following what I interpreted as gospel formulae, I would avoid pricking myself on any of life's thorns.

I patterned my life after my mother's, though with her encouragement, I determined to graduate from college. By attending the Y every semester, summers included, I could graduate and then marry at age twenty-one. By then, certainly, one of my missionaries would return and confess his eternal love for God and me before angels at a temple altar. We would drive off into a sunset glowing with all the blessings inherent in living the full gospel life.

As I carefully plotted out the seasons of my life, however, I failed to consider that in the last days not only nature's seasons would be subject to change but my own life seasons might not come and go precisely as planned, either. In my teens, while my friends were maturing on schedule and beginning to date, I was a late bloomer who grew in only one direction—up! All the way through high school, I was inches taller than most of the young men and had the figure of a string bean, which was not then in fashion.

I felt ready and anxious to go on a mission at age nineteen, but by the time I was twenty-one and finally old enough for a mission call, other, more romantic interests held my attention.

When the bishop called me in, I had to readjust my thinking yet again. After returning from a two-year South German mission, I began counting broken engagements as fast as my girlfriends were counting new babies.

At age twenty-six, I had completed a bachelor's degree in English and political science at BYU, was certified to teach English in grades seven through twelve in Utah, and was well on my way to completing a master's degree in early American literature at the University of Utah, when Dan Bartholomew proposed—only six weeks before he was to drive back East to begin work at Bell Labs. I accepted his proposal and hurriedly sewed together my wedding veil in the halls of Salt Lake City's East High, where I was completing my student teaching. Without the last-minute stitching of my talented sisters, my dress would never have been finished in time for the ceremony.

After a Salt Lake Temple wedding, we moved to Illinois, where Dan also had a company scholarship to pursue graduate work at the University of Chicago. I struggled with my faith while deciding whether to follow Church leaders' suggestions to newlyweds about beginning and continuing families. (That was before First Presidency statements cautioned members to consider such factors as a mother's physical and mental health.) If family fertility on both sides was any indication, such suggestions were an invitation to count on a new baby every nine months up to and beyond my fiftieth birthday.

After prayer and fasting, Dan and I decided to follow Church counsel and welcome as many children into our family as soon and as often as he provided. I did not search out a teaching position in Illinois, because I was certain morning sickness loomed on the immediate horizon. Instead I took a secretarial job, making sure my employer understood that I planned to begin a typically large Mormon family and might soon be ill and bulging. Many months passed, however, and soon my fears of early pregnancy turned into anxiety that I would never be a mother.

Twenty-five years later I can report only two babies for all that concern and all those years of determined nonprevention. How grateful we are we did not postpone having children, because they came during years we were tempted to wait.

We tried to add to our family by agreeing on six occasions to receive foster children and babies, each with the hope of eventual adoption. Because we already had two children of our own, however, agencies seemed inclined to give us the less secure cases. Again and again, parents or guardians changed their minds. Three babies that did arrive were, at various stages, taken from our arms—one at an age old enough to be calling us "Mommy and Daddy."

I also experienced several miscarriages through the years, which drained our energies and hopes; exploratory surgery and several fertility doctors were also no help. Only those who have visited those doctors and clinics over years can under-stand the emotional price for those who dearly want children.

We allowed the grief of those disappointments and other stresses to settle into our marriage relationship, and at age forty-two I found myself separated from my husband, on the way to a divorce, and essentially responsible, after sixteen years of homemaking, for the support of our two young teenagers, who were in my custody.

Life was not at all what I had planned. I was aware of many of my faults and failings, but I felt I had tried very hard to live the gospel both inside and outside our home. In addition to the agony of our marital situation, I felt spiritually disillusioned and betrayed. What about all those promises and happy formulae in my patriarchal blessing and in the gospel teachings? Had I listened wrong? Perhaps I had drunk formula all those years because I could not yet stomach the plentiful meat, gristle, and string-in-the-bean also clearly defined by our leaders. But still, where was the ride into the sunset after the temple marriage? Where were the sunsets, period?

At the invitation of my bishop, I received a special blessing from my stake patriarch in New York shortly after my husband and I separated. I was told in this blessing that my life had been an example of faith, but I would yet learn much more about faith in my Savior. I felt a little insulted at that point in the blessing because I thought my faith was already very strong. The blessing continued, and then I heard the comforting promise that in not many years the clouds would part and I would bask in the sunshine of the Lord's blessings—words at that time incomprehensible to me.

Since that blessing, I *have* learned much about faith and about adjusting to life's changing seasons—whether balmy or stormy. First, I realized that my expectations had been inflexible. Our faith must be in the Lord, no matter what our circumstance. We cannot expect faith to eliminate the very difficulties that will prepare us to be more like him. I wish I had spent less time arguing with the Lord about his timing and my dissatisfaction with my circumstances and more energy trying to accept my lot. I appreciate a cartoon I saw showing an embattled warrior stretching trembling hands toward heaven, asking, "Why me?" From the thundering clouds comes the response, "Why not?"

It has taken years to understand what my beloved grandmother Zina Charlotte Chlarson Langford was trying to teach me whenever I tried to get out of a task or unpleasant assignment by asking, "Why do I have to?" She would respond, "Why is a duck." It was not a question. Her strange answer ended the conversation. It worked—and so did I.

The question is not, "Why, Lord?"—a way of ducking responsibility—but, rather, "What is thy will for me in this circumstance? Help me to be the best person I can be throughout this difficulty." No matter how much pain we experience, we can trust that if our prayers are humble and grateful, rather than bitter and angry, the Lord will fill our minds with creative ideas and our souls with energy to carry them out. If we are willing to do our part, in harmony with answers to prayer, the Spirit can ease our difficulties or enhance our ability to cope. Not only will our Father in Heaven relieve our anguish but he will provide opportunities that will strengthen us and lead to a significant measure of personal growth.

Second, I have learned to accept service opportunities that the Lord extends, no matter how incongruous the call may seem at the time. We certainly may discuss our particular challenges with the priesthood leader extending the call. He may change his mind; however, we need to keep an open heart and search our minds to find a way for the Lord to extend the blessings he sees will arise from a particular call. For example, I was asked to visiting teach a sister who had for some years declined to welcome the Relief Society sisters into her home. She was divorced and had been inactive for years; we did not seem at the time to have much in common. It took several visits before we were even admitted to her home; once we entered her door, she made it clear she had no desire for gospel discussion of any kind. I simply tried to be of service, to listen well, and to be a friend. One day, months later, she was the one to begin a gospel discussion—the first of many.

When I was separated from my husband, this sister became my dearest friend. She offered me a room in her home and peeked in carefully during the two days that I assumed a fetal position on the bed, refusing to eat and wishing to die. It was this dear sister who coaxed warm noodle soup down me, let me know she understood exactly how I felt, and assured me with empathy—not pity—that she had survived such a crisis, and so would I.

I enjoyed some of the most spiritual experiences of my life under her roof, which at one time seemed inhospitable to the gospel. Today this sister is active in the Church, makes marvelous contributions to her ward, and is a joy and inspiration to many. How I have repented of the day I ever said, "Why me, Lord? Why can't I just once visiting teach a normal, active member of the Church who will be like a sister?"

Further, my calling to the ward nursery of more than thirty toddlers paved the way, as much as my six years of college, to landing me a job teaching in a Scarsdale, New York, elementary school during the first year of separation from my husband. The second year of our separation, the money I earned teaching was not enough to pay the bills and the house payment. The children and I were strongly attached to our home, where we had lived for ten years. Staying there was important as we struggled for some degree of stability and continuity.

At the end of the school year, I reluctantly left teaching to accept a salaried job selling long-distance telephone service for a very small company that resold AT&T lines at competitive rates. As I went through their training programs, I knew I had a better way. My mission experience had taught me that each potential client must be approached with a plan tailored to meet specific needs, not pressed to adopt some rote company hard sell. I ignored the training instructions and earned customers' interest by engaging the understanding of human need and nature I had learned on a mission. It helped, too, to be convinced of the quality and value of my product. Within weeks I was outselling the other six salespeople combined. Soon I was doing the training, but as my success and our income escalated, so did my stress level.

I remember well what it was like those difficult two years. I got up at 5:00 A.M. to rouse our children (about four hours after they finally settled down), got breakfast, and transported them to seminary in Scarsdale by 6:00. While they were exercising spiritually, I speed-walked around the high school track across the way for forty-five minutes, often listening to scripture tapes, praying, or thinking. By the time the seminary hour ended, the school bus had left, so I then drove Laura and Dan to White Plains High, where they were the only LDS students. Then I had fifteen minutes at home to shower and get ready for work.

Our children also sacrificed during the separation. They both got after-school jobs and assumed more responsibility around the house. I returned home from work at 5:30 P.M. to begin the rounds of meals, housework, food and other shopping, and driving the children to evening church and school events. I also spent many hours and dollars with attorneys and counselors, working out the divorce, which was automatically to become final, under New York law, after two years of separation.

Desperately needing some peace and comfort in my chaotic life during this time of trauma at home, I attended a satellite broadcast of a fireside with President Ezra Taft Benson. As I listened to his ten points for parenting—which I recall were specifically directed to mothers in the Church—I was overcome by the contrast between the targeted ideals and what my own children were then experiencing, and I bolted from the meeting in tears.

At home, I locked my bedroom door, threw myself down on my bed, beat my fists upon the mattress, and indulged in some unsuppressed screaming. After two or three simmering days, in which I more than once shook my fist toward heaven in frustration, I finally humbled myself, knelt by my bed, and begged the Lord to forgive me. I pleaded for help to rout out those dark feelings. I asked him to help me understand why, when I felt I was doing all I could, my best effort was still miserably insufficient. Why were even more requirements being added to my mothering responsibilities when I felt I was already shouldering an impossible load? And what about the men in this Church, anyway? Why weren't they getting their ten points, too? (Had I listened more carefully through my pain, I might have heard President Benson's clear call to husbands as well.)

I do not now remember the exact words, but as I knelt that day the Lord etched this thought in my mind: "Sherlene, my dear, beloved daughter, the words of my prophet are not just another burden. They are a promise you can hold onto for strength. They are a blessing to you, if you are only willing to try your best. Why don't you quit trying to be your own savior and let your Lord carry your burdens? Take his yoke upon you—it is so much lighter than what you impose upon yourself." Joy and peace beyond description filled me. I felt forgiven of my sins, and my mind welled with creative ideas for managing this season in my life. Still beside my bed, I thanked the Lord for sharing this problem, and I enjoyed my best night's sleep in a long time.

I had previously tried unsuccessfully to get more flexible hours from my employer. Instead, he and his wife were demanding longer hours and even more production; they also had reneged on promised bonuses. I began interviewing for other positions and had the promise of a good job as a personnel manager in my back pocket before I went to bargain with them.

My husband, Dan, had also heard President Benson's broadcast and offered to bridge the financial gap, should I be caught between jobs. It was the most cooperative thing the two of us had done in nearly two years.

I went to my employer and let him know the value of my unpaid bonuses, agreeing to forgo that debt if he would pay me what I was worth for selling twice as much as the other employees. I asked him to halve my working hours for the same pay. I figured my Jewish boss should understand about prophets and explained that I was responding to the counsel of President Benson, who had requested that all mothers be at the crossroads for their children. I even suggested he send his wife home afternoons to be with their two children. I let them know I was prepared to leave for another job, if they could not grant my request.

My employer treated my request as ludicrous and refused even to consider it. He suggested that if I wanted to quit, I could put on my coat and leave immediately. I thanked him and his wife for the good times with the company and was halfway down the stairs when they called me back. Would I please review the accounts I was leaving behind, so they could plan reassignment? I took a deep breath and followed the Spirit, which said this was a chance to model Christian values. I discussed my active accounts with them for more than an hour. As I rose to leave, I was asked to wait in the coffee shop below while they consulted once more about my request.

I got my half-day at the same pay, allowing me to be more fully at the crossroads for our children. Better yet, my husband and I began negotiating, too. That amazing process, which renewed our marriage, began with a prophet's concern for the rearing of children. Thus I learned a third lesson, one I thought I already knew: Follow the prophets.

Now that I am fifty and have just returned to live in Utah after twenty-three years of life in Illinois, New York, and New Jersey, I can look with a sense of wonder at how much the Lord has blessed me over the past half century. Dan and I have put together our marriage, through a series of miracles that came in the wake of much individual and joint counseling, consistent personal effort on both our parts, faith exercised by our loved ones and leaders, the cooperation of our children, and priesthood blessings. The Lord has bound us in a love and unity I would not have believed possible only seven years ago.

We are blessed to have a returned missionary son, now a student at Brigham Young University, and a lovely missionary daughter, who writes from Ecuador of deep bonds of appreciation and love for her native companions. After witnessing miraculous conversions of the honest in heart, she tells us she has changed her mind about missions for young women being optional. Laura now thinks every woman who can should fill a mission. (This daughter used to label my handing out copies of the Book of Mormon as overzealous rabidity. She was probably right, but she seems happy to have caught the inclination.)

Life also has challenges at this age, but most of the time my heart is overflowing with gratitude for life's bounty. I am enthusiastic about challenges, enriched by abundant opportunity to learn and create, enticed by many avenues for service, and feel constant wonder at the grace Jesus offers me. I do not experience much fear in the face of trial, because I have felt myself in the jaws of hell and, through our Lord's mercy, did not get swallowed up, after all. Now that I believe in miracles again, the bad times pale in the face of remembered blessings. When we are in pain, all we can remember is that hurt. We need to remember that pain ends. New seasons do come.

To those who have not been so fortunate in putting their marriages together, I testify of hope. I have learned that our feelings have less to do with circumstance and more to do with attitude and understanding, practiced in faith. I deeply admire all the courageous single parents who step-by-step and day-by-day reach beyond perceived light with faith. I have empathy for the difficulty our single sister-parents face but find it unnecessary to pity those whom, through faith, the Lord can strengthen and so greatly empower. I know from my own experience that the Lord gives these sisters compensatory blessings of support and companionship. What comfort we can glean in the knowledge that we are not rendered helpless by life's tragedies. We can baptize negative feelings in our Savior's tears and rise to a new life in the arms of his love.

We can, at least ultimately, be grateful for life's pain, for only through opposition are we able finally to comprehend joy in all its rich measure. We can accept life's challenges with faith in the Lord's power to change human hearts—especially our own—when we exercise agency to invite him into our life. No personal challenge is beyond hope in Christ, when we are willing to do our part. We cannot enlist his power to abrogate another's agency, but we can yield our own hearts to him as our Savior and trust that good will follow not only in our lives but for those we love. With his help, we can write a revitalized final version of our personal history—string bean and all—and look serenely back at a life made abundant in the Lord's love and mercy.

FROM COOKIES TO CRISIS

EILEEN N. WHITAKER

My first child was still a baby herself, only nineteen months old, when her brother was born. She was quite precocious and very verbal. One day we had just finished making cookies together and had set them on the kitchen table to cool. Needing to nurse the baby, I sat down and said to Rachel, "Now don't touch the cookies." Even as I spoke, I knew I had made a mistake. A little light came into Rachel's eyes as she watched me very much occupied on the couch. She looked at the freshly baked cookies and then looked back at me. Moving as nonchalantly as a one-and-a-half-year-old can, she crept around to the opposite side of the table and slowly inched her little hand up over the tabletop to sneak a cookie. I was irritated but kept quiet. The tiny hand repeated the process, and my irritation increased.

The third time her hand crept upwards, I was angry. I didn't want to call her name, especially with a voice that might startle the nursing baby, but I wanted her to obey. I didn't want her to grow up thinking she could get away with disobedience! So I said audibly, albeit quietly, yet with as much anger as I could allow without upsetting the baby, "Heavenly Father, how do I teach this child to obey!" Distinct words came immediately

Eileen Newman Whitaker has served as a ward Relief Society president and in stake Relief Society presidencies. She is the author of *One Little Child,* a book of poems for preschoolers published by Deseret Book. She and her late husband, R. Michael Whitaker, are the parents of five children.

into my mind. I did not hear a voice, yet I knew I was being spoken to. I even felt an emotion of love mixed with humor at the situation and my anger. What was I to do to teach her to obey? "Nothing," I heard. "Just put the cookies away."

I had to chuckle. Of course I was being unreasonable to expect a baby to obey an order so beyond her ability. In fact, my very command had planted the idea to take them in the first place. I uttered a silent thank-you and called Rachel to bring me a book so that I could read to her while I nursed the baby. When I was finished, we shared a cookie and then put them away together.

That experience, seemingly small and unimportant in the eternal scheme of things, illustrated to me how very much our Heavenly Father cares about each of us, individually, all the time, not only when we are in trouble. He is indeed aware of every sparrow that falls. He knows each of us by name; he is in charge; he loves us. That awareness brings us peace. Somehow I have always felt that Heavenly Father was there watching me and listening to me when I spoke to him. And I speak to him often, both in formal prayer and in daily, silent, constant communication. I always have.

When I was young, I shared a room with my older sister, who was also my best friend. We played well together and loved each other. But I remember being irritated with her if she began her nightly prayer while I was still saying mine because I didn't want her interrupting us. Surely she must know Heavenly Father couldn't listen to her while I was talking to him! I always waited for her to finish before I began praying if she had started before me. I never verbalized that to her, but I was certain her prayers were being wasted if she tried to pray at the same time I was praying.

Thank heaven, that is not the way prayer works. Thank heaven, each of us could simultaneously say an individual prayer, and each one would be heard with our Father in Heaven's undivided attention—not only heard, but answered, correctly, without once having someone receive the response intended for a neighbor. God is all-powerful and all-knowing.

A favorite scripture hangs in a stitching of my creation upon the wall of my dining room: "I am the vine, ye are the branches: He that abideth in me, and I in him, the same bringeth forth much fruit: for without me ye can do nothing" (John 15:5). I began to understand this scripture when I was twelve years old. I had just graduated from Primary and was immediately called to teach Primary. Mature for a twelve-year-old, I felt excited to teach the CTRs. I knew I could do it. I put off preparing my first lesson, but I wasn't worried. I was a good baby-sitter and could come up with lots of things to do on the spur of the moment. I never opened my manual until the day of Primary. Needless to say, the lesson was a disaster. I could not control the children. Of that day my clearest recollection is of the children running wildly up and down the stairs in our two-story chapel in Falls Church, Virginia. I went home and bawled. I didn't ever want to go back. Thoughts of facing those children again terrified me. That entire week I prayed diligently and constantly for help. I prepared ardently. I had definitely begun to learn the "for without me ye can do nothing" part of the scripture on my dining room wall.

I did go back the next week, and things went miraculously well. I say miraculously, because I felt definite divine intervention on my behalf. The children were well behaved, and I was able to keep their attention and teach them. I have never since attempted to teach any kind of a lesson without invoking my Savior's help. Thus I learned to call upon the Savior to help me when I needed him, but I still needed to learn that I had to recognize my dependence on him even when I didn't know I needed him. I had to learn that I always need him.

The last three years of my life have taught me that lesson more deeply. Three years ago my world, which had always been safe and happy, began to fall apart. The Friday before Mother's Day, my sweet mother passed away after a long illness. Even though I knew she was going to die, I did not realize it was quite so imminent. Even if I had known, I don't believe one is ever fully prepared to lose a mother. Mother's Day was also my husband's fiftieth birthday. Though we celebrated Mike's birthday, it was a bittersweet day. In the back of our minds was an upcoming appointment I had insisted he make with our doctor. He kept assuring me that his continuous cough was only allergies, but I was worried. My instincts told me something was wrong. The next day, my fears were confirmed when X-rays showed that his lungs appeared full of tumors.

I had to face the week of my mother's viewing and funeral waiting for more conclusive tests but knowing in my heart things were bad. As I stood in line at my mother's viewing I kept thinking, "I know I am going to have to do this again soon, this time for Mike." My tears flowed freely at the funeral, but they were as much for the feared loss of my husband as they were for my mother. Seven months later Mike passed away. The doctors had not given us any real hope through treatment, so he was home the entire time of his illness. I felt extremely blessed to care for him myself. It was a sacred experience, more sweet than sorrowful, more sacred than sad, and certainly more tutorial than terrible. In saying that, I do not want to diminish in any way the difficulty of the ordeal. My days were spent in frequent weeping and continual prayer. My lessons in relying on the Lord were constant. Two of those sacred lessons I would like to share with you now.

At the time of Mike's illness, we were studying the New Testament in Gospel Doctrine class. Each Sunday we discussed the Savior's many miracles. I became full of questions about miracles. Yes, they are dependent upon faith, but in the face of seemingly equal faith, why are some miracles granted and some not? Why, at the time of the Savior's ministry and again at the time of the restoration of the gospel, were miracles so seemingly plentiful? And why, at times like the present, do they seem fewer? Was it because of faith alone? Does our knowledge of modern technology and medicine somehow unintentionally diminish our faith?

I often pleaded with the Lord, praying, "I know I have enough faith to have Mike healed. I know Mike has enough faith. I know thou canst do anything. I know it. Why are we not receiving a miracle? Why can't the beautiful blessings my husband has received be fulfilled?"

In my questioning, I was not angry nor adamant that our prayers be answered in the way we desired. I was not counseling the Lord or issuing ultimatums. Mostly, I was just curious. Why are miracles sometimes granted and sometimes not? One Sunday my answer came during Gospel Doctrine class, though not by the instructor or by a class member. The instruction instead came into my mind: miracles are granted when they will further the work of building the kingdom. They are not granted to fulfill the desires of those requesting them. Yes, they are preceded by and dependent upon faith, but they are not guaranteed by faith. If it does not further the work of the Lord, or will hinder it, the miracle does not occur. At the time of the Savior's ministry, many miracles were necessary to build and, equally important, to try the faith of those witnessing them. The same was true at the time of the Restoration. Miracles are not as requisite today. For us to learn faith in the Lord's will is now more necessary.

Another Sunday I was pouring out my heart to the Lord on the same subject. This time I was asking not the why of miracles but, May we please have one? Again I assured the Lord that my faith was sufficient, that I was able to accept his will, but if there was any way possible, could my deepest love and best friend be spared to remain with me and our children a few more years? Again, in the midst of my pleading, inaudible words full of love spoke to my mind, "Eileen, sometimes it takes more faith to let someone go than to receive the miracle."

At that point I knew my husband was going to die. I

needed to get on with whatever preparation I could make for myself and our children. I also knew I could not do it alone. I needed divine help and support. And I knew I would receive it. I also knew more deeply what I had always known. If we can learn to pray, "Thy will be done," and *mean it,* then we can survive whatever life experiences we have and remain peaceful.

Let me share another story. This one occurred when Rachel, the child in the cookie incident, was six months old. I had taken her in for an immunization. She was flirting with the doctor and showing off for the nurse, having a ball. She has always been a charmer. Suddenly, out of nowhere, she was jabbed with a needle, and a pain shot through her tiny thigh. She whirled around to face me, with an expression of pure anguish. Everything in her small demeanor asked, "Why? What on earth did I do to deserve that? Why did you let them hurt me?" Then she burst into tears. I could tell that most of her tears were not from the pain. She felt betrayed. I held her little body in my arms and rocked her. I soothed and comforted, but I could not tell her why what had just happened had happened. I could not explain to a six-month-old what an immunization is or why she had to have it or even that it was for her own good. And I could not explain that I had allowed it to happen because I loved her. All I could do was comfort and reassure her. She had the choice at that point to calm down and accept my comfort, or push away and throw a tantrum. She chose to be calmed.

As we drove home I thought how very much like all life's difficulties this experience was. Often when something completely unexpected and seemingly unfair is hurled at us, we are tempted to scream in anguish, Why? What did I do to deserve this? Just as I was unable to tell my infant why, the Lord cannot make us understand in our infancy. But he can offer comfort, peace, and love. It is up to us to accept it, or to kick and throw a tantrum and waste valuable time being angry and demanding to know why. Inner turmoil is one of the greatest deterrents to spiritual communication. If we can be still, we can feel the complete peace that comes without complete understanding, and it is sufficient.

Last year I stitched a sampler that I cherish. The first line of text reads: "First, faith in the Lord, Jesus Christ." Which is, of course, from the fourth article of faith. Faith in the Lord Jesus Christ has to be our foundation.

After some rows of decorative stitching, there is a quotation from Victor Hugo, which reads: "Courage for the great sorrows of life, and patience for the small ones. And when you have laboriously accomplished your daily task, go to sleep in peace. God is awake."[1]

And finally, after some more decorative rows, is the passage of scripture from Psalm 46:10: "Be still, and know that I am God."

One thing I have come to learn is that not only may I depend upon my Savior whenever I need him but I have to depend upon him. I cannot function without him. No one can. Every living being on this earth depends upon him for their every breath, for their very life. The tragedy is that few realize it. Many feel needlessly alone and abandoned and hopeless. He is there, but "the light shineth in darkness, and the darkness comprehendeth it not" (D&C 88:49). That is so sad. Realizing how completely dependent upon the Lord we are can bring tremendous peace. Our fears, our achings, even our unanswered questions and prayers can all be all right.

God is awake. He knows us by name, and he loves each of us. He cares about us from the cookies to the crisis. In him we can find peace. We can run to him for our refuge, but we will not need to hide in him, for if we abide in him we will be able to abound, to go forth and to be profitable servants, and to have joy.

I remember a comment made at a stake conference years ago by John M. R. Covey: "A fish discovers water last." As I pondered that somewhat strange comment, I realized that he was referring to the light of Christ. It surrounds and encompasses us. It is in and through all things. It allows us to move and think and have our being. It is to us as water is to fish, and profoundly more. Yet the world does not realize how powerful and vital the influence of the Savior is. The world has not yet discovered Christ. Without him we can do nothing. May we recognize him. May we accept him. May we love him and obey him. For surely then we can do all things.

NOTE

1. Ralph L. Woods, ed., *A Third Treasury of the Familiar* (New York: Macmillan, 1970), 452; punctuation of sampler differs slightly from the original.

CONSIDERING COVENANTS:
WOMEN, MEN,
PERSPECTIVE, PROMISES

JEFFREY R. HOLLAND AND PATRICIA T. HOLLAND

Patricia T. Holland: The Prophet Joseph Smith once wrote that the Holy Ghost "is . . . powerful in expanding the mind, enlightening the understanding, and storing the intellect with present knowledge. . . . As [it] falls upon one of the . . . seed of Abraham, it is calm and serene."[1] May we be "calm and serene" as we expand our minds and enlighten our understanding together.

Jeffrey R. Holland: One of the most important things I can bear testimony of is God's love for you. God is good, as any father worthy of the name will always be to his children. That fact has important implications for our making and keeping covenants. I worry that many sometimes feel detached from God, seem convinced that there is too great a distance between Kolob and Kanab. You fear that God in his heaven, with all of his urgent national and international, galactic and intergalactic business, is certain to be occupied with things other than your hopes and happiness.

I do not know exactly how he does it, but I testify to you

Jeffrey R. Holland and Patricia T. Holland are the parents of three children. Sister Holland has served in the Young Women General Presidency, and Elder Holland has served as president of Brigham Young University. Elder Holland is a member of the Quorum of the Twelve Apostles.

that he knows us and loves us individually and that he hears our prayers. My testimony is that *nothing* in this universe is more important to him than your hopes and happiness. Nephi wrote, "The Lord God . . . doeth not anything save it be for the benefit of the world. . . . He inviteth them all to come unto him and partake of his goodness" (2 Nephi 26:23–24, 33). When we pass through the veil, it will be thrilling to learn how God watches over us and cares for us, how he knows our every thought. For now it is enough to know simply that he does it. That seems to me such an important doctrinal concept. The Prophet Joseph taught that we could not fully exercise faith in God until we understood his nature.[2] It shouldn't need to be stressed that God is good, but sometimes in our extremity we seem to forget that. Through the cunning influence of the adversary, down through the ages we have lost something of that most encouraging doctrine.

PTH: That aspect of God's character—his absolute goodness—may be the single most important point to make when we discuss covenants. God wants us to be happy! He is eternally committed to our well-being and wants us to be committed to our ultimate happiness as well. The safety and surety of making covenants with God is anchored in the fact that he has prepared them for our exquisite joy. He won't hurt us; he won't trick us; he won't disparage or demean us. No one will be left alone or adrift or unanchored. Goodness in God means exactly what it means in us (only in his case even more so)—living up to the highest ideal, living up to the best that he is.

JRH: In the Book of Mormon, Ammon was teaching King Lamoni the gospel, specifically, the eternal plan of salvation or, as Alma later called it, "the great plan of happiness" (Alma 42:8, 16). As this plan was presented to his mind and to his heart, the beauty, safety, and protection of God's love and Christ's selfless sacrifice overwhelmed him. In that moment, Lamoni cried out, "O Lord, have mercy [upon me]; according to thy abundant mercy," and he fell to the earth as if he were dead (Alma 18:41).

PTH: After two days his servants prepared to bury the king, certain not only that he was dead but that his body was beginning to decay. The queen, believing in Ammon's spiritual strength, asked him to work a miracle, to raise her husband from the deathlike state he was in. I have always been touched that it was a wife, a woman, who stepped forward at a crucial moment and exerted such faith in behalf of her husband. In doing so, she reached a major turning point in Book of Mormon history. Ammon later said to her, "Woman, there has not been such great faith among all the people of the Nephites" (Alma 19:10).

JRH: The record says: "Now, this was what Ammon desired, for he knew that king Lamoni was under the power of God; he knew that the dark veil of unbelief was being cast away from his mind, and the light which did light up his mind, which was the light of the glory of God, *which was a marvelous light of his goodness*—yea, this light had infused such joy into his soul, the cloud of darkness having been dispelled, and that the light of everlasting life was lit up in his soul, yea, he knew that this had overcome his natural frame, and he was carried away in God" (Alma 19:6; emphasis added).

PTH: The light that comes into our lives in times of great personal need, the light that dispels the clouds of darkness and rends the veil of unbelief, the light that lit up Lamoni's mind to the point of spiritual transcendence and physical collapse is the marvelous light of God's goodness. It is the realization of divine compassion and mercy and long-suffering, once we begin to comprehend it, that lifts those oppressive clouds from our lives. It is his goodness—goodness that gives us a plan of safety and happiness, goodness that gives us a redeeming Brother even at unspeakable Parental cost, goodness that gives us help in times of daily struggle and nightly sorrow. The glory of such compassion lights up the soul and wrenches away fear, anger, and disbelief so majestically that we have to be, in effect, carried from the scene—much as Sidney Rigdon felt after witnessing the splendor of the vision we now know as Doctrine and Covenants 76.

JRH: That is why we can make covenants with such confidence, knowing with certainty God's power over darkness and danger and troubles of every kind. We should give gratitude from the depths of our soul for a plan of happiness that provides for escape from every personal mistake we have ever made and every dumb thing we have ever done. We should express eternal thanks for the pure, single-minded, divine goodness that can cover every concern, heal every wound, make up for every defect, and eventually dry every tear. That's the God and Christ and plan King Lamoni saw, and that is what stunned him so. It will stun us, too—by its strength and by its splendor—when our need is great enough, our faith strong enough, and our view clear enough to see it. In our hour of extremity, we will, if we keep our covenants, see the clouds of darkness lift, the veil of unbelief cast away by the hand of a Father who is eternally committed to our happiness.

PTH: Life holds a thousand and one challenges that can try our faith, or at least try our faithfulness. Some days it can be hard to keep going, particularly if we are already weary from long effort and feel we are struggling on alone. God has not and will not forsake us. That is one reason keeping covenants is so crucial, so central to the mortal experience. Covenants not only commit us to being unshakable in our devotion to God, they remind us God will always be unshakable in his devotion toward us. And though we may falter and make mistakes, he never falters. He never makes a mistake. He is ever faithful to us. That is the beauty and majesty inherent in the covenants we make with God.

JRH: Covenants are binding, supernal, consummate contracts between God and his children. They are the solemn promises of Deity—a God who always keeps his word—that heaven will pour out unmeasured blessings upon all who are faithful and honor the conditions of their pledge. An individual can swear an oath, but only when God reciprocates in kind is a covenant established.

We know that oaths are never to be spoken lightly, and covenantal language is of a higher order yet. By definition, covenants invoke the most sacred language we can utter in this world. This language establishes a bond and a relationship unique in the human experience. It is the means by which individuals in a fallen family make their way back to eternal splendor. It is the means by which each of us can be, in the Lord's own words, "a peculiar treasure unto me above all people" (Exodus 19:5). That is why keeping covenants will, as the scripture says, add "glory . . . upon their heads for ever and ever" (Abraham 3:26).

On those days when we think life is harder to bear than we can endure, and when we may think God has somehow forgotten us, that is the time most of all when we should remember our covenants. When God wants to remind us of the surety and permanence of our blessings, he speaks of sealing them, binding them, or, as Joseph Smith once said, welding them (D&C 128:18). These are muscular verbs, intended to convey a strong message. He uses the most powerful terms in our language when asking us to keep our promises and to believe he will keep his.

PTH: Why then do we so often feel, or at least say we feel, that God has forsaken us or has forgotten us or is unmindful of our concerns? Do we ever, even fleetingly, resent God or get angry with him or determine not to hear his voice? "Not my will, but thine, be done" is possible for us to say—and mean— only if we understand that God is totally committed to our happiness (Luke 22:42).

That is why Christ was very careful to say that he was a "good shepherd," not a bad or mediocre one (John 10:14). Bad shepherds lose their sheep and forget to feed them and leave them vulnerable to wolves and weather. But not Christ, and not his Father. If we will just agree to be part of the flock—by covenant—then we have their promise that we will never be forsaken or forgotten and will never be left on our own. In the end the promise is that Christ gave everything, including his life, for his sheep. That is the earthly counterpart to the same heavenly loyalty God the Father has always given to us.

JRH: That is particularly important to remember when we are not so much dissatisfied with God as we are dissatisfied with ourselves—and then blame him for it. So often we do not like the way we are or the way we look or the way we feel. We think we are weak and worthless and have made too many mistakes. Sometimes we don't remain faithful because we think we are beyond the grasp of divine help. We long to be like someone else who is less feeble, someone who has, we think, greater gifts of appearance or education or talent or opportunity. We grow discontented with ourselves, and then faith in everything else starts to falter. But we would certainly be happier if we understood that we are God's handiwork, divine art produced at his potter's wheel, and we must believe he is making what is best and most beautiful for us. We must trust God, including trusting what he does with us, knowing he is making something which will be not only to his glory but finally to ours as well. We can expect perfectly satisfactory explanations later about disappointments we may have experienced along the way.

My point is that it can be spiritually fatal to think wrongly about God. Such dim views of "the light of God's goodness" can immediately affect not only how we see ourselves but also his Church, his Church governance, his Church leaders, and our neighbors in and out of the Church. It can certainly affect how we see spouses, children, marriage, and other family matters. Wrong thinking about God can lead to a terrible breach, a severe separation, an ever wider gulf of doubt and unbelief. It can sap our strength as dramatically as does sin. That is why

101

the first great commandments in both Old and New Testament records ask us to focus on the true nature of God, specifically his love and compassion. Surely our erroneous, ungenerous views of God's love are every bit as wrong and idolatrous as creating a gold calf or some other graven image.

PTH: It seems to me obvious, though still not so easy to do, that submitting to God's will would be infinitely less difficult if we could accept the fact that he is longing to bless us, that his only desire is for our happiness. That realization can be a blinding, stupefying experience, as King Lamoni reminds us, but then we would not only submit gladly but enthusiastically embrace his will. We would greet his counsel and commandments with delight. Our hearts would spring out to meet them.

JRH: Brigham Young University Shakespeare scholar Bruce Young writes of the miracle it was for him to find a wife and to now be so thoroughly happy in marriage. He notes the problem in *The Winter's Tale* of a man whose marriage is breaking apart because he does not believe that anything, including his good and gracious wife, can really be so marvelously good. Surely God is a trickster and must be waiting to jerk the rug from beneath him very soon now, the character reasons. Such suspicion and self-interest will destroy virtually any life or marriage. The man is told that the marriage can be redeemed but only upon one unyielding, fundamental obligation. "It is required [that you] awake your faith," he is told.[3]

PTH: Brother Young then observed that it was just such lack of faith—his own fear and suspicion and doubt—that had kept him from getting married. He had friends whose marriages hadn't worked out, so what guarantee was there for him? Would he marry the wrong person? Would she eventually—or worse yet, immediately—stop loving him? The fears of two decades came to terrify him as the possibility of marriage seemed more and more imminent. Then he tells of this key to his happiness, which continues to this day: "I let go of my great burden of preconceptions, judgments, anticipations, and concerns and became—in at least one respect—as a little child."[4] The first step, he said, was to believe in the possibility of good things—surely one of the greatest of all children's virtues. Children believe everything is possible, and they believe everything will be good.

One of our challenges in making and keeping covenants is overcoming this kind of resistance to our own happiness. Yielding on such matters is often a painful, long-term process requiring us to take responsibility for the confusion, fears, and resentment we feel, realizing they are largely of our own making. But we must give them up—a hard thing for all of us who want to cling to everything we have ever created.

JRH: Such worries, fears, anxieties, such self-torment and self-pity set up overwhelming, potentially debilitating barriers to our happiness. They distance us from God, and they distance us from each other—from spouses, children, friends, almost everyone—and they keep us from seeing God's plan as it really is and ought to be.

Brother Young found himself resisting love, avoiding commitment, fearing disappointment, betrayal, all of which became for him a sort of miserable protection against the possibility of real happiness. "Having experienced such self-created conflict," he concludes, "I am struck by how closely critics of the Church resemble people upset with their marriage partners. There is, for both the critics and the dissatisfied spouses, the same combination of inexorable logic and essential blindness. Everything they see seems obvious to them. . . . But anesthetized to their own faults, [while] hypersensitive to the imperfections of others, they do not see the real and potential splendor in [those] with whom they are yoked. The dark things they see are too often the products of their own hearts. And the evidence of a spouse's willingness to love and give, like the abundant evidence of God's love and active presence in His Church, is easily ignored or forgotten."[5]

PTH: If we are willing to receive and remember it, there is always an abundance of evidence to sustain our faith, not only in a loyal husband or wife but in the Church and its leaders and in the reality and love and goodness of God. Love, marriage, and friendships of a hundred kinds are like membership in the Church. They require at the outset—and all the way through—an act of faith in what will bless and save us in the end. That is why covenants are so dearly and deeply important. We claim through them the promise that the darkness of night will disappear, that questions will be answered, and that in the final day, all will be well with us.

JRH: With that trust in God and the love we really must feel for each other as we make our way toward the celestial city, I wish to appeal to the women of the kingdom. Day in and day out, with large families or small families or no families at all, you render service to your families, to the Church, and to the neighborhoods and communities in which you live. Yours is a divine touch, and your history has been one of compassion, of conviction, of strength and stability. I have always been moved by Wallace Stegner's introduction to *The Gathering of Zion*. Of the Mormon pioneer movement into these uninhabited and often hostile regions, he said, "That I do not accept the faith that possessed them does not mean I doubt their . . . devotion and heroism in its service. *Especially their women. Their women were incredible.*"[6]

PTH: President Howard W. Hunter recently reminded us that the Savior particularly appreciated the company and comfort of women. Perhaps the women and children sensed more keenly who and what he truly was. Women remained to the very last, lingering in view of the cross—"many women," the Gospels record—ministering unto him as best they could, and it was the women who followed to mark where the Savior's body was laid (Matthew 27:55). To Mary, Christ first appeared as the resurrected Lord; to Mary, he entrusted the delivery to his disciples of the glorious message that he had risen. Quoting President Hunter: "As our Lord and Savior needed the women of his time for a comforting hand, a listening ear, a believing heart, a kind look, an encouraging word, loyalty—even in his hour of humiliation, agony, and death—so we, his servants all across the Church, need you, the women of the Church, to stand with us and for us in stemming the tide of evil that threatens to engulf us. Together we must stand faithful and firm in the faith against superior numbers of other-minded people."[7]

"It seems to me," he continues, "that there is a great need to rally the women of the Church to stand with and for the Brethren in stemming the tide of evil that surrounds us and in moving forward the work of our Savior. . . . Obedient to him we are a majority. But only together can we accomplish the work he has given us to do and be prepared for the day when we shall see him."[8]

JRH: It is as Martin Luther once said, "The kingdom of God is like a besieged city surrounded on all sides by death. Each man [and woman] has [a] place on the wall to defend and no one can stand where another stands, but nothing prevents us from calling encouragement to one another."[9]

I think the Brethren have seen some spiritual death near the gates of the city in past days, and perhaps they fear they will see more in the years ahead. Each of us needs to take our place on the wall and to call out encouragement to one another. I have my station, and Sister Holland has hers, and each of you has your own. None of us will stand in the place of any other, but like Gideon's valiant band, we can each stand in our own place (Judges 7:21). Together we can fight against the prince of darkness and the dangers of spiritual decay. Our covenants are our protection. Our strength will be in the Lord. Every woman, man, and accountable child will be enlisted "till the conflict is o'er."[10] We must stand true and call out encouragement to one another.

In Civil War days, a performer named Blondin astonished the nation by crossing the Niagara River on a tightrope. President Abraham Lincoln, facing a delegation of critics, said:

105

"Gentlemen, suppose all the property you possessed were in gold, and you had placed it in the hands of a Blondin to carry across the Niagara River on a rope. With slow, cautious steps he walks to the rope, bearing your all. Would you shake the cable and keep shouting at him, 'Blondin, stand up a little straighter; Blondin, stoop a little more; go a little faster; lean more to the south; now lean a little more to the north?' Would that be your behavior in such an emergency?

"No, you would hold your breath, every one of you, as well as your tongues. You would keep your hands off until he was safe on the other side.

"This government, gentlemen, is carrying an immense weight. Untold treasures are in its hands. The persons managing the ship of state in this storm are doing the best they can. Don't worry them with needless warnings and complaints. . . . Be patient, and we will get you safe across."[11]

PTH: In that same spirit our Church leaders carry an immense weight, and with our support they will get us safely through. I remember President Spencer W. Kimball speaking of some of the difficulties of the last days and saying that "much of the major growth that is coming to the Church in the last days will come because many of the good women of the world (in whom there is often such an inner sense of spirituality) will be drawn to the Church in large numbers. This will happen to the degree that the women of the Church reflect righteousness and articulateness in their lives and to the degree that they are seen as distinct and different—in happy ways—from the women of the world. . . .

"Thus it will be that the female exemplars of the Church will be a significant force in both the numerical and the spiritual growth of the Church in the last days."[12]

I believe the Brethren are looking to the women of the Church—the strong, valiant, ever-faithful women, the modern equivalent of those handcart-pulling women Wallace Stegner found so incredible—to be defenders of priesthood power. In times of difficulty and stress ahead, it will be the women of the Church, as well as the men, who will speak persuasively of God's plan, of his eternal government, and of his priesthood assignments. In the years ahead, some of the great defenders of priesthood roles for men will be women speaking to other women. A woman can speak to another woman in language men would not normally use and with a fervor men would not dare invoke. God has a view of women, who they are, what they do incomparably, and what eternally they will be. Women must seize that vision and embrace it, or they—and the human family with it—will perish.

JRH: Some confusion, or at least much discussion, is ongoing about gender and rights and priesthood. In the *Young Woman's Journal* of 1914, Elder James E. Talmage wrote a remarkable piece, with particular relevance to the 1990s. Noting the sacred and eternal role of both women and men, Elder Talmage said eighty years ago, "The status of woman in the world is a subject of present-day discussion and an element of current social unrest; it is, however, by no means a new topic. . . . [Woman] has suffered the greatest humiliation during periods of spiritual darkness, when the Gospel of Christ was forgotten. [But in the light of the gospel] woman occupies a position all her own in the eternal economy of the Creator; and in that position she is as truly superior to man as is he to her in his appointed place. Woman shall yet come to her own, exercising her rights and her privileges as a sanctified investiture which none shall dare profane."[13]

PTH: Of this equal honor but eternal distinction between men and women, Elder Talmage goes on to say: "In every organization, however simple or complex, there must needs be a centralization of authority, in short, a head. [God has placed man at the head of the household, alongside his wife as full and faithful partner,] and God holds him accountable for his administration. That many men fail in their station, that some are weak and unfit, that in particular instances the wife may be

107

the more capable and in divers ways the better of the pair, should not be considered as evidence . . . [of] unrighteousness in the established order.

"Woman should be regarded, not in the sense of privilege but of right, as the associate of man in the . . . home, and they two should form the governing head of the family institution, while to each separately pertain duties and function which the other is less qualified to discharge. Weakness or inefficiency on the part of either in specified instances must not be taken to impugn the wisdom by which the organization of the home and of society has been planned [by God]."[14]

JRH: Elder Talmage continues: "In the restored Church of Jesus Christ, the Holy Priesthood is conferred, as an individual bestowal, upon men only, and this in accordance with Divine requirement. It is not given to woman to exercise the authority of the Priesthood independently; nevertheless, in the sacred endowments associated with the ordinances [of] the House of the Lord, [it is clear how dramatically] woman shares with man the blessings of the priesthood.

"When the frailties and imperfections of mortality are left behind, in the glorified state of the blessed hereafter, husband and wife will administer in their respective stations, seeing and understanding alike, and co-operating to the full in the government of their family kingdom. Then shall woman be recompensed in rich measure for all the injustice that womanhood has endured in mortality. Then shall woman reign by Divine right, a queen in the resplendent realm of her glorified state, even as exalted man shall stand, priest and king unto the Most High God. Mortal eye cannot see nor mind comprehend the beauty, glory, and majesty of a righteous woman made perfect in the celestial kingdom of God."[15]

As the Prophet Joseph Smith continually taught, in this Church we *do* believe in a government and kingdom that ultimately are not of this world. Ours will not be a democracy or an oligarchy. Technically, it will not even be a theocracy. It will be in the millennial day a monarchy, with Christ reigning as King of kings and Lord of lords.

PTH: Under the priesthood order, both women and men are to seek the government of their King, a righteous, perfect, loving, thoroughly good king. That government, and the priesthood principles upon which a righteous king would administer it, have always existed. As the Prophet Joseph taught, "Priesthood existed with God from eternity, and will to eternity, without beginning of days or end of years."[16] Never let it be said of any Latter-day Saint man that he has contributed to the "injustice that womanhood has endured in mortality," to use Elder Talmage's searing phrase.

JRH: The Prophet Joseph taught, "It is the duty of a husband to love, cherish, and nourish his wife, and cleave unto her and none else; he ought to honor her as himself, and he ought to regard her feelings with tenderness. . . . [He is] not to rule over his wife as a tyrant, neither as one who is fearful or jealous that his wife will get out of her place, and prevent him from exercising his authority. It is his duty to be a man of God (for a man of God is a man of wisdom) ready at all times to obtain from the scriptures, the revelations, and from on high, such instructions as are necessary for the edification and salvation of his household."[17]

PTH: Unfortunately, not all men measure up to their assignment, but the principles are true, and the ultimate, ideal government of God is perfect. So we need to hold fast to our beliefs until—even if it is, as Brother Talmage says, "in the great beyond"—we fully realize the exalted ideal of women and men crowned with equal majesty.

Eliza R. Snow, who had firm opinions about most things, certainly made it clear that *she* was not going to be thrown off the track of her womanhood simply because of the inadequacy and foibles of men. More than one hundred twenty years ago she said that some women "are so radical in their extreme theories that they would set [for themselves an] antagonism to

109

man . . . [and] make [their sisters] adopt the more reprehensible phases of character which men present, and which should be shunned or improved by them instead of being copied by women."[18]

JRH: Eliza and virtually every other woman knows that her spiritual success and salvation does *not* lie in her becoming more like a man. Indeed, of late much of what I hear from women indicates that some would advocate the opposite course! But please, to remedy an ill, we don't throw the baby out with the bath water. We don't retreat from or alter what has been declared as the perfect government of God. One day, and we pray sooner rather than later, we will enjoy the perfect peace that surpasseth understanding—in gender issues as well as every other matter troubled by human inadequacy.

PTH: As Brigham Young University professor Alma Don Sorensen has written, "It must be admitted, as some of our critics claim, that sex discrimination exists among LDS people more or less as it does in the societies surrounding them. But the explanation for this discrimination does not lie at all in the belief system of the restored gospel but in the fact that we live too much in the world and fail to realize the equality between man and woman that living in the kingdom requires. The fact is that the doctrines and principles of the kingdom are the proper remedy for the unequal treatment of the sexes . . . not its cause."[19]

If we can help one another with our limitations in a marriage or in a family or in the Church, and not retreat from or damage the very truths, principles, and covenants that will one day fulfill and empower us beyond measure, then we will—both women and men—find that we have successfully traveled the path of progression from womanhood and manhood to godhood. Then we can sit "crowned with glory and majesty" like (and these are Elder Talmage's words) our "Celestial Parents," the "eternal Father and . . . the eternal Mother."[20]

JRH: These are not tranquil times, nor are they for the

fainthearted. But then we have just learned from Elder Talmage that 1914 was not so smooth a period either, and neither were those days along the Sweetwater and the Platte and the frozen passes of Wyoming. President Kimball spoke for all the difficult seasons of the Saints when he said, "To be a righteous woman is a glorious thing in any age. To be a righteous woman during the winding-up scenes on this earth, before the second coming of our Savior, is an especially noble calling. The righteous women's strength and influence today can be tenfold what it might be in more tranquil times. She has been placed here to help to enrich, to protect, and to guard the home—which is society's basic and most noble institution. Other institutions in society may falter and even fail, but the righteous woman can help to save the home, which may be the last and only sanctuary some mortals know in the midst of storm and strife. . . .

" . . . We have grown strong as a people because our mothers and our women have been so selfless. That ennobling quality must not be lost, even though some of the people of the world may try to persuade otherwise."[21]

PTH: Struggles and sifting among the Saints have been with us from the beginning and will inevitably be more pronounced with the hastening of the latter-day work. We face some difficult days ahead, days that will require faith in the goodness of God, in his plan and his government, in his leaders—especially the prophets and apostles of God. As women we are called to prepare for these days. Alma said that women and men were "to prepare their minds . . . that they may prepare the minds of their children to hear the word at the time of his coming" (Alma 39:16).

We would have to be blind and deaf not to see the devastation of society all around us and hear the desperate cry for fathers and mothers to turn homeward to "behold [our] little ones" there (3 Nephi 17:23). As for Church members, not even stake callings or Church meetings are to obstruct our focus on home, family, and the strengthening of our children.[22]

111

JRH: A recent newsmagazine article points to a "pattern of neglect" in American parenting. The piece concludes, "The best thing that society can do for its toddlers is to make 'parent' an honorable title again. No job is more important, yet no job is more often taken for granted. We teach work skills but not life skills, how to change a carburetor but not a diaper, how to treat a customer but not a [child]. Becoming a parent should be . . . a source of pride, and not remorse. Only then will our children be safe."[23]

PTH: I have always wanted to speak about being a mother. I have served the Church in a variety of ways, just as you have. And I have been blessed all along the way, just as you have. But I would like to say that all I have ever really wanted to be is a mother. I was thrust into the public eye during our years at BYU, and I fulfilled those public assignments. It was my duty, and they were wonderful years. Even now, as the wife of a General Authority, my life is more public than I prefer. But my husband's calling is an unequaled and profound privilege for our family. We have never been more blessed. Yet all I have ever wanted to be is a mother, to have as the psalmist said, a "quiver full" of children (Psalm 127:5). Such was not to be our lot in life. We were blessed with three perfect children; the others we hoped for never came. (As I say this, I know very well some of you have not yet had any children at all.)

My happiest thoughts and my highest hopes are to someday, somewhere, on some green and grassy piece of God's celestial realm, sit with my children and grandchildren crowded around me for as far as I can see and tell them of the love I feel and speak with them of eternal things. I long for that sense of family and home; it is the most motivating force in my life. I wanted it in our early married life, I want it now, and I want it in the world to come.

Our eleventh article of faith allows all to choose their religion and worship as they wish. In that same spirit, if I may pursue the path I most long for and the one I hope to savor through eternity, I choose home and mothering and woman-hood, now and forever.

JRH: My responsibilities as a father are all that have been out-lined for mothers, and perhaps even more. It seems to me that if more fathers would focus on their marriage, home, and family with anywhere near the intensity they focus on their careers, we would not have nearly so many women trying so frantically to get away from that marriage, home, and family. As someone said recently, too many mothers in America are dead tired because too many fathers in America are deadbeats. I am not here to berate fathers, but I do believe God will hold us accountable for our performance as fathers, sons, and brothers, and not for how we did as doctors, lawyers, and corporate chiefs.

The community, the nation, the world are crying for lead-ership in the home, stability in the family, safety for our chil-dren. And what do some men do? Stay a little longer at the office! That's a little unkind of me, and unfair to many good men, but I am trying to make a point. Society has some prob-lems, and too often men have been part of that problem. A sig-nificant portion of the challenges women and children face in the world today will not be healed or helped or resolved until men are more of what God expects them to be—good and gentle and compassionate and reliable. In short, more as he is.

Some of the most distressing experiences Sister Holland and I faced after our devotional addresses at BYU were the small but inevitable handful of students, semester after semes-ter, who would come up to the podium afterwards, or some-times later that night to our house, and say, "But I cannot com-prehend a Heavenly Father who is good or loving or kind—because my earthly father has been none of those things to me. How can I get from where my father has left me to where you say my Heavenly Father wants me to be?"

And so, at least for some, the vicious cycle continues, with too many men trying to be superior at everything but what mat-ters most—being a husband and father. I pray I can do better in

113

that responsibility, the task in life I reverence and cherish the most. I pray I can merit the love my wife and children have always given me. They mean more to me than life itself. I desperately want my children to see at least something in their earthly father that would encourage their belief in a dependable, compassionate, and loving God. Certainly my children's view of their earthly mother has already prepared them to behold the splendor and strength of their Heavenly Mother one day.

PTH: Women of covenant can be a powerful force for righteousness in this world. It is our nature to kindle spirituality within every sphere of our influence. We are bearers of light, even as John saw the woman in his marvelous revelation, and I know we can be the instrument for conveying that light from one realm to another and another and another (Revelation 12:1). That is at the heart of our "sanctified investiture," which none shall dare profane. Let us reach out enthusiastically for our assignment and rejoice in our God-given appointment. As we do so, we will enjoy divine rights and powers and privileges surpassing any other earthly satisfaction.

JRH: May God bless you in this the true and living Church of the true and living God. May you feel the arms of his love and protection around you, and his angels on your right hand and on your left to bear you up in time of need. May all of your deepest, heartfelt longings be met, all your wounds be healed and sweet peace be yours now and forever. I promise you that your covenants will be a source of strength and satisfaction and safety to you. Through keeping them we can all rejoice in the triumph of the Savior of the world, including his saving of our personal world and all we hold dear within it.

NOTES

1. Joseph Smith, *Teachings of the Prophet Joseph Smith,* sel. Joseph Fielding Smith (Salt Lake City: Deseret Book, 1977), 149–50.

2. This is, for example, the basic premise of the Prophet Joseph Smith's *Lectures on Faith.*

3. Bruce Young, "The Miracle of Faith, The Miracle of Love: Some Personal Reflections," in *A Thoughtful Faith: Essays on Belief by Mormon Scholars,* ed. Philip L. Barlow (Centerville, Utah: Cannon Press, 1986), 260.

4. Ibid., 262.

5. Ibid., 272.

6. Wallace Stegner, *The Gathering of Zion: The Story of the Mormon Trail* (New York: McGraw-Hill, 1964), 13; emphasis added.

7. Howard W. Hunter, "To the Women of The Church," *Ensign,* Nov. 1992, 96.

8. Ibid.

9. Quoted in Lewis Spitz, *The Renaissance and Reformation Movements* (Chicago: Rand McNally, 1971), 335.

10. "We Are All Enlisted," *Hymns of The Church of Jesus Christ of Latter-day Saints* (Salt Lake City: The Church of Jesus Christ of Latter-day Saints, 1985), no. 250.

11. John Wesley Hill, *Abraham Lincoln: Man of God* (New York: G. P. Putnam's Sons, 1927), 402. Quoted in Boyd K. Packer, *The Holy Temple* (Salt Lake City: Bookcraft, 1980), 168.

12. Spencer W. Kimball, *My Beloved Sisters* (Salt Lake City: Deseret Book, 1979), 44–45.

13. James E. Talmage, "The Eternity of Sex," *Young Woman's Journal,* Oct. 1914, 602.

14. Ibid.

15. Ibid., 602–3.

16. Smith, *Teachings of the Prophet Joseph Smith,* 157.

17. Joseph Smith, "On the Duty of Husband and Wife," *Elder's Journal of The Church of Jesus Christ of Latter-day Saints,* Aug. 1838, 61.

18. Eliza R. Snow, "Woman's Status," *Woman's Exponent* (15 July 1872): 29.

19. Alma Don Sorensen, "No Respecter of Persons: Equality in the Kingdom," in *As Women of Faith,* ed. Mary E. Stovall and Carol Cornwall Madsen (Salt Lake City: Deseret Book, 1989), 52.

20. Talmage, "Eternity of Sex," 603.

21. Kimball, *My Beloved Sisters,* 17, 19.

22. For another very recent example of the repeated counsel given on this theme, see Neal A. Maxwell, "'Take Especial Care of Your Family,'" *Ensign,* May 1994, 88–91.

23. Steven V. Roberts, "Neglecting Children—and Parents," *U. S. News and World Report,* 25 Apr. 1994, 10–11.

SEPTEMBER

MARILYN BUSHMAN-CARLTON

We've circled back.
With color seeping from our cheeks and hair,
being that couple we once were,
just the two of us,
seems again a possibility.
September is knowing we can't return;
    it is not wishing to.
We move enriched by five sprigs
remarkably like us,
and never farther than their daily news.
Like a checker kinged,
we order the same meals at restaurants,
prefer violin symphonies,
revive in green scenery,
charge up with deep talks,
mental sparring—
the good list
    outweighing what we cannot change,
    and growing.
Some say September signals the end;
we slow because our bodies do.
We've learned that pausing helps us see.
We bend toward, and cherish,

Marilyn Bushman-Carlton received her bachelor's degree in English from the University of Utah. Her first volume of poetry will be published in 1995. Sister Bushman-Carlton teaches poetry workshops at Pioneer Craft House in Salt Lake City. She and her husband, Blaine L. Carlton, are the parents of five children.

the few things we're sure of.
What moves me now
is not the quick, impatient energy
that started us,
but sure moments:
    your easy *I love you* to a son,
    your tears at a daughter's leaving.
    It is affirmation in your eyes;
    the antics of your mind,
    your understanding
    when even I cannot explain.

And postscripts:
    your smell,
    the soothing ritual
    of peppermint lotion on my feet,
    the hope of winter
    with you.

PUZZLES AND PROMISES:

COVENANTS AND THE

SINGLE WOMAN

MARY-MARGARET PINGREE

I pulled out the bundle of letters and flipped through them. One from Brighton High School caught my attention. There was something vaguely familiar about the address written in script on the front. Curious, I ripped open the flap and pulled out a slightly yellowed piece of white notebook paper.

"Dear Mary-Margaret," the letter to me, from me, began. "I'm writing this letter to you from my freshman English class at Brighton High School. A few years from now, I thought you might be interested in what my life is like."

The letter went on to tell about my best friend, Danielle, and David, the boy I liked (funny, I can't even remember his last name now). It listed my favorite class (algebra!) and some current world events. In a fifteen-year-old way, the letter bemoaned my five-foot-nine-inch frame, because I was taller than all the boys, and reminded me that I detested school lunch.

Reading the letter ten years later, I found the most interesting passage was my teenage prediction about the future. Here

---

Mary-Margaret Pingree received her MBA degree from the Kellogg Graduate School of Management at Northwestern University and is a marketing manager at O. C. Tanner Company in Salt Lake City. She has served in the Church with the young adults.

is how the letter concluded: "This is what I believe will happen in my future:

"1. School: I will go to college and graduate in four years.

"2. Marriage: I will get married when I am twenty-two.

"3. Children: I will have five children."

As I refolded the letter, I mused that the boyfriend might be long forgotten but my expectations were not. To my surprise and some others' concern, my life has not turned out the way I expected it to when I was fifteen. That is true for everyone, but I think Latter-day Saint singles feel particularly sensitive to how their lives defy expectation. Whether never-been-married, divorced, or widowed, singles often feel frustrated and blocked in their desires to fulfill their covenants. We worry that we are barred from the full gospel life.

Our frustrations come not only from how reality is different from our expectations but also from the emphasis that others place on marriage covenants. Not long ago, in a conversation with an LDS business associate, I mentioned that I was speaking at a women's conference on the topic of single women and keeping covenants. He laughed and said, "What is there to talk about? *You* haven't made any covenants." Perhaps my single status led him to overemphasize the importance of one particular covenant—marriage—to the exclusion of all the other covenants Latter-day Saints make. I have found this perspective to be quite common among members of the Church. Its narrow focus is understandably frustrating to singles.

Let me suggest a broader way to look at covenants. First, it is important to consider carefully the purpose of covenants, rather than focusing on the performance of specific covenants. Covenants are made through symbolic actions, but our being immersed in water or partaking of bread and water is not the purpose of covenants. The purpose is to help us develop a relationship with God. God makes covenants with us because he loves us and wants us to draw closer to him. In the Book of Mormon we read, "And he loveth those who will have him to be their God. Behold, he loved our fathers, and he covenanted with them" (1 Nephi 17:40). Each covenant, whether it be tithing or baptism or sacrifice, draws us closer to our Heavenly Father. He promises us blessings when we obey him.

Occasionally, at a particular point in our lives, one covenant may be difficult or impossible for us to fulfill. Rather than dwelling on our frustration with our circumstances, we can use another covenant to bring us closer to God.

Another insight that might broaden our perspective regarding covenants is to avoid thinking of covenants as events that take place in a linear sequence. Our natural inclination is to organize events so that they make sense to us. Because of our educational background and social training, we typically think of life as a sequence of events. We chart significant events along a time line, such as birth, learning to walk, and starting school. At eight years of age, children reared in the Church record their first covenants—baptism and confirmation. Those who decide to go on missions in their youth record a second covenant between ages nineteen and twenty-one—the endowment. The expectation is that next, probably somewhere in the midtwenties, a person should be recording marriage and the sealing covenant.

But covenants aren't necessarily meant to be fulfilled in a particular order. In fact, some covenants, such as tithing, the Word of Wisdom, and honoring the Sabbath, are less likely to be recorded on a time line because they are not initiated with a specific ordinance. Consequently, I don't think a time line is the best model to use in evaluating our covenant-making progress. I prefer to think of keeping covenants as putting together the pieces of a puzzle. There is no particular order or way that we need to put it together. Some people like to start with borders; others work on color groups. If part of the puzzle becomes difficult, we don't stop dead in our tracks and quit. We work on a different part of the puzzle. Eventually, we'll all complete our puzzles, but we'll do it in very different ways, ways that match our personalities and our individual circumstances. Thinking about covenants in this way helps us realize that the keeping of covenants isn't really that different for single, divorced, or widowed women and men. It is simply a matter of doing the best you can to keep your covenants in the circumstances that you happen to be in at the moment.

I would like to share a few examples of how my particular circumstances as a single person have affected my ability to keep covenants. For me, one of the most difficult things about being single is feeling alone. All of us—married or single—feel lonely at times, but single people may face this uncomfortable emotion more often and, perhaps, more acutely. For me nothing compares with loneliness; it is a most painful emotion. I was reminded of this recently when I called a single friend of mine who has a successful career working for a large corporation in Chicago. She had spent the weekend alone. I could hear the despair in her voice as she described how lonely she felt. It reminded me of the time I felt most alone.

Immediately after my graduation from college, I accepted a job in Cairo, Egypt. It was an internship with an American company that specialized in software training. I was hired to do some programming and assist with their marketing efforts. On the plane, I began to realize how alone and isolated I would be in Egypt. I would not understand the culture nor have much of a support system to rely on. I would not have my family, and I would have very little contact with them, because it often takes hours or even days to place telephone calls. I would have no friends or acquaintances there. And because it is illegal for Egyptians to be members of the Church, I would have very little contact with Latter-day Saints.

I stepped into a taxi at the airport, feeling completely isolated and out of place. I stared out the window in bewilderment at the mass of humanity surging around me. To my right, two small boys bounced along in a three-wheeled donkey cart.

I cringed as one of the dirty boys smiled at me through black, toothless gums. When we stopped in Tahrir Square, an old woman hobbled to the cab window, shoved a rusty can inside, and muttered something I could not understand. I recoiled quickly and hugged my overnight bag until we entered the suburbs. While my cab slowed to a stop, I noticed a cardboard village laid out haphazardly on the sidewalk. Barefoot children in ragged *gallebeyahs* (tunics) were chasing each other amid mounds of garbage that smelled of filth and sewage. Loneliness engulfed me as I paid the cab driver and moved toward the dilapidated houseboat on the Nile that was to be my home for the next three months.

The weeks passed, and my loneliness intensified. Then one day, I read in Proverbs this familiar passage: "Trust in the Lord with all thine heart; and lean not unto thine own understanding. In all thy ways acknowledge him, and he shall direct thy paths" (Proverbs 3:5–6). This scripture suddenly made me see my situation in a new light. I realized that because I had always had someone else to lean on, I had never truly trusted in the Lord. I had never had to. Now because I was so completely alone, I had a unique opportunity to develop a deeper relationship with my Heavenly Father. I recommitted myself to regular prayer and scripture study, covenants that I had been neglecting. My loneliness in this instance was a blessing because it prodded me to remember my baptismal covenant to always remember the Lord and to rely on him as my support.

Several years after my return from Egypt, I began a graduate program in business at Northwestern University in Chicago. My graduate school experience provided me with another opportunity to learn about covenants. In my program were five hundred students from very diverse backgrounds. Some had just come from Wall Street; some had been farmers in Arizona. Some were Roman Catholic or Protestant; others were Buddhists or Sikhs. Some were from North or South America; others were from Asia or Africa. As we got to know each other through group projects and hallway conversations, it was quite natural for us to discuss our backgrounds, beliefs, and lifestyles. These discussions forced me to explore my own belief system, to really question what I believed and be more thoughtful about the covenants I had made and will make.

I was constantly confronted with fulfilling my covenant to obey the Word of Wisdom. Social activities at business school revolved around parties and usually alcohol. It was easy to understand the purpose of the Word of Wisdom when I saw people drink excessively. It was more difficult to justify my abstinence to my best friends, who were careful to drink responsibly. They were people whom I respected and admired.

I remembered that the purpose of covenants is to develop a stronger relationship with God. Maintaining a consistently close relationship with God is more likely when there is no interference from such substances as alcohol. Understanding that made obeying the Word of Wisdom easier for me. My experience in business school, which might not have occurred had I married earlier, led me not only to contemplate the purpose of the Word of Wisdom but also to see more clearly the purpose of covenants in general.

A final example of how my circumstances as a single person have affected my ability to keep covenants relates to the covenant of the Sabbath. Until recently, I have been living with others who don't share many of my values. In many ways I enjoyed the exposure to new ideas, but that also presented certain challenges. For example, keeping the Sabbath Day holy was—and still is—hard for me. I need to remember that keeping covenants is like putting together a puzzle. Right now, this piece is more difficult for me. In time, my circumstances will change—this challenge will fade and a new one will take its place.

There are two ways I can approach this challenge. I can feel frustrated and discouraged that my circumstances make this covenant more difficult for me than I perceive it to be for others. Or I can realize that the purpose of covenants is to bring me closer to God, not to make my life hard. Focusing on the purpose of the Sabbath invests the day with its meaning: to create, through a sacrifice of time or an interruption of secular patterns, a relationship with God.

As a fifteen-year-old Brighton High freshman, I had no idea how the puzzle of my life would develop. The opportunities I've had and the challenges I've faced have been more diverse than I ever imagined. No, I'm not married, and I have no children yet. But even though I have not put together the puzzle in just the way I thought I would, my experiences have given me a multitude of opportunities to develop my relationship with my Heavenly Father. I believe that God has created a plan that allows each of us, through covenants, to put together our own puzzles. Some of us start with the edges; some with the blue pieces; some wonder if they are following any pattern at all. The important thing is not how the puzzle comes together but that with God it does.

SCAPEGOATING

AND ATONEMENT

C. TERRY WARNER

Jacob admonished his fellow Saints: "Look unto God with firmness of mind, and pray unto him with exceeding faith, and he will console you in your afflictions, and he will plead your cause" (Jacob 3:1). When the Lord came to earth, he fulfilled this promise in person: "And it came to pass that when he had thus spoken, all the multitude, with one accord, did go forth with their sick and their afflicted, and their lame, and with their blind, and with their dumb, and with all them that were *afflicted in any manner;* and he did heal them every one as they were brought forth unto him" (3 Nephi 17:9; emphasis added).

The world seems not to believe that he has such powers. In connection with one problem after another—depression, homosexuality, and abuse, to name only a few—I have, over the years, heard the solemn warning: This kind of challenge has nothing to do with spirituality or morality, righteousness or repentance. Only a scientific, professional approach has any hope of dealing with it. And yet when I have heard such talk, I have thought of the Source to whom we must look for healing

C. Terry Warner received his doctorate in philosophy from Yale University. He has been a visiting senior member of Linacre College, Oxford, and has served as dean of the College of General Studies at Brigham Young University. He is bishop of a Provo, Utah, ward and is married to Susan Lillywhite Warner, a counselor in the Primary General Presidency. They are the parents of ten children.

and consolation in our afflictions. It is of him that I would like to speak.

I have read that Masai tribal doctors ask their patients not "Where do you hurt?" but "Whom have you wronged?" I do not know whether that is true, but it doesn't matter much if it isn't, for the same sentiment, pertaining to at least some afflictions, can be found in the scriptures. "My disciples, in days of old, sought occasion against one another and forgave not one another in their hearts; and for this evil they were afflicted and sorely chastened. Wherefore, I say unto you, that ye ought to forgive one another; for he that forgiveth not his brother his trespasses standeth condemned before the Lord; for there remaineth in him the greater sin. I, the Lord, will forgive whom I will forgive, but of you it is required to forgive all men" (D&C 64:8–10).

This passage makes three amazing statements: First, when we refuse to forgive others, we do them wrong; we sin against them. Second, this refusal to forgive causes us, who do the wrong, affliction: we are sorely chastened for it. We suffer from doing wrong to others, as the Masai doctors are supposed to have said. Just how we suffer is an issue I will address later. Third, the Lord counts our refusal to forgive a greater sin than whatever trespass we are refusing to forgive. These truths can be restated in this simple maxim: "It is not the wrong that others do to us that harms us most, but the wrong we do to them."

We may resist these truths, especially if we have not yet fully forgiven those we believe have offended us. If I am unforgiving, I am certain my problems are the fault of those whom I refuse to forgive. "How false," I may argue in my heart, "to say *I'm* responsible for my unhappiness! And how unfair! For I just *know* that I'm the victim. I'm the one suffering. How can I be blamed if I'm the victim?" Many put forth this objection. Some push it to an extreme conclusion: "In effect, I am being told, If bad things have happened to you, it's your fault! What of those who suffered unspeakably in the Nazi death camps? What of children who undergo horrible abuse? What of any suffering at all? How can the victim be responsible?"

This argument distorts the passage quoted from Doctrine and Covenants 64. That scripture does not imply that we are responsible for the events that happen to us. It implies instead that we are responsible for how we respond to these events, for how we choose to let them affect us. Christ himself and Joseph sold into Egypt and Joseph Smith in Liberty Jail, great leaders eternally, suffered terribly without recrimination or resentment and so too have others less well known.[1] They sought no occasion in their hearts against their abusers but forgave, even in the very moment of their suffering. We have little to say about many of the events that befall us, but much to say about how we experience them, how we understand them, how they influence us.

This distinction miraculously opens up a bright window of opportunity, the opportunity of forgiveness. It permits us to remember wrongs done to us without believing they have damaged us irreparably, without feeling helpless or hopeless. We can remember those wrongs without retaliating in our hearts, without writhing in animosity and vengeance. Forgiving, we avoid doing ourselves terrible harms. And repenting of our refusal to forgive, we put an end to such harms.

In a book subtitled *The Spiritual Advantages of a Painful Childhood,* Wayne Muller writes: "To let go of the ones who hurt us is to let go of our identity as the one who was hurt, the one who was violated, the one who was broken. It often feels like the bad guys are getting off scot-free while we are left holding the bag of pain. But forgiveness is not just for them. . . . Forgiveness . . . allows us to be set free from the endless cycle of pain, anger, and recrimination that keeps us imprisoned in our own suffering."[2]

Thus forgiveness transforms us in a marvelous way. It might be called an end of the worst, most damning kind of

127

affliction, or, equally, the beginning of a journey that leads to the most exalted joy. The Savior's gift of himself makes this transformation possible. The price he paid for sin, including the greater sin of refusing to forgive, is infinite; and that means, among other things, that no suffering lies beyond his power to redeem, no sorrow cannot be turned into joy. That means—I put the case boldly—that even the worst horrors perpetrated by humankind, the death camp tortures, the abuse of innocent ones, scalding hatred toward the perpetrators—all can be redeemed on this simple condition: that the individual, *whether the one who has suffered or the one who has made others to suffer,* repents completely, which includes retaining in his or her heart no hardness toward any creature, no refusal to forgive.

Writes C. S. Lewis: "Not only [Heaven] but all this earthly past will have been Heaven to those who are saved. Not only [Hell], but all their life on earth too, will then be seen by the damned to have been Hell. That is what mortals misunderstand. They say of some temporal suffering, 'No future bliss can make up for it,' not knowing that Heaven, once attained, will work backwards and turn even that agony into a glory. [Others take pleasure in sin,] little dreaming how damnation will spread back and back into their past and contaminate the pleasure of the sin. . . . What happens to [the Saved] is best described as the opposite of a mirage. What seemed, when they entered it, to be the vale of misery turns out, when they look back, to have been a well; and where present experience saw only salt deserts memory truthfully records that the pools were full of water."[3]

Christ offers us spiritual advantages to be found in the afflictions through which we pass in this life, if we will accept them without resentment or hard feelings. Every experience can be redeemed in him: "*All things* work together for good to them that love God" (Romans 8:28; emphasis added).

Suffering without vengeance—does it not conform to the example of the Atoning One? Does it not overcome evil with

128

good? Is it not the way of those who become saviors on Mount Zion? In choosing this way, and in no other, we can find a fulness of joy.

Speaking to the eleven apostles of his impending suffering and death and of the hatred and persecution and scattering and affliction and sorrow they would endure, the Savior promised: "Ye shall weep and lament, but the world shall rejoice: and ye shall be sorrowful, but your sorrow shall be turned into joy. A woman when she is in travail hath sorrow, because her hour is come: but as soon as she is delivered of the child, she remembereth no more the anguish, for joy that a man is born into the world. And ye now therefore have sorrow: but I will see you again, and your heart shall rejoice, and your joy no man taketh from you. . . . These things I have spoken unto you, that in me ye might have peace. In the world ye shall have tribulation: but be of good cheer; I have overcome the world" (John 16:20–22, 33).

However broad the offense or deep the sorrow, Christ bears away our sins, lifts from us their destructive effects, enables us to let go of our hardness. In ancient Israel the workings of this healing process were symbolized by a curious and wonderful element called the scapegoat, which was included in the sacrifice ritual of the Day of Atonement. The high priest offered both a sin offering and a burnt offering for himself and his house and the same offerings for the congregation of Israel. In addition, he also sent one goat, the scapegoat, alive into the wilderness, to bear away the sins of the people symbolically. Except by those without understanding, this animal was not thought actually to remove the congregation's sins but to call to remembrance and point the way to that pure and perfect Lamb of God who would, in the meridian of time, remove their sins. This he would do not just ritualistically but actually, once and for all (Hebrews 9:6–28). I believe it is through participating, by belief and act, in this real sacrifice that we live the one

129

true religion, the one plan that actually relieves us of the pain, unfairness, and deep sorrow of life. We can call it "the religion of atonement."

From almost the beginning of time we have had a counterfeit of this religion. It also claims to rectify injustice and compensate for pain, though unlike the religion of atonement, it cannot deliver on its promises. This counterfeit religion, like the religion of atonement, features scapegoating, but not the kind of scapegoating that points toward Christ's sacrifice. Often this other scapegoating has been played out in community religious rituals. In these rituals, the uncleanness of the community is projected onto a particular creature or creatures, sometimes an animal, sometimes a human being. The scapegoat, a surrogate or substitute for all offenders, is sacrificed, or driven out from the community. It serves as a kind of sponge to absorb the guilt and uncleanness of the whole community.

In the most commonly cited examples, this rite of purification takes place in a formal ceremony, such as the mock warfare enacted among the Dinka people that gradually becomes a united frenzy as the participants actually strike a cow or calf tied to a stake.[4] In other cases, the community conducts this grim proceeding quite unaware of its ritualistic character, as in the Salem witch trials. It might be said of all such cases that accusers despise in the animal or person accused—the scapegoat—the evil they sense in themselves and cannot deal with directly. On the surface, they punish the offenders; on a deeper level, they desperately try to purify themselves.

Many of us practice the religion of scapegoating daily, when we find fault, condemn someone (even if we say it only to ourselves), or try to dig the mote out of another's eye. We may say we are only trying to help the other person "straighten up," or to teach that person an important lesson, or pay that person back for what he's done. But in the scapegoating pattern, the truth is that we want to make someone else pay for our miseries; we desire that because we do not feel clean ourselves, and without quite realizing why, we feel compelled to fixate on the sins or shortcomings of someone else. At least momentarily, finding another to blame relieves us, or at least distracts us, from the necessity of examining ourselves. We pin our hopes on establishing someone else's uncleanness so that we won't have to face up to it in ourselves.

Contrast this religion of scapegoating with the religion of atonement. In the religion of atonement, we don't feel compelled to scapegoat in order to find justice and bring relief from guilt; the Savior fulfilled the demands of justice by suffering the effects of sin. Because we believe he paid for every sin, we do not desire to exact payment for whatever we have suffered. Instead, we are able to forgive freely, seeing even those who have wronged us with compassion. We let go of enmity, much as one whose boat has capsized might let go of a satchel of belongings that is dragging him or her underwater, might let it simply float away as obviously the lesser of two losses. For us, what Christ endured on our behalf is enough, and therefore we want for nothing.

Dennis Rasmussen, author of the remarkable book *The Lord's Question,* has written: "To hallow my life [Christ] taught me to endure sorrow rather than cause it, to restrain anger rather than heed it, to bear injustice rather than inflict it. 'Resist not evil' he said in the Sermon on the Mount. (Matthew 5:39.) Evil multiplies by the response it seeks to provoke, and when I return evil for evil, I engender corruption myself. The chain of evil is broken for good when a pure and loving heart absorbs a hurt and forbears to hurt in return."[5]

Many, including people who have been wronged in the most severe ways, have come to this light. I spoke not long ago with a woman who six years earlier had recalled having been abused sexually by her father when she was a girl. She had worked with a psychiatrist for most of those six years. Despite her efforts, she had gained no fundamental relief, no healing. "I feel as if I am a set of pipes that are clogged. Life,

131

the joy of life, does not flow through me." I asked whether she had forgiven her father. She said she had thought she had but wasn't sure, because still she had no peace.

Then I asked her, "Have you sought his forgiveness for your hard feelings, your resentment, toward him all these years?" She had not. It had never occurred to her to do so. I suggested that forgiveness consists not of forgetting what happened but of repenting of unforgiving feelings about what happened.

A light went on in her face. She pondered for a few moments and said, "I'm going to do that." The next day she told me she had written a letter to her father, asking his forgiveness. "I saw that by blaming him I was refusing to forgive, refusing to admit that he too had suffered in his life and needed my compassion," she said. "Now that I have done this, I feel free for the first time in my life. This morning, life is flowing through me, and it is sweet." Since then she has written me twice, letters filled with happiness. In one she said of her father, "Last week I even asked his advice, and he was shocked and pleased."

The two options I have described, scapegoating and forgiving, define the two available religions, the world's two fundamental conceptions of salvation. We continually choose between these two religions: either we accept Christ's payment for the losses we have suffered at others' hands, or we refuse it by demanding that they be made to pay for those losses. If we refuse it, we believe his suffering either does not apply to the offense we have suffered or is not sufficient. His sacrifice as the Lamb of God seems irrelevant to us. Inconsolably resentful, we want a scapegoat. Our offender, or at least someone on this earth, must pay the difference, make up for what we have lost.

That kind of talk suggests what the Lord might have meant when he said that scapegoaters—those who "sought occasion against one another and forgave not one another in their hearts"—are guilty of the greater sin (D&C 64:8). How can someone who refuses to forgive an injury be doing something worse than the person who perpetrated the injury? If we ask the question that way, we are unlikely to arrive at the answer. But if we ask what can make one sin greater than another, then we see that it is not how much blame it deserves (the Lord, after all, is scarcely interested in blame) but instead the degree of scapegoating in it, which is to say, the degree to which it rejects Christ's atonement. The rejection of the Atonement, it seems to me, is what makes an unforgiving heart so sinful. The sin of refusing to forgive involves us in the sin of refusing to accept Christ's forgiveness. As President Spencer W. Kimball wrote, "He who will not forgive others breaks down the bridge over which he himself must travel."[6]

Surely that is part of what the Lord meant when he said that his disciples who would not forgive one another were "for this evil . . . afflicted and sorely chastened" (D&C 64:8). What could be a heavier affliction, a sorer chastening, than the self-amplified misery of one who will not accept the relief the Savior offers from the corrosive emotion of resentment, the agony of a vindictive, hopeless heart?

Serious abuses seem not to be decreasing. Indeed, more and more of them are coming to light, of a kind that past generations often dared not name. They are perpetrated by the strong upon the weak. In too many instances the horror of the abuses has been so great that no adjectives at our disposal suffice to express it; it is unthinkable. They strike near the heart of everything most holy in life—everything critical for human wholeness. No one can seriously question whether exposing and trying to prevent such abuses is the right thing to do.

The issue I am concerned with is not whether we should oppose abuse; we must. I am concerned with how. Some, no doubt with good intentions, are resolutely unforgiving, contending that some abuses are simply too heinous to be forgiven. It would be wrong, they say, to let the offenders "off the hook." Or they say that the victims of such abuse cannot forgive, no matter how they might wish to, because the damage inflicted is too great.

This position assumes that forgiving someone requires that we pretend whatever they have done to us never happened. It assumes that our forgiveness of our abusers is designed to release them from bondage rather than to release ourselves—as if it had nothing to do with whether or not we accept the gift of the Atonement. The freedom that forgiveness brings is not, at least initially, for the forgiven; it is for the forgiver. It concerns not what the perpetrator did in the past but what the victim is doing now. Understood this way, forgiveness releases us from the thrall and anguish of the resentment that accompanies the belief that one has been irreparably damaged; it becomes an opportunity for sweet liberation. The horror happened, yes; but through forgiveness we find in Christ consolation, meaning, increased sensitivity, purification, and even feelings of pure love.

It may help to offer one example of the scapegoating mentality from among the many prevalent in our contemporary culture.[7] I refer to some adherents of the so-called "recovery" movement that has gained great popularity in recent years. (I do not speak of all of them by any means; there, as elsewhere, it is usually not the program or cause they support that makes particular individuals suspect but the motivation and attitude with which they support it.) These adherents describe, correctly, how the violated child suffers at the hand of abusive caretakers terrible feelings of humiliation and anger and is simultaneously taught by those same abusers to feel ashamed of having those feelings. The brilliant ethnologist Gregory Bateson called this contradictory set of expectations a "double bind": the expectations of the abusers both provoke and forbid the child's resentment. They coerce the child into hiding resentment behind outwardly "good" behavior that will please and pacify them.[8]

That makes the child an unwitting conspirator in the family's cover-up of the abuse. Many children in such a situation work doggedly to keep the family in equilibrium, despite constant tensions or outbursts from others; they deny even to themselves that anything might be wrong. But always these children harbor a deep sense of discomfort about their own worthiness and acceptability. They may become "addicted" to the counterfeit reassurance they get from pleasing others. In the vocabulary of the recovery movement, these children are said to avoid feeling the anger and resentment their abusers have aroused in them. They are said to be "in denial." They produce a false public self—or so the recovery movement says—to protect and to hide the private, angry, "real" self. The public self feels constantly driven to prove itself and win approval, as if trying to gain absolution for deep shame. This self seems to have no identity apart from others' opinions. But, of course, the shame and self-doubt abide, because the good opinion of other people never silences the haunting parental voices that say, "You can't," "It's your fault," "You aren't worthy."

The scapegoating mentality shows itself not so much in the foregoing diagnosis of the problem (though I think this diagnosis is deeply flawed) as in the remedy that some of the recovery movement adherents prescribe. According to them, to recover from the condition I have just described, the victim must acknowledge and fully feel long-suppressed anger. Only by so doing can the victim "come out of denial" and be liberated from the emptiness, fear, self-loathing, or other problems left in the wake of the abuse. Indeed, in many cases moving from this stifled condition to open anger temporarily brings with it a promise of relief, as if a new day were dawning. The freshly recollected or reconstructed abuse explains just about every personal difficulty or self-disappointment the individual has experienced; it feels like a repudiation, once and for all, of reliance on a damaging relationship; it goes a long way toward

135

settling old scores. Is this not a pathway of escape from all that has gone wrong before? How could it not lead to something much better?

But the promise is illusory. Some victims, once embarked upon this journey that starts with anger, at last let their anger go and forgive their victimizers, often after long and difficult struggles; they abandon their initial path for a better one. In these cases, though certainly not in all, feeling angry may have served an important purpose temporarily. I have seen a few such instances but think they are in the minority. Those who indulge in anger without letting go of their identity as victims, and instead resolutely continue to accuse, grow increasingly miserable. You may have observed this yourself if you know an abuse victim who has taken the scapegoating "remedy" to heart. By attempting to put right the past wrongs, the individual who begins as scapegoat burns with increasing resentment and thereby takes up the role of scapegoater. He or she becomes a wrongdoer and bears the scapegoater's unwanted burden of conscience and desperate need to expend a continuing effort to justify a hard, retaliatory heart. Exchanging the role of scapegoat for that of scapegoater changes nothing fundamentally; it brings no end to retaliation and sorrow. Those who make this exchange must cling to their miseries as evidence of having been violated, and in some cases they "act out" their anger, becoming overt victimizers themselves. It is in this pattern that some abused children become abusers when they grow up.

Compare this counterfeit solution with forgiveness, as illustrated in the following true story. For most of his life, Samuel exhibited symptoms that would have led many therapists to assume childhood abuse even before talking to him about his history. Much of the time he was sunk in deep depression, a kind of utter darkness of spirit that often completely incapacitated him. He had been put up for adoption by his biological parents, and his adoptive parents were highly dysfunctional individuals who apparently could not relax their concern for their own agendas enough to nurture or to love him. Like many other victims, this was a child whose shocking introduction to this life was cold, systematic rejection and mistreatment. So harsh was his self-loathing that, though a believing member of the Church, he became involved in what he himself considered despicable sexual activities. Professionals labeled him an addict. He spent a great deal of time with psychiatrists who for years medicated him heavily with very limited success. One day he appeared at my door and asked me to help him. I told him I would stay by his side but wanted him also to consult with David Hamblin, a psychotherapist in private practice who believes in the religion of atonement as much as I do and who played an important role in what happened next.

The following week Samuel came to see me and recounted a significant event. That morning, he had been pondering a recurrent dream in which he found himself in an abandoned house—the furniture gone, the windows boarded up. The waning light of sunset filtered through the windows. He became aware of beings moving outside the house—vampires, scratching to gain entrance. As he continued in this reverie, he found himself reliving the dream, even though now he was awake. He realized this was the house of his grandparents, and in his mind he went out on the veranda, where he encountered his adoptive father, as a man in his early thirties, smiling.

The two men walked together onto the lawn and sat down to talk. Samuel felt a desperate yearning for his father to give him a blessing, to provide some of the care and love and emotional sustenance of which Samuel felt he had been deprived. As they sat there, his father put his head on Samuel's shoulder and then diminished in size, becoming smaller and more vulnerable than the adopted son sitting by his side. All of a sudden Samuel realized that his father was the one who needed a blessing. For the first time ever, he felt compassion for this man. Precisely with the advent of this feeling, the Savior appeared and silently held both father and son in his arms and,

137

for the first time ever in his life, Samuel felt the Savior's love for him. He spent the hours before he came to see me that day walking in the mountains, weeping profusely, in a release, both painful and joyous, of pent-up feelings for which he did not even have a name.

"I anticipated that I would one day need to go through some sort of process of excusing my father for how he treated me," Samuel said. "But that is not at all what happened. Instead I came to the realization that he needed me even more than I needed him, and I had closed my heart toward him. This, I had to confess, I had always known in some deep and unadmitted way. I felt a tremendous sense of regret, not because I knew during my growing-up years what to do for him, but because I had not been able to help him. What left me in this moment was my conviction that my parents were to blame for my condition. Yes, in one sense they had misused me, but they could not have done better than they did. I remembered with great sorrow something I had once been told: that my father stuttered as he was growing up and his father took him to the basement and beat him to get him to stop.

"My problems have been rooted in a willful insistence on paying the price for all my troubles myself. By judging myself so ruthlessly, I kept myself from admitting that it was really my father I resented, and this I'm sure was a kind of cover-up. It allowed me to excuse myself for closing myself to my father and his needs. Being the mistreated and deprived one, I couldn't be expected to reach out to him. Opening myself to the Savior would have ruined that excuse. In long hours of introspection, I have figured out this much, at least——that my savage judgments upon myself are in some way connected with unwillingness to open myself to the people I blamed for my problems. That is why I am convinced that my refusal to let the Savior bear my burdens has in a certain way been willful——even though that would have seemed preposterous to me a year ago. I began to

138

feel his love for me the moment I opened myself to love my father."

Samuel's story reinforces a profound truth about the unforgiving condition. It's a kind of trap. From inside it, the doctrine of forgiveness just doesn't make sense. Before letting his heart be touched by, and forgiving, the person he was blaming, Samuel could not see that blame was not the issue; he could not comprehend the meaning for him of the doctrine that the Lord has satisfied every debt we owe to one another. To him, blame *was* the issue—the only issue.

To be convinced, as scapegoating victims are, that someone is to blame is like living in Flatland, a country of only two dimensions where it is impossible to comprehend the possibility of a third dimension.[9] That is why, when I commend the therapy of forgiveness, those caught in a scapegoating outlook will tend to think that forgiving absolves the perpetrator of responsibility. As Wayne Muller suggests, saying that blame is not the issue sounds to them like saying the perpetrator should be let off the hook. And since in their minds blame *is* the issue, refraining from blaming the abuser must mean that the victim ought to be blamed for the abuse. "You are blaming the victim!" they often say.

We need to realize that they cannot, at least for the moment, see any other possibility—because it simply does not compute with them that the therapy of forgiveness blames no one. We would be wrong to find fault with them; we would be unforgiving. If we judge them, we ourselves will be caught in just such a box as they are, unable to see that we too are rejecting the therapy of forgiveness without realizing it.

Samuel's story also helps us appreciate a second truth—that forgiveness may not be easy to extend. No work is more demanding or, I believe, more significant. It heals individuals; it heals families; it heals generations united by blood or adoption. To forgive another might take years or become the work of a lifetime, and that is just as it ought to be.

139

Wendy Ulrich, a consultant with a background in psychology who says that "we deserve to forgive," writes that the process must not be cut short. As heart-wrenching as it may be, we need to pass through the difficult experiences that lead us to realize, by suffering them, the painful consequences of sin. This process, Ulrich says, "clarif[ies] our efforts not to repeat them" and enables us to "more fully appreciate what Christ endured during the Atonement."[10] Her work acknowledges the immense difficulty of coming to forgiveness without watering down the absolute need for it. She quotes President Gordon B. Hinckley approvingly: "If there be any who nurture in their hearts the poisonous brew of enmity toward another, I plead with you to ask the Lord for strength to forgive. . . . It may not be easy, and it may not come quickly. But if you seek it with sincerity and cultivate it, it *will* come."[11]

A terrible storm seems to be gathering on the horizon of our future. In increasing numbers, children are accusing their parents of rejecting, mistreating, or even violating them. Often the accusation comes after the children have reached adulthood. No doubt in many or most cases the recollections are true. But even when they are false, the mere accusation creates a presumption of guilt, just as it did in Puritan Salem. Today being accused of any kind of child abuse damns a person in the public mind.

It compounds this problem that the family takes sides, and hatred spreads like a contagion. Neighborhoods and even communities can become hideously divided. Perhaps the only thing as poignant as listening to a story of child abuse is listening to the story of parents completely broken and a family utterly shattered by allegations of abuse. A public accusation that is true shatters a family; a false one creates a tragedy at least as great. Although I don't want to deal here with the issue of false accusation (a number of responsible researchers have been writing with alarm on this subject[12]), I do want to point out what everyone who has ever exchanged accusations with another person knows: once we begin scapegoating, it becomes easier and easier to exaggerate and even contrive offenses.

What I have been addressing is whether scapegoating is constructive when the accusation is true. Many who encourage identifying the perpetrator and "feeling all their anger" typically insist that the victim avoid all contact with the perpetrator, even if the perpetrator is a parent. We must, of course, do everything necessary to prevent child abuse from recurring, but some think that means adult survivors of abuse must avoid all contact with their parents. They say this strategy is essential for the individual's healing. But following this advice virtually precludes forgiveness and reconciliation from the start. Is this not the same pattern as believing that a great cause justifies using oppressive methods—a kind of abusiveness in reverse?

What could be more demonically ingenious than to infect a noble cause—in this case, opposition to abuse of children—with ignoble motives? How could Satan strike a more telling blow than to enlist us in a counterfeit solution, one that in the end only increases the enmity among us? Unless we are vigilant, we not only will see but will ourselves foster division and sorrow within the human family and think we are doing God a favor.

To ensure that this never happens, we should always remember who established the scapegoating pattern: Satan, "which deceiveth the whole world," was "the accuser of our brethren" and "accused them before our God day and night" (Revelation 12:9–10). The religion of scapegoating will claim to end the cycle of enmity and suffering by setting things right once and for all. But we must not be deceived. We would do well to remember the Buddhist saying: "Hatred never ceases by hatred; but by love alone is healed. This is an ancient and eternal law."[13] "Therefore, renounce war and proclaim peace, and

141

seek diligently to turn the hearts of the children to their fathers" (D&C 98:16). There is no real peace, ever, without forgiveness.

Whereas the religion of scapegoating seeks to turn many of us against our parents, the religion of atonement calls us all to turn our hearts towards them, even in their weakness and sins. Whereas scapegoating teaches us to refuse to reconcile, the Savior said that to come unto him we must be reconciled (3 Nephi 12:22–24). He commands us, if we would be his and enjoy the peace that passes understanding, to become of one heart, one with another (D&C 35:2; 38:27). He lives to help us do so.

True Christianity, the religion of atonement, is not merely one road to salvation among many others; it is the only road. The alternative, scapegoating, sets individuals against one another, giving each a sense of justification in refusing to be reconciled. Though religions call certain scapegoating rituals "atonement," unless these rituals "[point] to that great and last sacrifice" of Christ (Alma 34:14), they provide at best only a temporary and deceptive sense of purification; the cleansing they proffer is illusory—a psychological trick, a communal self-deception, an empty ritual. No real payment for sin underwrites the promissory note conveyed in these rituals.

On the other hand, Christ's willingness to allow himself to fully feel the effects of all the harms we have done to one another offers us the only actual, rather than merely ritualistic, atonement, the only actual payment for those harms. That entitles him and him alone to forgive us for inflicting such harms, to cleanse us from our guilt, and to convey to us, in an intimately individual and personal way, assurance of his having done so.

We have only to accept the payment and the forgiveness (which means renouncing all scapegoating claims against each other and repenting of the sins that make us want to make such claims) in order to be relieved of sorrow and discover peace. "For this is thankworthy, if a man for conscience toward

142

God endure grief, suffering wrongfully. For what glory is it, if, when ye be buffeted for your faults, ye shall take it patiently? but if, when ye do well, and suffer for it, ye take it patiently, this is acceptable with God. For even hereunto were ye called: because Christ also suffered for us, leaving us an example, that ye should follow his steps: . . . Who, when he was reviled, reviled not again; when he suffered, he threatened not; but committed himself to him that judgeth righteously: Who his own self bare our sins in his own body on the tree, that we, being dead to sins, should live unto righteousness: by whose stripes ye were healed" (1 Peter 2:19–21, 23–24).

Only the real Atonement offers a truly cleansing power; only when forgiveness flows from acceptance of that atonement does the mercy in it respect the divine law of justice. As the scripture says, without a real atonement, "all mankind were lost; and behold, they would have been endlessly lost were it not that God redeemed his people from their lost and fallen state" (Mosiah 16:4). The religion of atonement and the unconditional forgiveness required to participate in it contain the only power to heal humankind.

NOTES

1. Viktor E. Frankl, *Man's Search for Meaning* (Boston: Beacon Press, 1992); Corrie ten Boom with John and Elizabeth Sherrill, *The Hiding Place* (New York: Bantam Books, 1974); Jacques Lusseyran, *And There Was Light*, trans. Elizabeth R. Cameron (New York: Parabola Books, 1987).

2. Wayne Muller, *Legacy of the Heart: The Spiritual Advantages of a Painful Childhood* (New York: Simon & Schuster, 1992), 10.

3. C. S. Lewis, *The Great Divorce* (New York: Macmillan, 1946), 67–68.

4. See René Girard, *Violence and the Sacred,* trans. Patrick Gregory (Baltimore: Johns Hopkins University Press, 1977), 97–98.

5. Dennis Rasmussen, *The Lord's Question* (Provo, Utah: Keter Foundation, 1985), 63.

6. Spencer W. Kimball, *The Miracle of Forgiveness* (Salt Lake City: Bookcraft, 1969), 269.

7. See, for example, John Taylor, "Don't Blame Me!" *New York,* 3 June 1991, 26–34; Joseph Epstein, "The Joys of Victimhood," *New York Times Magazine,* 2 July 1989, 20–21, 39–41.

8. Gregory Bateson, "Toward a Theory of Schizophrenia," in *Steps to an Ecology of Mind* (New York: Ballantine Books, 1972), 201–21.

9. Dillon Inouye introduced me to this idea, found in Edwin A. Abbott, *Flatland* (New York: Dover Publications, 1952).

10. Wendy L. Ulrich, "When Forgiveness Flounders: For Victims of Serious Sin," in *Confronting Abuse,* ed. Anne L. Horton, B. Kent Harrison, and Barry L. Johnson (Salt Lake City: Deseret Book, 1993), 353.

11. Ibid., 347; emphasis added.

12. See, for example, Carol Tavris, "Beware the Incest-Survivor Machine," *The New York Times Book Review,* 3 Jan. 1993, 1, 16–17; David Rieff, "Victims, All?" *Harpers Magazine,* Oct. 1991, 49–56.

13. From the Dhammapada, quoted in Muller, *Legacy of the Heart,* 12.

COMPLEXITIES, COVENANTS,

AND CHRIST

CHERYL BROWN

Such sweetness comes whenever Latter-day Saints gather, whenever we have moments of any kind away from a "lone and dreary world," whenever in the grace of God we are able to touch one another, to share. Whether at Women's Conference or rough camp, at Education Week or general conference, together we laugh, cry, yearn, ache, and sing. We ponder deep and profound doctrine, talk about the trying and the trivial, feel the need to rise—both out of the seats that just don't seem to fit our bodies and out of world circumstances that just don't seem to fit our spirits.

When we head back into our normal lives away from those safe harbors of fellowship, sisterhood, and inspiration, we know circumstances will be different. We know that seeing and doing what's right seem simpler and easier when we are together, that both become much more complicated and difficult when we are on our own, facing the complexities that constitute part of normal life.

The Lord understands those complexities but nevertheless invites: "Lift up thy heart and rejoice, and cleave unto the covenants which thou hast made" (D&C 25:13). Can we also come to understand the complexities of our lives and how our

Cheryl Brown is associate dean of the College of Humanities and a member of the Department of Linguistics at Brigham Young University. She served a mission in Chile, has taught Book of Mormon for several years, and co-chairs her ward activities committee.

145

covenants relate to them and our capacity to rejoice? Can we come to an appreciation of the covenants and also to an appreciation of the One who invites us to cleave unto them and rejoice?

I believe the answer to those questions can be a resounding "Yes!" We can understand the complexities of our lives, our covenants, and our Savior better, and we can rejoice more. But in order to do that, we need the perspective of a different time, a time before the veil dropped over our understanding, a time when the Lord "laid the foundations of the earth," and we all, with full understanding but no mortal experience, "shouted for joy" (Job 38:4, 7). The reason for our joy is revealed in more detail in Abraham 3:24–25: "And there stood one among them that was like unto God, and he said unto those who were with him: We will go down, for there is space there, and we will take of these materials, and we will make an earth whereon these may dwell; and we will prove them herewith, to see if they will do all things whatsoever the Lord their God shall command them."

Do we understand the implications of these passages of scripture? We shouted for joy about a test! We wanted this opportunity because we knew what it meant. We knew that this life was the school of godhood. Although we had not experienced how difficult mortality would be, we knew the Lord's work was "to bring to pass the immortality and eternal life of man" (Moses 1:39). We knew our Father's curriculum was designed so that we would learn to make the kinds of choices he makes, to have the kind of compassion he has, to be the kind of person he is.

We were not fooled by Satan's great lie that we could enjoy eternal life, God's type of life, without learning how to make choices on our own. When our Savior stepped forward, covenanted to offer himself and to lay the foundations of the earth so the plan could go forward, we shouted for joy.

And now the schoolwork is upon us. According to

President Spencer W. Kimball, we each have different assignments—different missions in life, ones to which we previously agreed. In the general women's meeting in September 1979, he said: "Remember, in the world before we came here, faithful women were given certain assignments. . . . While we do not now remember the particulars, this does not alter the glorious reality of what we once agreed to."[1] The Savior covenanted to fulfill his mission; we covenanted to fulfill ours. And the tests were laid out. Because of what we are trying to become, the training is complex and the tasks and tests often difficult, even though they hold promises of great joy and fulfillment.

Though we all have different tests (I sometimes think of mine as a series of "story problems"), the nature of the tests seems to be common to us all, falling into two categories—tests of understanding and tests of time. Probably all of us would be more than happy to deal with the complexities, the disappointments, the unfulfilled expectations of our lives if we just understood better what they were about. If only we could see the causes and purposes behind illnesses, disappointments, difficult relationships, early deaths, and heartaches of all human kinds, we could both endure and handle them better. But not understanding, we are tested "to see if [we] will," of our own free will and walking by faith, "do all things whatsoever the Lord [our] God shall command [us]" (Abraham 3:25). These are tests of understanding.

The tests of time are of two types. One type seems to be a daily quiz in which we must decide each day what we are going to do with the twenty-four hours the Lord has given us. The second type is related to the tests of understanding. In the complexities of our lives, in our trials, even if we don't understand all of their causes or their purposes, we could endure if we knew when they would end. Young women would quit fretting about not being married if they were sure that in two years from today they would be married. Mothers would move steadily forward if they knew that their wayward children

147

would be fully active in just six and a half years. The elderly would be patient in suffering if they knew the pain would end by October 25 or some other definite date. Even without understanding, we could handle many of our complexities better if we knew exactly when resolution was coming. But we don't, and so we are tested to see if we will do whatsoever the Lord commands under those conditions for as long as he sees fit.

Tests of time. Tests of understanding. Tests of this well-designed mortal earth where the veil blocks our understanding and where we come from eternity to dwell in time. These are complexities.

Covenants. Baptismal covenants, sacramental covenants, temple covenants, marriage covenants. The covenants we make on this earth are designed to lead us through our complexities and help us decide what to do when we do not understand, or when demands press upon us, or when we feel as if we cannot hold on one second longer. We are invited to lift up our hearts and rejoice and to cleave unto the covenants we have made. They are sure sources of guidance and strength. One covenant we repeat almost every week specifies the means by which that guidance and strength come: "They . . . eat in remembrance of the body of thy Son, and witness unto thee, O God, the Eternal Father, that they are willing to take upon them the name of thy Son, and always remember him, and keep his commandments which he hath given them, *that they may always have his Spirit to be with them*" (Moroni 4:3; emphasis added). This one covenant assures us that as we commit ourselves to following the Son, we can always have the Spirit to be with us—and the Spirit can guide us to see where we most need to put effort when we don't understand what a particular test is all about, and the Spirit can comfort us when the need for endurance seems too long.

Christ, through whom we make our covenants, understands fully their purposes. He also fully understands the complexities of our lives not only because he helped fashion the plan for this earth but also because he experienced the tests and complexities of mortality himself. Before Christ's birth, Alma spoke in prophecy: "And he shall go forth, suffering pains and afflictions and temptations of every kind; and this that the word might be fulfilled which saith he will take upon him the pains and the sicknesses of his people. And he will take upon him death, that he may loose the bands of death which bind his people; and he will take upon him their infirmities, that his bowels may be filled with mercy, according to the flesh, that he may know according to the flesh how to succor his people according to their infirmities" (Alma 7:11–12). Christ himself speaks of his experiences: "Which suffering caused myself, even God, the greatest of all, to tremble because of pain, and to bleed at every pore, and to suffer both body and spirit—and would that I might not drink the bitter cup, and shrink" (D&C 19:18). These are some of the very last words he uttered in his final hours: "My God, my God, why hast thou forsaken me?" (Matthew 27:46). Does he understand us when we suffer and shrink at our tests? Does he know what it feels like when we cannot bear one second more? Does he know what it means to have to go forward without fully understanding how all the pieces fit in our missions, our lives? Does he know what it means to cleave unto a covenant when things are the darkest, the hardest? I believe that even Jesus Christ had to have faith in Jesus Christ.

Because our Savior experienced mortality, we can trust that he understands how hard it is to lack understanding and yet to hold on through time. He understands personally how difficult tests can be. But, more important, through the keeping of his premortal covenant, he has made it possible for us to keep ours. His example shows us the way; his atonement redeems us from our weaknesses, faults, and failings. As Alma instructs and promises: "Come and fear not, and lay aside every sin, which easily doth beset you, which doth bind you down to

149

destruction, yea, come and go forth, and show unto your God that ye are willing to repent of your sins and enter into a covenant with him to keep his commandments, . . . and whosoever doeth this, and keepeth the commandments of God from thenceforth, the same . . . shall have eternal life, according to the testimony of the Holy Spirit, which testifieth in me" (Alma 7:15–16).

I once climbed with a group of friends to the top of Lady Mountain in Zion Canyon. The trail was treacherous. There were steep dropoffs in places. There were places where trail-builders had cut steps into the side of the mountain or placed chains for climbers to hold on to. After working our way up the difficult trail, we finally reached the "almost top." We could see the top, but reaching it required a leap across a very deep chasm, a chasm which, although narrow, plunged dangerously to the valley floor.

For many years the climb up Lady Mountain has been for me an analogy of how our Savior and our covenant relationship to him work. My part of the covenant relationship is the climb up the mountain. Although it can be dangerous and difficult, I must persevere. Although there are some slips and occasional backtracking to return to the trail, I climb. And even though I keep climbing, I will only reach the "almost top," where, because of my sins, there will be a chasm between where I am and where I want to go.

That is where Christ's part of the covenant relationship comes in, because "it is by grace that we are saved, after all we can do" (2 Nephi 25:23). He has been on the trail before us and with us, building the path, placing commandments and covenants, easing the climb all the way up. And when we reach the top and see the depth of the chasm created by our sins and the justice of God, Christ is there, the sure hand across an unfathomable separation. He reaches out because, in his covenant with us, he has promised to lift us across.

He says in Isaiah, "Can a woman forget her sucking child,

that she should not have compassion on the son of her womb? yea, they may forget, yet will I not forget thee. Behold, I have graven thee upon the palms of my hands" (Isaiah 49:15–16). Those hands reach out to us in the midst of our complexities. As the children's song states:

> His promises are sure;
> Celestial glory shall be [ours]
> If [we] can but endure.[2]

Celestial glory will be ours if we cleave unto the covenants that we have made with him who has engraven us on the palms of his hands. May we remember and rejoice in his promise as we head toward our eternal home.

NOTES

1. Spencer W. Kimball, "The Role of Righteous Women," *Ensign,* Nov. 1979, 102.

2. Naomi Ward Randall, "I Am a Child of God," *Children's Songbook* (Salt Lake City: The Church of Jesus Christ of Latter-day Saints, 1989), 3.

151

ALBANIA, A LABOR OF LOVE

CHARONE H. SMITH

I am a registered nurse, and my husband, Thales, is a pediatrician. He and I had always hoped to use our medical skills in a third-world country, and our opportunity came in 1992 when the Church called us as humanitarian missionaries to Albania. Most people have trouble placing Albania on the map, which is not surprising considering its half-century of self-imposed isolation. This tiny Balkan state, about the size of Maryland, is bordered on the north and east by the former Yugoslavia and on the south by Greece. It was ruled for more than forty years by a ruthless Stalinist dictator, Enver Hoxha, who regularly employed terror, political purges, and paranoia to control his people. Citizens who dared, even remotely, to criticize his totalitarian regime were declared enemies of the people, removed from their jobs and homes, and either killed or, with their families, sentenced for life to labor camps. Eventually Hoxha severed links with Yugoslavia, the Soviet Union, and China, all former allies. In 1967 he outlawed all forms of religion and wrote atheism into the nation's constitution. Schoolbooks were altered to teach that there is no God.

Hoxha died in 1985, but his successor, Ramiz Alia, kept communism alive. A flood of refugees fleeing to Italy and

---

Charone Hellberg Smith is a registered nurse who has been active in community affairs and state politics. She and her husband, Thales H. Smith, a pediatrician, are the parents of seven children. Together they served as two of the first LDS humanitarian missionaries in Albania.

student protests at home finally forced Alia to make some mild reforms. Then in 1989 the overthrow of the Ceausescu regime in Romania served as a catalyst for Albanian youth to begin their own relatively bloodless revolution. Albania started to open its doors to the outside world. At that time Elder Dallin H. Oaks and President Hans B. Ringger of the European Mission went to Tirana, the capital of Albania, to see if the country would accept LDS humanitarian service. The government was interested in receiving technical assistance in health care, business administration, and English language instruction. In the fall of 1991, my husband and I, along with Melvin and Randolyn Brady, were called as the first missionaries to Albania. We entered the communist nation in February 1992 as humanitarian missionaries. We were not to proselyte, though we were free to answer any questions about our religion.

When we arrived there, Albania's poverty had become pervasive and endemic. Over half the people were unemployed. Housing and food shortages had forced two and sometimes three generations of a family to live together in very small apartments. Those who were lucky enough to have jobs earned the equivalent of nineteen to thirty dollars a month. Shortages were rampant. The infrastructure of the country was dilapidated, especially in telecommunications, transportation, roads, industry, and agriculture. Many industrial plants were working at 5 percent capacity, struggling with outdated machinery and shortages of raw material.

The four of us rented a small apartment from Anastas and Sophia Suli. Fortunately, three family members spoke English, and the family was kind, friendly, and helpful. Even so, we felt very much like we were camping out. Electricity and water were available only erratically, food was quite scarce, and I got used to standing in bread lines. We adjusted, however, to the local routine. The Sulis had been very concerned that we arrive before the election, because there had been much rioting and some deaths during the April 1991 election. Thinking our stay would be short, they were astonished to learn that we intended to stay for eighteen months and at our own expense.

Melvin Brady taught free-market economy in the economics department at the University of Tirana, and Randolyn taught English. Thales and I were assigned to a dystrophy hospital, which dealt with cases of malnourishment in the very young. There we found about eighty infants and children, the oldest only two and a half. Most were ailing children of poor peasant families.

Conditions at the antiquated Russian-built hospital were horrendous. Windows were missing, and it was bitter cold. We found rooms of children swaddled like infants, even the ones who were two or older. Some could not sit or even hold up their heads. All of the children avoided eye contact, and I did not see one smile. Everything was gray—the faces, the clothes, the walls. We were overcome but didn't realize we were crying until the doctors showing us around said, "Please, don't cry." How could we not cry, seeing the complete lack of physical and emotional stimulation, human beings treated more like objects than precious little children?

We spent the first two weeks establishing trust with the doctors and staff (we were careful *never* to criticize), deciding where to begin, and praying for help and insight. Though we were overwhelmed, we began where we could. Thales worked on the skin diseases that were prevalent and made sure the children's formula provided adequate nourishment. I began working to improve the physical and emotional state of the ten children assigned to me. It soon became evident that I could serve most effectively working full time at the dystrophy hospital. Thales spent one day a week at the hospital, checking the sick children and lecturing the doctors on medical problems related to the children, such as skin diseases and developmental pediatrics. The rest of the week he spent at the pediatric hospital and the medical school, where his training and talents were desperately needed. At the medical school he consulted and presented lectures on what had happened in the field of pediatrics during the last quarter of a century. Their pediatric textbook was twenty-five years out of date.

Hardly knowing where to begin, I exercised the children, worked on their range of motion, talked and sang to them, held and loved them. The staff thought this kind of personal involvement was a little crazy, but when in time the children started to respond—began smiling, gaining weight, sitting up— the doctors were amazed. They had no idea that was what the children needed!

A scarcity of water in the hospital made difficult conditions even worse. Taps worked only two or three hours early each morning, and hospital workers hurried to fill containers for the wards, laundry, and kitchen. Consequently, baths were few and far between, and diapers were changed only on a schedule, regardless of need. Doctors and nurses couldn't believe I would hold and love a child who was soiled.

Diarrhea was rampant, especially in the summer months, as were hepatitis, salmonella, and giardia. Infrequent bathing resulted in constant skin infections, particularly scabies. Because soap as well as water was scarce, we had a continuing struggle to get nurses and doctors to wash their hands. Rats, flies, and cockroaches bred everywhere. There were no bottles; the babies were fed from metal cups because that's all there was.

I rejoiced when the Church humanitarian service sent truckloads of supplies to help in the dystrophy hospital as well as the pediatric and maternity hospitals. We received great quantities of hand and washing soap, insecticide, water containers, diapers, bottles and nipples, clothes, blankets, and much-needed medical and cleaning equipment. Toys for the children came also, but most were quickly stolen by nurses whose own children needed toys too.

I tried to teach many things by example, and I did learn some Albanian so I could communicate. Most of the time,

155

however, I worked alone. Four months after we arrived, young proselyting missionaries came to Albania and helped with the children once a week. Some of the staff responded to what I taught them; many did not. I was surrounded by apathy and exhaustion. The Albanian women worked very hard to earn about nineteen dollars a month in the hospital. They rose very early to get water for their cooking and washing at home; by the time they got to the hospital, they were already tired. One nurse said, "I know you're disappointed that we don't do more of what you've taught us, but we're so tired." Some of that exhaustion is depression. They see no way out of their circumstances.

The long years of political oppression (censorship of thought, expression, conscience, and individual liberties) plus the difficult economic situation have pushed most of the Albanian people into a spiritual numbness. Despite these problems, however, we were able to make a significant change in the physical appearance of the hospital and in the well-being of the children. When we left, many children were smiling and active. All but three of the first eighty had returned to their homes.

We formed close bonds with the Albanians during our stay. People at the hospital and the university were very aware of what we represented and showed us great respect. We learned to love and respect them also and had a difficult time leaving in August of 1993.

Now serving humanitarian missions in Albania are two nurses and a physician and his wife. The nurses are working at the dystrophy hospital, where wives of the senior missionaries also help.

A free election in March 1992 resulted in the nation's first democratically elected president, Sali Berisha. We have rejoiced to see the fledgling democracy develop and the economy gradually improve. But even with those positive changes, Albania has far to go. Unemployment is still estimated at 50 to 70 percent. Small, free-enterprise businesses are developing now, but there is still no major industry.

Perhaps most promising of all, religion is making a come-back. Because Albania was under the Ottoman Empire for five hundred years, it is about 70 percent Muslim. About 20 percent of Albanians are Greek Orthodox, 10 percent are Catholic, and The Church of Jesus Christ of Latter-day Saints has a wonderful beginning—three branches with 130 members. The people need faith—faith in God, faith in themselves, and faith in their country.

We learned a great deal from our experience. We are now keenly aware of need and suffering and of opportunities for service all around us—even at home. Returning to the United States was a far bigger adjustment than leaving. We have so much, and the Albanians have so little.

I once met Mother Teresa, who is Albanian. She said to me, "We cannot love God and man and do nothing to lessen human suffering." To have had a chance to lessen some of the suffering of precious Albanian children has been a great bless-ing in our lives. This indeed was a labor of love.

A SUMMER TOGETHER
IN GUATEMALA: A LEAP OF FAITH

RAE JEANNE MEMMOTT

M ost people who are striving to be spiritually in tune will at certain times in their lives know without question what the Lord would have them do. Taking my children to Guatemala during the summer of 1991 was one of those experiences for me.

I am a single parent of four children. My oldest daughter, Megan, turned seventeen while we were in Guatemala; my other two daughters, Mandy and Maren, were ages fourteen and twelve; and my son, Mason, was age ten. As my children had approached and entered adolescence, I became very concerned about some of their attitudes. I was also concerned by a growing lack of harmony in our family, especially during the summer months. I determined to do whatever was necessary to break the usual summer routine of wasted time and complaints that our family never did anything fun.

Two main issues seemed to be at the heart of the children's complaints. First, they felt deprived. My husband and I had separated when our oldest child was eight years old. The children and I continued to live in our affluent neighborhood,

Rae Jeanne Memmott, a single mother of four, is associate professor of nursing at Brigham Young University with a special interest in international nursing. She has worked with the homeless, the terminally ill, and the severely and persistently mentally ill. Sister Memmott serves as a Relief Society spiritual living teacher in her ward.

where our loving friends and neighbors sustained us in truly exceptional ways. Nevertheless, the children were very aware that their friends spent vacations at family condos in Hawaii while we drove our used station wagon (a real embarrassment) to California to stay with friends for our vacations. They seldom forgot that their clothes were mostly hand-me-downs, however lovely. The second issue was a sense of entitlement, or the attitude that it was their right in life to have the things that they wanted. The notion that most of us don't get all that we want but can still be grateful and happy with what we have was foreign to them. Instead, they complained that life wasn't fair and implied that someone ought to do something about it.

Though I realized my children's attitudes were not unusual, I was deeply concerned. During the 1990–91 school year, I fasted and prayed earnestly for guidance. At the same time, I looked closely at our family to discover our common strengths. I also reviewed my own life for themes that might indicate what the Lord would like me to do. In time I began to feel impressions. In April I called the children together. "I feel we need to do something different this summer that will allow our family to help someone less fortunate than we are," I told them. "Would you be willing to go to another country and work with children in an orphanage?" The power of prayer is truly amazing. Without hesitation they all said yes.

The story of how we got to Guatemala is long and involved but truly miraculous. We were blessed at every turn. Each time I thought or was told that I must be crazy—that getting us all to Guatemala was an impossibility—inner strength, encouraging words, or resolution of a financial crisis kept our plans in motion. I learned things about faith that I had never known. Familiar scriptures took on new meaning for me: "Wherefore, dispute not because ye see not, for ye receive no witness until *after* the trial of your faith. . . . For if there be no faith among the children of men God can do no miracle among them; wherefore, he showed not himself until *after* their faith" (Ether 12:6, 12;

emphasis added). Verses 17 and 18 continue, "And it was by faith that the three disciples obtained a promise that they should not taste of death; and they obtained not the promise until *after* their faith. And neither at any time hath any wrought miracles until *after* their faith; wherefore they first believed in the Son of God" (emphasis added). Many, many times as I made preparation, a leap of faith was necessary; there simply was no other way. To have refused to step ahead until things were more certain would have meant that we would not have gone to Guatemala. I pressed forward because the one thing I knew for certain was that, for whatever reason, we were supposed to go.

Such was the case as I determined where to go and how to get there. Early in our planning it seemed that I would need to do one of two things: either find an orphanage we could reach in our "much loved" station wagon, such as one just over the border in Mexico or else secure a short-term job with the World Health Organization so that my salary could cover a good share of our expenses. All my efforts in both those directions proved fruitless, so I continued exploring other possibilities. One evening as I visited with a neighbor about his archaeological expeditions to Guatemala, I asked if he knew of any orphanages there. When he replied, "Many—there are many," I was filled with an inexplicable sense of joy and excitement. This was where we were to go. I began calling airlines and travel agencies and discovered that we could cut the airfare to Guatemala City in half if we flew from Los Angeles instead of Salt Lake. Even so, my projected summer income would cover no more than the monthly bills at home plus a little for living expenses in Guatemala. I had no savings for airfare. As I struggled to find a way to purchase the tickets, I remembered a small life insurance policy I carried; perhaps the company would allow me to take out a loan against the policy. On inquiring, I discovered that the amount they would lend me was just enough to cover round-trip airfare between Los

Angeles and Guatemala City for the entire family. In my mind that was not a coincidence.

We arrived in Guatemala City on July 3. We knew no one, spoke only a few words of Spanish, had no place to stay, and were even uncertain where we were going to volunteer. (I had spent a great deal of time and energy trying to arrange all of those details, but as one arrangement after another fell through, I decided to board the plane and solve such problems as we went.) Bruce Brower, a friend of a friend, had consented to meet us at the airport. He drove us to Antigua, where I felt we should stay, and generously helped us find a place to live. Our home for the next six weeks consisted of two small rooms in a not-so-nice *posada*, or inn. One room had three single beds with just enough room to walk between them, four wooden hooks on the wall, and a small, wobbly wooden table. The other contained two single beds and a rather basic bathroom with a cold-water-only sink, a small mirror, a toilet, and a shower with an electrical device in the shower head that sometimes heated the water to lukewarm.

The afternoon of our arrival in Antigua, we arranged to volunteer at Hermano Pedro's, a huge urban facility that houses disabled people of all ages. We chose to work Monday, Wednesday, and Friday afternoons with mentally and physically disabled children, ages two through ten, most of whom were orphans. When we first began our volunteer work, we planned to stay all day, but the volunteer coordinator accurately warned us we probably couldn't last for a whole day. Many of the children couldn't walk. Some didn't understand games as simple as rolling a ball back and forth between two people. Others were so demanding of our attention that we couldn't move without three or four children hugging and pulling at us. As we soon discovered, the work was more taxing than we had imagined.

Certain things we never adjusted to. One of them was the orphanage odors. Ten-year-old Mason was particularly sensitive to odors and would say, "Mom, I just don't think I can go there." I would respond, "Well, I think you can go just one more day." So he continued, one day at a time.

Many of the employees were attendants, not professionals, who spoke no English, did not understand our jumbled attempts at Spanish, and were very likely intimidated by us. They gave us no direction and for the most part ignored us. It became clear that we needed to make our own assessment of the children's needs and develop our own plan of action. We quickly learned that what the children needed and wanted most was our love and attention. We found simple games and activities that helped diminish their disabilities. Learning to color in a coloring book, something none of the children had ever done, taught eye-hand coordination. Walking or running in the corridors exercised unused muscles and taught balance for those who could not walk on their own. Taking turns on the slippery slide encouraged social skills.

Randy, a five-year-old boy who had been born blind, simply wanted my son to hold his hand and run him around the courtyard. He had been afraid to run by himself for fear of bumping into something. So he would run Mason around the court until Mason could run no more. Randy's broad smile and giggles registered his delight with the simple act of running. When we would leave for the day, Randy would stand in his crib and cry. I was concerned about his distress until I realized that his tears were mainly a reaction to my youngest daughter's voice and manner. Each day as we prepared to leave, she would take Randy by the hand, lead him out of the courtyard, and say mournfully, "It's okay, Randy. Don't feel bad. I promise we will come back again." Of course, Randy didn't understand a word of what she was saying; however, he knew we were leaving and could tell by the tone of Maren's voice that it was a very sad occasion. With some coaching, she was able to tell him good-bye in a more positive, cheerful manner. In turn, Randy cried less when we left.

Many of the children never spoke, but their radiant smiles and wiggles of delight as we approached their cribs were more than enough to guarantee our return. Judy never stopped smiling as long as we stayed nearby. All she ever demanded of us was to be held. Sylvia, whom the other children nicknamed "Cheena" because her slanted eyes made her look like a China doll, best loved a ride in a wheelchair, usually off-limits to her for some unknown reason. Otito, an energetic, mischievous two-year-old, had arrived at Hermano Pedro's as an infant in a critical state of malnutrition. The director of nursing paraded him around the entire facility when we dressed him in Oshkosh overalls, a brightly colored T-shirt and Teva sandals, all contributed by neighbors at home. Because he was not accustomed to wearing shoes, the Tevas caused him to tip and teeter as he walked. The combination of his obviously proud grin and unsteady gait sent the staff, who loved him dearly, into fits of laughter.

A small boy with Down's syndrome became unit sentinel. He would begin shouting, "HOLA! HOLA!" (the one word he spoke clearly) when he saw us coming through the courtyard gate. In response, other children would begin shouting and rushing to greet us, but the Hola! sentinel made certain he was always the first to reach us for a hug.

Our memories of such treasured moments are many. To say we came to love those children does not adequately express the depth of our feeling for them.

Our experiences in Guatemala included much more than our work at Hermano Pedro's. Some of the experiences were painful and uncomfortable. We found it hard to constantly remind ourselves not to drink the water or eat certain foods. And we all felt some degree of culture shock and homesickness during our first couple of weeks in Guatemala. Megan had the toughest time and swore that she would walk home if I didn't get her out of there. But I couldn't get her out; I simply did not have the means to do so. She thought she was going to have an emotional breakdown until she met a handsome young man who began "hanging out" at our *posada.*

We all made many new friends, including the family who owned the *posada,* members of the LDS ward in Antigua, owners of the restaurants where we ate each day, teenagers and musicians who congregated at the central square in the evenings, and an LDS Hispanic family from Texas who own a business in Guatemala. Some of those friendships will be life-long. We didn't have the funds to tour the country, sightseeing and shopping, but we did something much more valuable. We were taken into the culture of Guatemala by our friends.

Six weeks after our arrival, it was time to return home. No one wanted to leave. We cried all the way to the airport. The children insisted we had to come back, "no matter what." My son said, "I'm not just coming back. This is where I'm going to live."

We had learned an important lesson. Happiness does not depend on clothes, car, house, or money; it depends on people. Our interaction with the people we came to know, including each other, created our happiness in Guatemala. We learned we can like—even love—those who are different from us, even when we can't speak the same language. We also learned that going to Guatemala didn't solve all of our problems. We still have problems, some of them very serious. Although my children still ask for things that they don't need and that we really can't afford, they know in their heart of hearts that they are not deprived. And I know that they know.

I'm certain that I do not yet know all the reasons that we were supposed to go to Guatemala. I only know that we were to go. I am most grateful to have been reminded in such a powerful way that the Lord will always provide the way for us to do the things he would have us do—if we will proceed in faith.

FROM NAUVOO TO RUSSIA:

THE REACH OF RELIEF SOCIETY

VERONIKA EKELUND

When the Relief Society was organized a little more than 150 years ago in Nauvoo, one of its objectives was to help those in need and distress. To honor that objective in celebrating the Relief Society's sesquicentennial anniversary, sisters all over the world were encouraged to serve in their communities. My ward in Stockholm, Sweden, was no exception. The Handen Ward is a tightly knit unit with competent, loving leaders and much love among the members. Under the leadership of our bishop, Bertil Rydgren, we have learned how to cooperate and accomplish.

As stake Relief Society president, my job was to explain to the wards in our stake how the sesquicentennial anniversary was to be celebrated. All agreed that the idea of a service celebration was excellent, but everyone wondered: What can we do that will be meaningful, that will edify both the giver and the receiver?

In the Handen Ward, Relief Society president Ingrid Jusinski and her counselors thought long and hard about their project. In Sweden we hear a great deal about the suffering of the people in the former communist nations and their urgent need

Veronika Ekelund has served as stake Relief Society president in Stockholm, Sweden. She and her husband, Mats Ekelund, are the parents of four children. Sister Ekelund is a homemaker and teaches early-morning seminary.

for help. With that in mind, Relief Society members contacted the Russian Orphanage Association in Stockholm, whose sole objective was to link needy orphanages with individuals or organizations willing to help. The association's needs were very great, and we were asked to sponsor an entire orphanage in Syktyvkar, the capital city of the forested Republic of Komi, a twenty-six-hour train ride north of Moscow. Ten months earlier, the director of the orphanage in Syktyvkar, having heard about the association in Stockholm, had written a letter pleading for help. At that time the association had been unable to find a sponsor, and the director's letter had gone unanswered. None of us had ever heard of Syktyvkar, but we found it on the map, so we assumed it must exist. This would be our project.

To proceed, the Relief Society next needed Bishop Rydgren's approval. He and his counselors decided to present the project to the ward council; they, in turn, resolved to proceed under the following conditions: the project had to be realistic, and the entire ward must participate.

We began collecting donations. When we learned that during the previous winter the children had attended school in shifts because they did not have enough warm clothing, winter wear became a priority. The Relief Society and the Young Women presidents were assigned to sort through donated items, weed out the rubbish, and organize what was left. The elders quorum and Sunday School presidents were assigned to find out about visa and customs regulations. The Young Men president was to arrange transportation for the donated goods and for whoever might accompany our shipment to Syktyvkar. The Primary president acted as secretary for the committee, and the high priest group leader and the activities committee chairman helped announce the project and encouraged ward members to take their donations to designated members' homes.

The collection exceeded our wildest expectations. One sister and her nonmember neighbor donated five carloads of supplies, mostly clothing. Another family convinced a local firm to donate one thousand packages of liquid soap. Yet another family donated twelve twenty-five-pound sacks of powdered milk. We gathered such things as a refrigerator, three sewing machines, tools, clothes, shoes, skis, ice skates, and toys. When we learned that the orphanage had to eat each meal in four shifts because they didn't have enough tableware, members came in droves with plates, utensils, cups, and pots.

With the collection well under way, the committee began investigating every possible scheme for transporting the goods to Syktyvkar. One wild plan hatched another. "We can charter a plane," someone suggested; but that was out of the question with a price tag of at least thirty-thousand dollars. What about driving the goods there ourselves? Several ward members (including myself) have chauffeur's licenses, so this proposal did not seem unreasonable. We could drive through northern Sweden, cross Finland, and then continue across northern Russia to Syktyvkar, a distance about as great as from Salt Lake City to Mexico City. That idea died, however, when we discovered that certain military regions are off limits and no roads cross through the northern part of Russia in the direction of Syktyvkar. Perhaps we could ship the goods by boat to St. Petersburg and then drive from there. Once again the answer was no. We were told there are altogether too many bandits along that stretch of highway—bandits who would stop at nothing, including killing, to get at a shipment.

The bishop was now very grateful that the committee had decided not to contact the orphanage before everything was settled: transporting the goods might be impossible. If members would be at risk, Bishop Rydgren would not permit the project to continue. My husband, Mats, refused to give up hope and reminded us of the warm feeling we had received when praying about this project. We were committed to our project—to the children at Syktyvkar—and we believed that if we persisted, we would find a solution to our transportation problem.

167

One day it occurred to us that if our Muscovite friend Svetlana, a business colleague of Mats's, agreed to help, we could ship the goods to her, and then she could forward them to Syktyvkar. We contacted her, and she agreed to help us. All we needed to do was to find a shipping firm that forwarded goods to Moscow. That was simple enough. No firms shipped to Syktyvkar, but many shipped to Moscow, and soon we had reserved half the space in a big truck to Moscow.

Bishop Rydgren gave his consent for the project to continue, and we contacted the orphanage for the first time, through Svetlana. When they understood why we were calling, they were overwhelmed and cried with joy. They had given up all hope of receiving help. We decided that representatives from our committee would fly to Moscow, en route to Syktyvkar, and pick up Svetlana, who besides providing a solution to our transportation problems, would serve as an interpreter at the orphanage.

The truck arrived in Moscow as planned and unloaded the goods at a customs depot. Svetlana was to pick them up and see that they were loaded onto the train to Syktyvkar. She had arranged for a truck to transport the 258 boxes and the refrigerator to a garage where they would be safe until it was time to take them to the train the following day.

Not everything in Russia runs as smoothly as we are accustomed to in the West, however. When Svetlana arrived at the customs depot, the personnel there would not release the goods to her. Additional forms, she was told, would have to be supplied from Sweden. Many precious hours ticked away while Svetlana negotiated to solve the problem.

But Svetlana is both decisive and resolute. Ten minutes before the customs office closed (but altogether too late according to the personnel who work there), she produced the documents needed and convinced the staff to release the goods. When Svetlana had informed Jekaterina, director of the orphanage, how many boxes were coming, Jekaterina had dispatched three of the oldest children from the orphanage to Moscow to help load and guard the boxes. By the time everything was finally loaded onto the train, only two seats—those for Svetlana's husband and brother-in-law, who had volunteered to accompany the shipment—remained. The children had to spend the entire trip, which lasted twenty-six hours, sandwiched in a twenty-inch-high space between the goods and the roof.

During this time Svetlana learned from the children much more about Jekaterina, the forty-five-year-old director of the orphanage, and about the staff who help her and the children. The orphanage housed about sixty-eight children from widely different backgrounds. One six-year-old girl and her two younger brothers had been at the orphanage about two years. One day, some time after their father had died, the young girl returned home from school to find that her mother had locked her brothers in the apartment and left—for good. The girl could not get in, and her brothers could not get out. By the time news of this situation reached Jekaterina and she convinced the authorities to break into the apartment to save the children, two days had already passed.

Half of the children in the orphanage have no parents; the others have parents who are incapable of caring for them because of illness, mental disabilities, or imprisonment. The only man at the orphanage is an electrician. On each of the three occasions when ward members subsequently visited the orphanage, numerous children followed the men everywhere, pulling and tugging at them or trying to climb onto their backs. These children have practically no male role models, and they dearly love it when men show them some attention.

Before Jekaterina went to the orphanage, all the children had been separated into age groups. Often biological brothers and sisters lived apart in separate groups in different areas of the orphanage. Jekaterina wanted the children to have the most homelike, secure, and harmonious environment possible, so she immediately set about reorganizing the entire operation, creating new groups called families. In this new organization, biological brothers and sisters always stay together.

Today, each family group at the orphanage consists of approximately fifteen children with three daytime and two nighttime "mothers." Each family has two or three bedrooms and a living room of its own. The complex also has large cultural halls where all can assemble to dance, sing, watch or act in plays, or read poetry (the performing arts play a central role in the Russian culture).

Jekaterina and her staff love the children they serve and do all that they can for them, even taking some risks. In 1986 they wanted to give the apartments and the orphanage a sort of face-lift, to make them comfortable and cozy so that the children would have a home they could be proud of. Jekaterina realized, of course, that it would do no good to ask her superiors for money for such a project. So, rather than asking, she simply took the budget for the year and bought paint brushes, paint, wallpaper, and curtains. By April the orphanage was completely renovated. They now had a cheerful, renovated orphanage but no money to buy food. What could the political committee do about that? Nothing! Children have to eat, and the committee was forced to give them more money.

Meanwhile, as the train sped northward from Moscow to Syktyvkar, my husband and the Handen Ward's Relief Society president, Ingrid Jusinski, had embarked on a flight from Stockholm to Moscow. Once in the air, they discussed how blessed we were and how wonderful that our plans had at last come together. Finally—imagine it!—they were on their way to visit the orphanage. The flight to Moscow went quickly. Svetlana met them at the airport, and after many hugs and Russian kisses (that is, on the cheek), she excitedly told them about all the problems with customs, trucks, and the train. She was so relieved to have the shipment safely on its way. Together they set out for Syktyvkar, full of excitement.

When the group arrived, they were met by Jekaterina and a very happy delegation from the orphanage. Jekaterina reported that the goods had arrived, and that just minutes before the delegation left the orphanage, the last of the boxes had been unloaded and locked in her office. No one was to touch anything before Mats and Ingrid arrived to hand over the goods officially.

In the following two days as the Swedish delegation distributed their offerings, numerous bands of friendship were tied, and many tears of gratitude shed. Hearing about our visit, a local television station in Syktyvkar came to film the story.

The orphanage "mothers" were particularly thrilled with the sewing machines—now they could sew all they wanted for the children. One girl in her early teens who received a long brown coat was so elated that she completely forgot that others were watching her. She stood for a while smiling to the mirror and then began dancing pirouettes with a bliss that suggested she had been transformed into the most beautiful of princesses. Ingrid could not hold back her tears to see how this young girl could find such joy in a used coat.

On one of the evenings when Mats and Ingrid were there, the children and their mothers put together a cultural program. The children sang and danced Russian dances as well as their own special regional dances. The high point of the visit, however, was when everyone sat together on the floor and Mats taught them about our Father in Heaven—how he loves us and wants the very best for each and every one of us. The children sat completely absorbed in this message. When Mats finished, no one spoke. No one wanted to let go of the Spirit that they all felt.

Some talked about taking the children to visit Sweden, though with sixty-five children and fifteen leaders that seemed an impossible idea. Impractical or not, the idea would not go away.

Once Mats and Ingrid were home again, Bishop Rydgren

called the ward together for a fireside. Mats and Ingrid related their experiences, showing pictures and a videotape. When the ward saw and heard what joy their efforts had brought, they wanted to do more. "Why not bring the children to Sweden for Christmas?!" There it was again, that same idea. But how? We already knew that chartering a plane would be too expensive. Someone suggested flying the children to St. Petersburg and meeting them there with private boats—but crossing the Baltic Sea in small boats in the middle of the winter would be too risky.

In Russia, Jekaterina and Svetlana also began to work on finding a way. They contacted an oil company in the region that had earned surplus profits during the year. According to Russian practices of the day, all surplus profits had to be paid to the national government. The president of the company liked the idea of sending the children to Sweden, saying, "I'd rather send the children to Sweden than the money to Moscow." He chartered a plane and paid the bill.

When we heard, we could hardly believe it. The children were coming! We had to organize ourselves quickly. With the bishop's approval, ward members agreed to house two or three children and/or a leader. Jekaterina had to arrange passports and visas for everyone. Because visas are issued solely to persons who have received a personal invitation, we sent an official invitation by fax, naming all sixty-five children and fifteen of their leaders. At the same time, we contacted the Swedish embassy in Moscow, explaining our plans and asking them to prepare for the eighty persons who would soon be applying for visas. That made the job a little easier for Jekaterina.

The committee had their hands full again. The Primary and Relief Society presidents compiled a list of families the children could stay with. Other committee members put together a program for our guests during their visit. The group was to arrive on a Saturday and return the following Wednesday. On Sunday, out of consideration for the children, who were completely unfamiliar with church meetings of any kind, we decided to shorten our meeting schedule to a special sacrament meeting. On Monday evening we organized a ward family home evening Christmas party.

The paperwork was finally completed at both ends, and the children arrived as planned on Saturday, December 26. Happy and full of expectations, they were also nervous about riding the bus to the church where they would meet their host families—people they had never seen before and whose language they could neither speak nor understand. Of course, the children were not the only ones who were anxious or who had questions. We members waited nervously at the church, asking ourselves, "What have we got ourselves into? Will we be able to communicate? Will the children feel secure? Can we give them the warmth and love they need?" When we finally met, however, all doubts were soon replaced by happy feelings.

One host family noticed that their little guest, named Dima, could hardly see a thing, even with his glasses. The host family telephoned Mats and asked if they could take Dima to have his eyes examined and possibly even to buy new glasses. And what about any others in the group who have problems seeing? A quick dialogue with the Russian leaders revealed that twelve of the children wore glasses or had poor eyesight.

Would it be possible, we wondered, to get an appointment to examine twelve children in the next two days? We could always try. We contacted several doctors, but none of them could fit the children into their schedules. On our last attempt, we called the eye division in one of the larger hospitals in Stockholm. A receptionist listened as we explained our request. "Wait a moment," she said. "I'm going to talk to the chief." After what seemed like a very long wait, she returned and asked if the chief could call us back. Yes, that would be all right.

Fifteen minutes later, the chief called and asked for more information about our group. Then she explained, "The entire staff and I had scheduled a two-hour meeting tomorrow,

173

during which time we do not have any patients booked. We have discussed the matter and have decided it is more important to examine your Russian guests, so if you can bring them here, we will look at them." All twelve children were able to have their eyes examined.

They needed it, too. Two of the children who wore glasses did not see very well with them; the exam revealed that they had perfectly good vision without their glasses. Two others, who were thought to need glasses, also had perfectly normal eyesight. But the remaining eight children needed new eyeglasses. With prescriptions in hand, we took those children to an optician to choose new frames and have new lenses made. When Dima took off his glasses, the raw sores on the bridge of his nose started bleeding. His old glasses were so thick and the frames so heavy that he had to use rubber bands to keep them in place. When his new glasses were ready and fitted, he could hardly believe he was wearing glasses at all, they were so light! And he could see clearly for the first time in his life.

That same evening everyone gathered at the stake center for the family home evening Christmas party. Since Russians do not have a Christmas tradition, we wanted to show the children and their leaders how and why we celebrate Christmas. To start with, some of our young people acted out the nativity scene, while Helena, one of our young women, read the story from the Bible. After each verse, Helena paused to let a nonmember, a Russian-speaking classmate of hers, read the same verse in Russian. We shared some of our other Christmas traditions, too, including Lucia, the queen of light, and several songs and dances that everyone could follow.

On Tuesday, a member telephoned Mats to tell him that the owner of a second-hand shop had heard about our visitors and wanted to donate some clothes. Mats, Jekaterina, Ingrid, and a few others went to visit the shop. To everyone's surprise, the owner had sixty-seven sacks and twelve boxes full of perfectly good clothes that she wanted to donate. The children returned to Russia with much besides their new eyeglasses.

Last summer, three families from the ward traveled to Syktyvkar to celebrate the orphanage's twentieth anniversary. The children were wild with joy to have their friends from Sweden with them again. During this visit, the question of continued help to the orphanage came up. Jekaterina responded, "You have given us so much already. Thanks to you, we now have all that we need. What we would like from you in the future is your love, your friendship and knowledge, and above all else, we want your smiles.

"When we have dark days here," she continued, "and I can assure you, at times it feels like we cannot go on, I gather the children around me and we talk about our friends in Sweden. We talk about all you have done for us, and in particular, the joy that radiates when you smile. We believe that joy comes from your faith. Please, give us your smiles. And your faith."

Mats took that opportunity to teach them again about the gospel of Jesus Christ. The Spirit was present; they all felt it, and there was not a dry eye when Mats finished speaking to them and then blessed their home. Afterwards, one of the children, who had just been taught to pray, offered a closing prayer.

We will always be grateful to our Relief Society leaders for encouraging us to celebrate the sesquicentennial through service in society. Serving the Swedish Orphanage Association has been a rewarding project. Mats once said, "I wonder who received the most: those in Syktyvkar or we in the ward?" This project has given us wonderful, unforgettable memories. In cooperation with and under the leadership of the priesthood and together with the other Church auxiliaries, we women *can* perform miracles. And in this day and age, miracles are truly necessary.

ACROSS A LIFETIME OF FRIENDSHIPS: "NO MORE STRANGERS AND FOREIGNERS"

ANN N. MADSEN

Across a lifetime of friendships I have come to believe that all friendships are long-term. Life is eternal. So are our friendships. Eternal, meaningful friendships, of course, presume commitment and loyalty as well as tolerance and respect. Joseph Smith provides a model. He said, "Mohemetans, Presbyterians, &c if ye will not embrace our religion embrace our hospitalities."[1]

I have been lucky enough to travel widely, but I don't feel that traveling is necessary to make friends from far and near. Some of my faraway friends I met right in my own home-town—they came to me. Others I met in their hometown—I went to them. Let me tell you about a few of them.

Gordon Roland Smith of Chelsfield, England, was seventeen years old when his friend sent an ad to a Salt Lake City newspaper for a young woman pen pal. My MIA—now called Young Women—adviser brought the ad to our class one evening, and I decided to answer it as a missionary venture. I

Ann N. Madsen is the mother of four, including an Indian foster son. She teaches in the Department of Ancient Scripture at Brigham Young University and has taught at the BYU Jerusalem Center for Near Eastern Studies, where her husband, Truman G. Madsen, was director. She served as Relief Society president in the Jerusalem Branch.

was fourteen years old, and World War II was in progress. Our correspondence began immediately, and we wrote about once a month. Soon after we began writing, Gordon joined the RAF, the British Royal Air Force. He seemed so mature and intelligent and educated, and I worked over each of my replies to try to match his thoughtful and interesting prose. We exchanged photos and our youthful philosophies about war and peace. As subtly as I could, I was introducing him to the gospel. He shared his dreams with me of being a painter. He sent me sketches and watercolors, which I framed and have hanging in our home today. When the London Temple was built, he stood in a queue for hours to see it so that he could report all the details to me. We exchanged books and other small gifts. What an education the correspondence was.

After several years, when I married, we mutually decided to keep writing. Then he married, and we each began our families. During that busy time, we wrote less but never lost touch. Once we even spoke on the phone when my husband and I had an unscheduled layover at Heathrow Airport. Gordon was by then the assistant headmaster in a boys' school—I thought of Mr. Chips—and I was an exuberant American. Our conversation was a stereotype of what you would expect from a staid Englishman and an uninhibited American. Since then—I think that contact helped us want to meet face to face—my family has visited his family, lodging with them for a night or two at their country cottage named Melilot, and they have stayed with us in Provo. Our children know each other, and we have shared some defining moments in our lives. One such time the Smiths were our guests in Provo when we were assembling a memory quilt for my daughter Mindy's marriage. Gordon's wife, Marjory, had earlier sent a particularly lovely square. She and I were crawling on the floor trying to piece this king-sized quilt perfectly and were having difficulty with only one spot. Gordon wandered in, saw us hard at it, and suggested, "Truly artistic creations are never perfect." I say that to myself often.

He and I still write after forty-seven years. We still share our philosophies of life. He is a follower of the teachings of Emanuel Swedenborg. Our sweet friendship continues to be one of the joys of my life.

In 1973 I accompanied my husband, Truman, who was on Church assignment, to Hong Kong and China. In the tiny town of K'Liao in south Taiwan, I first met Julie Wang, a sixteen-year-old who had recently joined the Church. At our first meeting, she ran toward me, arms outstretched to hug me. "You are the first really Mormon sister I have ever seen!" she cried. We became fast friends. She was full of questions, and though her English lacked a little here and there and my Chinese was nonexistent, we communicated heart to heart, often with few words. When the time came for us to leave, I almost couldn't. We both cried. I searched through my purse for any little gift or memento I might leave with her, but my simplifying for travel had left no nonessentials. I had brought a pink felt-tip pen to use for my Taiwan journal so I could recognize it quickly. (Pink for Taiwan, orange for China. I was so organized!) That priority vanished, and I gave her the pink pen along with my home address. For the first few months of our correspondence, each of her letters and aerograms was written in that easily recognizable pink.

We loved writing to each other. "I hope you have a fun vacation in California," she wrote. "The ocean is so much fun! When you are in California I will go down to the beach and you can call from there and I can call from here and the clouds and birds will carry our messages of concern and love across the wide waters." About two years after our visit, she came to stay with us for a month. I took her with me to help teach my MIA Maids, and I remember so well how she taught them to pray. I asked her just to tell them how she talked to Heavenly Father. She said, "I say, 'God, this is Julie Wang.' Then I wait, and he says, 'Yes, Julie?' Then I tell him thank you for all the beautiful world, and I mention what I could need."

Julie moved to Toronto to go to school and there married a fine Canadian lawyer, not a Latter-day Saint. She now has four beautiful children and has become less and less active in the Church, but she wrote recently that she wants to regain her earlier faith. Of course, I tell her honestly how that can be done. I recently found all her letters written with the pink pen and will send copies along to her soon. We write regularly, and she always calls me on my birthday. While we were living in Jerusalem, during my five-year teaching assignment at the BYU Jerusalem Center, Julie and her husband, John, visited there for a convention and we had a good visit. We said to each other, whoever would have thought that a woman born and reared in a valley in the Rocky Mountains would meet a young girl born in Taiwan and that they would later see each other in Jerusalem. What a triangle on this shrinking globe!

I first met Sister Diodora Monachi of Greece in Jerusalem just a year ago. I interviewed her for a book I was writing on the lives of various women who live and work in that stress-filled city which knows neither war nor peace.

We sat in the sunshine at the Greek Orthodox patriarch's summer residence on the Mount of Olives, sipping fresh lemonade and sampling the wonderful white cheese produced there. Kittens played at our feet as she unfolded her life as a nun before me. By the time the two-hour visit was finished, we were fast friends.

Some of my favorite memories are of our walks on the Mount of Olives and working together either at her beautiful, walled compound or mine. When the time came for me to return to Utah, she helped me pack my office and my home, and we laughed and cried together as I prepared to leave Jerusalem, a city I had loved for many years. As I sorted a few things to give away, she told me how happy she had been on the day she gave away everything to become a nun. Back in Utah, when I opened the boxes and files she had so lovingly packed, I found notes, tender messages in simple Greek, which

179

she knew I could read, such as *Agape en Christos* (love in Christ).

In her last letter she wrote: "Many warm regards to your children and grandchildren. You must send us at least two each year, so that we get to know them all one day!" I would like nothing better than to have all my children and grandchildren know her.

As you think to begin a friendship with someone who lives far away, you might keep the following ideas in mind:

Be open to the adventure. Be "color"-conscious and delight in diversity. Advice I received in Relief Society as a young wife transplanted to Cambridge, Massachusetts, for my husband's doctoral program still rings true: "Now don't you Utah girls come here and hold your noses for four years wishing you were back in the only true West where things are done right! Absorb this wonderful culture. Learn New England cookery; get to know your Yankee neighbors. Take something home besides your husband's Ph.D."[2]

Remember that language need be only a small barrier. All of my friends know some English, some much less than others, yet we manage. Brigham Young University president Rex Lee has spoken of becoming "fluent in the universal language of love and friendship."[3] Don't be put off by such unusual clothing as clerical collars or habits. Remember Paul's moving declaration to the Ephesians, "But now in Christ Jesus ye who sometimes were far off are made nigh by the blood of Christ" (Ephesians 3:13). Those wearing such uniforms are likely to share with you a strong commitment to values and a God we can all worship according to the dictates of our own consciences. We allow all men and women that privilege, according to the eleventh article of faith.

Keep in touch and visit whenever possible. Write letters, phone, fax. They're all worth the money. Send photos; share new insights, joys, and sorrows.

We leave soon for a trip to Israel via Boston, London, and

Spain. In each of these places, we will be visiting friends—in London, my pen pal Gordon and his wife, Marjory. On the phone last week we agreed to meet under the clock in Charing Cross Station. The first time we met, Gordon carried one of my husband's books under his arm so we would know him. We joked about not needing that this time. In Spain, a new friend, Ubald, and his family will show us around Barcelona for a day. And in Israel are the many dear friends we made during our years there.

Express love. Care. Lift. Look always for the highest in your friend and in yourself; then point it out. I remember well how I reached for my highest as I wrote that first letter to Gordon. I still do.

Pray for each other. Prayers are faster than faxes and heard equally from any corner of this wonderful world. Prayer unites us.

In a short time my husband, two of my granddaughters, and I will be flying to Israel. Who is waiting for us there? The list is long, but among them is my gentle friend Diodora. I can hardly wait to hug her and stroll with her again on our Mount of Olives with her black habit blowing in the breeze. I will tell her of this women's conference. She will tell me of her days. We will both come away enriched.

NOTES

1. Joseph Smith, *Words of Joseph Smith,* ed. Andrew F. Ehat and Lyndon W. Cook (Salt Lake City: Bookcraft, 1980), 162.

2. Betty Hinckley taught me this invaluable lesson more than forty years ago.

3. Rex E. Lee, opening remarks to BYU-Relief Society Women's Conference, 28 Apr. 1994, unpublished.

TRUST MENTORS

JOANN SHIELDS

Shortly after graduating from law school, I moved into a downtown Salt Lake high-rise and planned to do little more than sit in the hot tub and be a business litigation lawyer. My yuppie madness did not survive the second Sunday in my inner-city ward when I was called to be the only Sunday School teacher for all youth from twelve to eighteen. That did not seem tough because only one came, but the bishop had bigger ideas. He handed me a list of twenty-five other young people who had either disappeared or never materialized. Almost every name had a pathetic margination, such as "runaway," "had baby," "on drugs," "ward of state," or "severe psychological problems." The bishop gave me carte blanche marching orders: "Do whatever it takes. Just bring them back."

I set out with cookies, balloons, and a fun's-a-poppin' attitude about how much these misused kids would just love the Lord and the Church once they were safely gathered into the fold. I found ten of them, who started attending church and other activities regularly. Throughout my seven years—including four as Young Women president—of working with youth in my ward, maybe one hundred fifty troubled youngsters passed through my modest stewardship.

I quickly discovered that most of their parents (or whatever older person happened to be in charge of them) had all the

Joann Shields is a Salt Lake City lawyer specializing in business litigation. She served a mission in Quebec, Canada, and is a member of the Young Women General Board.

adult behavior characteristics of angry two-year-olds. One mother and grandmother nearly came to blows over treats I took for my class members, so I learned to make enough for the whole family. Even then it was a fight for a bite. Perhaps treats were a genuine scarcity, but I couldn't help thinking of Ecclesiastes 10:16: "Woe to thee, O land, when thy king is a child."

I soon discovered that *all* the young people I was teaching suffered from some type of abuse, and many had been abused in every way: sexually, emotionally, spiritually, and physically. In time I learned how dear and precious they are, especially to the Father, who performed countless little and big miracles to help them feel his love and choose his life. And they did grow. But they did not stop running away, having babies, becoming wards of the state, or developing psychoses; rather, their fledgling church lives flew against the ice storm of their home lives. I do not have comfy, cozy tales about many of these young people. To date, most have not survived the storm.

I learned many things from these lost lambs. They were not inherently bad. They had not voluntarily given up their innocence; it was systematically stolen by the very people who should have been protecting it, by the immature adults who had become their enemies rather than allies and guides. The daily rip-offs and betrayals were like stab wounds to these young souls. When I tried to teach trust in God, their glazed responses were uncomprehending.

News magazines tell me that these youth are the "X Generation"—the no-sense-of-self-or-others generation. I think they are partially the soul-dead generation. They are not just in my ward; they are everywhere.

The look and state of no-being does not go away with the passage of time, just as an untreated virulent disease does not stop its rampage. I see the same death trance in the YWCA's battered women when I lead monthly discussions of their legal

183

options. I hear the description of the "X" condition when I sit on legislative domestic violence advisory councils.

I have now been involved with these youth and other abuse victims for nearly ten years—long enough to see something far more powerful than even their most excruciating pain: healing through a return to innocence; that is, through learning to trust someone and ultimately God. They heal as they develop a strong internal reality.

I have watched the Lord heal the inner and design the outer lives of the seriously injured as they regain trust in him. Usually trust in God comes through first learning to trust another person. I coined the term *trust mentor* to mean someone who teaches another how to rebuild trust.[1] Trust mentors can be parents and others who have themselves learned to trust and be trustworthy. I think that is what attaining adulthood is all about—every day acting more as the Father, the nurturer, and less as the enemy, the destroyer.

What role do adults have in teaching young people to trust God? I have discovered that people tend to get their perceptions of the Father and the Savior all mixed up with their perceptions of people. For instance, during my mission I noticed that several investigators described God with the same adjectives they used to describe their fathers. (My discovery illuminated how spiritually mature fathers really can stand in the place of God on earth.)

Some investigators had the feeling God was always playing fatalistic tricks on them or had set things in motion and then lost interest. Uncoincidentally, those people had been tortured or abandoned by their fathers. They could not comprehend a Father who was fair, much less kind, generous, and forgiving. We suggested to them the message the scriptures fairly shout: *Try him and see.*

My mission experiences merely introduced me to the emotional wasteland of chronic distrust. Distrust was *the* soul-rotting issue for *all* the troubled youth I taught. They did not trust God because they did not know enough about him—had not had enough experiences with him. They did not trust people because they knew *too* much about them—had had too many hideous experiences with them. And they lived totally outside themselves; they had no inner life—just pain and momentary release from pain. I began to see why the Father could forgive them completely for what they did to try to escape that pain and defend themselves from more of the same.

I may not always be a quick study, but when I started working with these youth, I received some on-the-spot spiritual tutoring that boiled down my job to one task with two prongs: to teach them to trust—me, with forgiveness, and the Father, without restraint.

I say "me, with forgiveness" because I finally began to realize the weight of gaining their sacred trust. My flibbertigibbet days were over. I suddenly had a truckload of promises to keep, truth to tell, fairness to mete out, confidences to guard, judgment to withhold. My heart was right and my mind was ready, but in the crucible of the moment I knew I sometimes let my charges down. I tried so hard and apologized so profusely that after a while most of them would pat me on the arm and say something comforting like, "That's okay, Joann. We know you're kinda spacey."

My mental and emotional archives are full of snapshot moments of what I call a *trust nexus,* or a trust link—that moment when the drops of a young person's experiences with me finally filled the seemingly abysmal cup and spilled over into genuine trust and finally love.

To one fifteen-year-old young woman, almost every human touch had been what D. H. Lawrence called "trespassed contacts, from red-hot finger bruises, on [the] inward flesh."[2] Naturally, she cringed and stiffened when hugged or patted even lightly. I, on the other hand, was and am a confessed serial hugger. I also know everyone needs appropriate physical affection, so I kept trying to show it to her in small, nonthreatening ways.

Establishing trust is no small thing. It is hard won and easily lost. I knew and taught this young woman four years before she reached a finger out to me, and Gumby had nothing on my bending and stretching in her direction for that entire time. For every activity I picked her up first and took her home last so I could talk to her. My jovial best self rarely met with more than her monosyllabic answers: "Yes," "No," "Nothing," "I dunno." One night she started talking a little. While I was taking her home, she told me her family had had to put their dog, also named Joann, to sleep because she was worn out. After sympathizing, I joked, "Well, now I see the writing on *this* Joann's wall"—meaning me. She shot back, "Oh no, I'm going to keep this Joann forever." I squeezed her hand and prayed for more.

A while later the Young Women were having a video party at my house. Without saying a word, this young woman sat by me, put her arm through mine, and laid her head on my shoulder. Although I was exulting inside, I hardly dared inhale or exhale for fear of dispelling her temporary relapse into innocence. This trust nexus led to many more. Several weeks later she announced from the church pulpit she liked hugs; next July she will be at the same pulpit bidding her missionary adieus. Meanwhile this young woman is earning straight A's in college biology, thanks to someone in our ward family who became a trust mentor by offering to finance her entire education at a time when he barely knew her name.

Gaining the trust of another young woman was equally demanding. She had been betrayed and brutalized by so many "adults" that she constantly interpreted others' reactions as negative. Anytime I was not beaming with relentless delight, she looked terrified and cried, "Why the crusty?" The slightest shift in tempo left her feeling ditched.

I did not have to wonder where she was on the trust scale, because she told me rather trenchantly. At our first meeting, she suddenly turned toxic and hissed, "I don't like you. I don't want to be here. You're no different from any other person. If I tell you anything, you'll use it to stab me in the back. Besides that, God hates me." I found myself modifying my missionary suggestion and just saying, "Try *me* and see."

Not so simple. This young woman called me at all hours with what seemed to be an outrageous trust obstacle course. I learned she had a superior mind but disordered thought processes. She reminded me of a kaleidoscope that was constantly being violently shaken instead of gently turned.

The trust nexus finally came after I invited her to my law office and helped her prepare a mock trial for school. We made charts, created evidence (ethically, of course), formulated arguments and examination, and practiced in my firm's moot court room. As we worked, I noticed she was gradually becoming rational and quite witty. I kept telling her (and truthfully so) that she had the makings of an analytical legal mind, and she said she might go to law school.

One night after much of her abrasive, defensive behavior had taken a rest, we talked for the first *real* time about the Lord and the Church. The Holy Ghost filled my office and her mind. The nexus was made—not just with me but with the Father. I felt like a link chaining two radiant pearls. That was three years ago. Last week I received a telephone call from one of this girl's new friends who said, "I want to join your church. Can you tell me where it is and when it starts?"

Those are "nexus" stories, and there are many more. But I could tell twice as many "no-nexus" tales. Sometimes the young people simply were not around long enough to form bonds. Our class often included new young women who would not say where they lived because it was the homeless shelter. They would attend church meetings and activities for two or three weeks, I would adore them, and then they would be gone—where, I will never know. How they will form a trust nexus with the Father only he knows. I have, however, seen him work mighty powerfully every moment he has their slightest attention.

What is my one-line message in all this? I suppose it would be a variation on President David O. McKay's motto: "Every member a trust mentor." I am not an unusual person in any way, but I have seen the Father do unusual things when I put my personal integrity on the line to help teach trust in him.

Not only am I ordinary but apart from law I am not a professional anything. A trust mentor, however, is anybody who tries to be faithful and trustworthy and who helps link young people to their Father. I often think of Michelangelo's detail from the ceiling of the Sistine Chapel entitled "The Hands of God and Man." We can fill the space between that reaching grasp.

Unfortunately we can also be "distrust mentors" and unwittingly widen the gap between the Father and his children. My lack of professional training about the human psyche does not deter me from making a few comments about how adults destroy trust and ultimately harm a young person's relationship with God—something that disturbs me intensely.

1. *Failing to teach about God and the atonement of Christ.* Adults must teach youngsters the truth about the Father and the Savior and help them erase human foibles (including their parents') from their understanding of deity (Moses 6:55–62; Ezekiel 18). Because God himself gave us scriptures specifically to help us learn about him, it is spiritual abuse not to pass these truths on to our youth. Through the scriptures young people can be *continuously taught* and *helped to experience* the unalterable facts that God:

- *Can*not (not *will* not) lie (Numbers 23:19; Titus 1:2; Hebrews 6:18).
- Forgives freely (Nehemiah 9:17; Psalm 86:5).
- Can do anything (Matthew 28:18; Luke 1:37; Alma 7:8).
- Protects constantly (Psalm 3:3; Hebrews 13:5).

• Loves everyone the same no matter what (1 Nephi 17:35; 2 Nephi 26:33).

• Stands by to meet physical and emotional needs (Matthew 6:8; Philippians 4:19; Mormon 9:27).

• Can see the past, present, and future all at once (2 Nephi 9:20; Moses 1:6; Abraham 2:8).

• Knows his children intimately (Ezekiel 11:5; Job 23:10; Psalm 139:3) and has planned a charmingly individualized course of events for each one (Words of Mormon 1:7; Ephesians 1:11).

• Answers *every* prayer in the way that is best for each child (Jeremiah 29:11–13); his noes are as loving as his yesses (1 John 5:14–15).

Young people need to know God's will would be their will if they were omniscient too! Only then can youngsters form their own relationship with the Father independent of their family relationships and all other life elements. That independent relationship could greatly ease the individuation process that naturally occurs during adolescent years as teens seek to identify themselves apart from their families.

Once young people feel the Lord's pleasure, they will not be desperate to please others. The difference is palpable. It is easier to please God than to please people.

2. *Shaming.* Literature on dysfunctional families has plenty of definitions for shaming, but I think it could be summed up as "life in the penalty box." The young person is always in trouble, has always done something wrong. Pretty soon they just *feel* wrong, even when they're doing right. I simply do not know how adults expect the Holy Ghost to speak through a conscience that has been treated equally brutally for leaving dirty dishes in the sink as for stealing cars. When everything feels like sin, nothing feels like sin.

Embarrassed or terrified by young people's misbehavior, adults often desperately resort to shaming in an effort to change it. Shaming changes nothing except trust and relationships, and

189

it destroys them. Shamers might win the little power struggles, but they always lose the child. Even more important, adults must avoid interfering with the Lord's correctional inner work through a lively conscience, which thrives when emotions function in the way they were designed.

3. *Poor role modeling.* At a public event I overheard an exchange that crystallized my thinking about poor role modeling. Long before the program started, a boy stood by his chair just looking around. A grandmother with an obviously tissue-thin nervous system screeched at him to sit down. He screeched back, "You sit down." She screeched even louder, "Don't you dare talk to me like that!"

Young people are regularly punished for merely repeating precisely what they have heard constantly since birth. Such hypocrisy staggers their mind and distorts their view of adults and authority of any kind—from law enforcement to church leaders to the Lord.

I suggest that in any situation, the adult's response is more important than the youth's. After moving through all their developmental stages, young people will eventually respond to others the way their parents responded to them. My seven-year-old niece has already learned emotionally generous responses, such as "Terrific idea" or "Good point." Sometimes it is hilarious to listen to her, because she sounds like an adult— a non-one-upping adult.

We grown-ups simply need to figure out how God responds, which is set out clearly in the scriptures and illustrated by life experience. We must also demonstrate that prayer and scripture study are *real* conversations with the Father and bring *real* solutions to life's never-ending dilemmas.

4. *Preaching that life is unfair.* I cannot believe how often I hear that life is unfair. Saying that life is unfair is tantamount to saying God is unfair. I can think of few defter ways to deny his hand in all things. Let us not be confused. Man can be unfair,

but God is fair (Ezekiel 18:25, 29). Young people need to know they may have reasonable expectations in life.

When I started working with the youth in my ward, my belief that life was fundamentally fair was shaken to the roots by what I was learning about their inner worlds. I could not help asking in my prayers, sometimes a bit angrily, why a young person with whom I worked had been required to suffer devastating blows before even getting started.

After one such prayer, I opened my Book of Mormon, and the first scripture I read was the description of Judgment Day found in Alma 12:15: "We must . . . stand before him in his glory, . . . power, . . . might, majesty, and dominion, and acknowledge . . . that he is just in all his works, and that he is merciful unto the children of men." The scripture then told me why he is just: "He has all power to save *every* man that believeth on his name and bringeth forth fruit meet for repentance" (emphasis added). That includes all the seriously wounded in this life—*especially* the seriously wounded (Matthew 9:12). In short, though improvements such as education are *an* equalizing factor, the Atonement is *the* equalizing force in life. Thus to teach that life is unfair is to distort the Atonement's powerful reality.

I never again plagued God about justice, because I have seen his merciful spiritual healing, which makes life fair—inwardly and outwardly. I instead recommitted myself to being a trust mentor with renewed faith that postnexus work is largely the Lord's. As T. S. Eliot put it, we "take no thought of the harvest, but only of proper sowing."[3]

5. *Valuing externalities and materialism.* Many adults are much more interested in appearance than in reality; consequently, families can look much better than they feel. I have seen young people with highly developed false selves because the adults in their lives demand perfection, which is fatal to the developing soul. In this life we are all developing souls from

191

cradle to grave. *Perfection* in the scriptural sense means "fully developed" (Matthew 5:48, note b).

On the other hand, *perfectionism* is a thirteen-letter code word for "highly conditional love," which, of course, is not love at all. The adult is saying, "I will love you if you should meet the unattainable expectations that I have made up so I will look good. And by the way, my expectations could change with my fears, so don't get too attached to anything."

Conditional love mangles and poisons a young person's reality, particularly the inner reality, and arrests natural development. The deadening upshot is the sense that everyone, including God, is impossible to please. One way or another, young people will rush to the arms of someone who can be pleased, even for a minute. My compassion for unwed mothers grew as I heard several say they looked to their babies for just a little love. Unfortunately, it is supposed to be the other way around. Those tiny babies are going to have a tough time trying to keep their mothers happy for the rest of their lives.

Materialism has its own nasty little insatiability: There will never be enough, because someone out there will always have more. In my work, I have seen spiritually sick zillionaires cadging for fifty cents and walking with cleats over the families for whom they are allegedly chasing it.

Only God's unconditional love breaks that cycle of unmeetable needs, but a trust needer's total acceptance by a trust mentor is usually the first step.

6. *Controlling every little thing.* I have known adults who collapse at the thought of leaving even the slightest decision to a youngster's prayers, because they do not themselves trust the youth or the asking and receiving process. In reality they do not trust God. So they end up telling a youth exactly what to do, how to feel, what to become—and all may be contrary to the young person's personality and life course. That fear-driven craziness meets only the adults' ego needs—until rebellion sets in. When I hear about a youth's "deviant" behavior, I cannot

help wondering how they were treated—what they are rebelling against.

Controlling adults do not stand in God's place; they try to stand in front of him. By setting themselves up as the ones to please in every instance, they obscure young people's sense of their relationship with God and his plan for their lives. The irony is that youth accept most readily the values of those who accept them most completely. When acceptance is complete, belief in God and personal morality are in the air a family breathes. Control suffocates all that.

Adults can help young people make mature decisions by suggesting they ask the Father themselves and by telling stories and more stories about the miracles he has performed. Even when adults do pray for young people, they often repeatedly ask the Father to do something *for* youth, when he wants to do something *in* them.

I recently had a dramatic experience that helped me see more clearly how adults can either support or impede young people's trust in God. One of my young women is astonishingly brilliant but has few resources to finance her education. During her senior year, she started receiving scholarship offers, including a full ride to a local university. As something of an afterthought, she applied to Vassar College, a very prestigious institution. Not only was she among the six hundred accepted from thirty-eight hundred applicants, but she received such a generous academic scholarship and other aid that Vassar moved down a few cloud banks into her stratosphere. I was so ecstatic when she told me that I broke into Steve Martin jive-limbo routines, nearly poking my eye out. Not everyone shared my response. Some well-meaning adults rushed in to provide this young woman with a reality check: What was she thinking? She could never get the money to travel there, let alone live. That was the kindest one. I had a feeling that the others were just ill-disguised ways of asking who she thought she was to go to an Ivy League school.

At bottom was *their* reality they were checking. Not one suggested that she ask the Father, and he is the only one who can see her future! Finally she cleared out the naysayers, and, amid all the hubbub, fasted, prayed, and received a powerful answer from the Father himself. Part of the answer was the continuous playing in her mind of the song from Disney's *Aladdin,* "A Whole New World."

Later that young woman will need to remember that experience; she will need to know the Lord placed her at Vassar and he will keep her at Vassar. When her plane lifts off next Thursday morning, so will she.

Does she know the Lord did all this? You bet. He made it unmistakably clear, not because he needs her praise but because he wants her trust.

First and last, as adult trust mentors, we should teach youth to expect more from God and less from people—to seek his approval first, knowing anyone who is attuned will approve too. Always, in Paul's words, "not as pleasing men, but God" (1 Thessalonians 2:4). When helping young people develop resilient inner lives, perhaps our own mentoring goal should not be to try harder but to trust more. As Hannah Whitall Smith said: "Thy part is to yield thyself, His part is to work."[4]

On the eternal path, young people might need fewer stop signs if adults obeyed more yield signs. Perhaps by yielding our will to God's will for them, we could "x" out the "X" in this generation. Through trusting in God we could create a whole and holy new world.

NOTES

1. Psychologist Erik Erikson describes a set of three essential developmental tasks or stages of growth an individual must pass through to become a morally and emotionally mature adult. The first and foundation task of childhood is learning to trust and to feel that the world is a safe place. Early caregivers should be instrumental in helping children to acquire this vital sense of security and hope upon which further moral and emotional development

depends. See Erik H. Erikson, *The Life Cycle Completed: A Review* (New York: W. W. Norton, 1982).

2. D. H. Lawrence, *Selected Poems* (New York: Viking Press, 1959), 113.

3. T. S. Eliot, *The Waste Land and Other Poems* (New York: Harcourt Brace Jovanovich, 1934), 83.

4. As quoted in *Bless Your Heart* (calendar), Series II (Edina, Minn.: Heartland Samplers, 1990).

TEMPERATURE TAKING

MARILYN BUSHMAN-CARLTON

My daughter and I talk often
on the phone
now that she is away for the first time.
She calls, or I do,
to pass news from different sides
of the country: she asks how
to adjust a high altitude recipe,
I need a copy of her pasta sauce,
she tells me her brother wrote,
she passed her anatomy exam.
I say it's quiet here, ask where
she gets groceries, if she went to church.
Her father, the practical,
sees decimals, pictures himself
in debtor's court, says our topics
are trivial. I think of those TV shows
where the hoodlums hold a daughter ransom,
call and tell the parents
where to leave the bag of dough.
The detective's advice is always this:
try to keep the other party on the line
long enough to get a good connection.

Marilyn Bushman-Carlton received her bachelor's degree in English from the University of
Utah. Her first volume of poetry will be published in 1995. Sister Bushman-Carlton teaches
poetry workshops at Pioneer Craft House in Salt Lake City. She and her husband, Blaine L.
Carlton, are the parents of five children.

SHARING THE SCRIPTURES IN OUR FAMILIES

ELIZABETH HUNTINGTON HALL

My children range in age from eleven to twenty-four. As they have matured, they have come to value the scriptures and use them with ease and comprehension. I feel gratified, but in truth I cannot take much credit for this development. The scriptures are so vital, valuable, and powerful that their mere availability can result in their becoming beloved. When I asked my eldest son, Tracy, how he would advise parents who wish to teach the scriptures to their children, he joked, "Tell them to leave their kids alone!" Although he spoke in jest, his response was food for thought.

Very often the best teaching has an invisible quality. As my brother John says, "It's like the air you breathe!" I have heard that children who see their parents reading at home—or even pretending to read—become better readers than children whose parents don't model reading. When our children see us using the scriptures regularly and matter-of-factly in our lives, they can have no more powerful lesson.

So, when we take time to enjoy sharing the scriptures with each other, the "lesson" takes root and blooms naturally. I use the word *enjoy* deliberately. Coercion and shame have no

Elizabeth Huntington Hall has worked as a library reference clerk and an editor. She and her husband, H. Tracy Hall Jr., are the parents of nine children. Sister Hall has served as a Primary president, teacher of the marriage and family relations class, and ward music director.

place in the teaching of our children. Any spirit of coercion or fear, or even simply anxiety arising from our sense of duty or of guilt about teaching children, makes them so uncomfortable that they cannot learn. I even recommend that if children are bored by an approach, stop. Children are born innocent, and their interests are an endowment from God. Normally, anything that interests a child is good, and if followed to its end will lead to God and his creations. Children are naturally interested in the scriptures, especially and appropriately in the stories that fill the scriptures.

My sister-in-law Bonnie was reading to Joe, her three-year-old son, about Adam and Eve from the illustrated Bible stories published by the Church. As they read about the expulsion from the Garden, Joe interrupted to turn the pages back to an earlier picture of Adam and Eve in the Garden. He pointed to it and said, "They're not real." Bonnie said, "Oh yes they are, honey. They're the first man and the first woman that Heavenly Father put on the earth." Joe said, "No, they're not real, 'cause they didn't eat that fruit yet." Had he understood the story? I think so!

Jean Piaget, that great scholar of children's cognitive development, learned from his skillfully constructed experiments that until children reach a particular level of physical brain maturation, they cannot comprehend certain kinds of ideas and tasks. One of the abilities they lack, he has said, is the ability to decenter, that is, to see another person's point of view. Later researchers found, however, that when Piaget's experiments were restructured to a narrative form, so that the information was presented as a story, very young children could often comprehend many complex ideas that they had not understood as abstractions. They even understood those requiring decentering.[1]

In one of my very favorite books, *The Man Who Mistook His Wife for a Hat,* Oliver Sacks contrasts the "paradigmatic" (abstract, precept- or principle-based) mode and the "narrative" (storylike, or concrete) mode: "Though [they are] equally natural and native to the expanding human mind, the narrative comes first, has spiritual priority. Very young children love and demand stories, and can understand complex matters presented as stories, when their powers of comprehending general concepts, paradigms, are almost non-existent. It is this narrative or symbolic power which gives a sense of the world—a concrete reality in the imaginative form of symbol and story—when abstract thought can provide nothing at all. A child follows the Bible before he follows Euclid. Not because the Bible is simpler (the reverse might be said), but because it is cast in a symbolic and narrative mode."[2] The older I become, the more impressed I am by the structure and composition of the scriptures.

The process a baby goes through in learning to talk provides a model of one kind of invisible teaching. We rarely make a conscious effort to teach children to speak, yet we assume they will eventually speak, and in almost all cases our confidence is justified. If you saw parents chastising their six-month-old baby for not repeating *sesquipedalian* on cue, you would be dumbfounded. You'd certainly know the parents were either naive or misguided. You might also predict that the infant's normal speech acquisition would likely be delayed. As teachers we tend to take a baby's nature more into account than we do an older child's or an adult's. In fact, we sometimes fail to recognize how much alike the learning styles of babies, children, and adults actually are.

So how do babies learn to talk? They are simply exposed to people talking to each other. Gradually, almost mystically, they begin to make sense of the sounds and to imitate certain ones that other people respond to. (Even more mystifying is the ability of very young children to form sentences that no one has ever modeled for them.) The people around the baby who are talking to each other will also talk to the baby. That too encourages language acquisition. What if we waited to talk to or in front of babies until after they could understand us? They'd never learn to talk. Modeling and imitating precede understanding. And one level of understanding precedes another, which is why we can read a passage of scripture repeatedly and yet on the tenth reading, or the hundredth, suddenly grasp something in it that we never saw before.

Studies also show that children whose parents believe babies understand them actually begin talking earlier than other children. Speech is also encouraged when parents use the babies' own terminology mixed in with the rest of the modeling speech. In other words, sometimes accepting baby versions of words can increase their confidence so that they talk earlier and more fluently. Ridicule of any kind at any stage can stop progress.

Wordplay and language play increase our power in speech and in every other language acquisition skill. Every great tool is also a toy. Our appreciation of the scriptures becomes more profound when we find our deepest life needs addressed there, but with our innocent children it begins in our freedom to enjoy not only the exciting adventure stories but also the funny stuff.

No family Christmas pageant at our house is complete without someone dressed in a sheepskin labeled "Haste" because, of course, the shepherds "came with haste." Once every few years, if we get especially carried away, Mary and Joseph attempt to climb into the manger along with the tiny Jesus, for do we not read that when the shepherds arrived they found "Mary and Joseph and the babe lying in a manger"? But in that very same pageant last December our sixteen-year-old son, Alex, playing the announcing angel, choked back tears as he recited the angel's glorious words of joy. Playful laughter doesn't block deeper feelings the way an enforced solemnity would.

We also love to refer to the prophecy concerning Santa Claus, found in Zechariah 2:6, "Ho, ho, come forth, and flee from the land of the north." But perhaps our favorite is that passage in which Abinadi seems so apparently ingenuous: "And it came to pass that after the space of two years that Abinadi came among them in disguise, that they knew him not, and began to prophesy among them, saying: Thus has the Lord commanded me, saying—Abinadi, go and prophesy . . . " (Mosiah 12:1).

We have had some fun, and that fun takes us a long way, but our experience in sharing the scriptures in our family has not been a smooth, unbroken success story. We know that some approaches are mistakes because we have made them. Our children, thankfully, have never rejected the scriptures, but sometimes we have made family devotionals pretty miserable for them.

I want to make a distinction here between rejecting the scriptures and questioning or even doubting them. Questioning and doubting are necessary parts of the learning process, and we ought to react to them neutrally, without anxiety. Saying, "I don't know; I've never understood that myself," is a good response if it's true. We don't want them to fear expressing their questions and doubts to us. If they wish, we can help find scriptural answers from the Topical Guide, can ask more knowledgeable friends, can pray together, and so forth. Even if a family member does reject the scriptures, either because of mistakes you have made or from causes beyond your control, never, never, *never* attempt to force compliance to family scripture study or to a certain view of the scriptures. To do so is to follow Satan's plan.

To fully expect the attendance of all family members at scripture study is appropriate, but expectation differs from coercion. For instance, family policy may be that all the family attend, and you can encourage participation: "We need you to come," or "We won't make anybody come, but we hope you will choose to come." Teaching them that they have a choice is as important as any single other lesson we can share with our children. But as for using anger or manipulation or physical force—don't! Tell a noncompliant family member privately from time to time how much you miss him or her, share personal experiences or other truths in a nondidactic way, pray for that child and for yourself, but, above all, listen and respect his or her agency.

We have had children who chose not to attend Church meetings or family devotionals for a time, but they have always come back, and they come back stronger because to do so has been their own choice. You may feel anxious or worried that you are failing. You may even be alone in your desire to share the scriptures in your family, but be careful not to fall into a pattern of judging or feeling critical of those who may not yet understand the value of the scriptures.

When I have those kinds of anxious or desperate feelings, it has become a sign to me that I need to stop and gather my energy. Several scriptures are especially strengthening and comforting to me, and I sometimes recite them, almost like a mantra or a litany. They include, "Be still, and know that I am God," "There is no fear in love; but perfect love casteth out fear," and "For God hath not given us the spirit of fear; but of power, and of love, and of a sound mind" (Psalm 46:10 or D&C 101:16; 1 John 4:18; 2 Timothy 1:7).

I still have no clear picture in my mind of how to make formal family scripture study work all the time. We take one approach for a while, and then we move to another. If the goal is to love and comprehend the scriptures, I can tell you some things that have helped to foster that ideal in our family, besides our treasured scripture jokes.

One favorite occasional activity is to draw pictures as we read a story from the scriptures. This works, by the way, only if Mom and Dad draw, too. To see the different interpretations is interesting, and these pictures are so precious to us that we have saved them. Also fun is to take passages of scripture, one for each participant, print them at the top of blank sheets of paper, and then distribute them. Each family member draws a picture trying to represent the passage assigned to him. Then, of course, we try to guess the passage illustrated. Once one of our daughters made a "scripture cake"; in this recipe game, the ingredients, such as "4 cups Leviticus 6:20," are deciphered from the scriptures listed.

We have taken subjects of interest to us and found every scriptural reference we could on that subject. How many gemstones are mentioned in the scriptures? How might the Bible and the Book of Mormon differ in their mention of gemstones? How many times is the word *ice* mentioned? What about snow? We like to track the foods, or fish, or kinds of wood that are mentioned. I once tackled a very satisfying personal project in which I listed every reference to females in the Book of Mormon. I read the entire Book of Mormon, noting each reference as I went, and I have shared some of the things I learned from that study with my family over the years.

We also love to study the words and grammar of the scriptures, and we go to great lengths to track down meanings for words and passages. We have saved for reference some extremely valuable articles published in the Church magazines. Remember that Shakespearean English is essentially the same as King James English, so information you find about one helps with the other. In fact, familiarity with the King James Version of the Bible from early childhood facilitates understanding Shakespeare.

Singing scriptural passages is another favorite family activity. I remember most easily passages of scripture that I have sung, such as those wonderful passages in Handel's *Messiah*. Robert, our nineteen-year-old on a mission in Portland, Oregon, delighted us recently with a tape recording of a song he had written for a baptismal service. He had set a passage from Isaiah to music with a lovely melody and guitar accompaniment. I hope we have more of those—that's an activity I'd like to encourage!

When I asked my twenty-three-year-old nephew, Daniel, to share with me his childhood memories of the scriptures, he instantly replied, "My tapes! My parents bought me a set of tapes I could listen to at bedtime with my own headset. I loved them. I memorized those tapes. They're where I learned to love the scriptures. I want to go home and find them—I haven't had them out for so long." When I asked his mother about the tapes, she commented, "Daniel was such an active kid, and nothing settled him down at night like those tapes."

My eldest son, who at first said, "Leave your kids alone," later offered some serious thoughts. He learned on his mission never to ask yes/no questions and to ask a question only when he did not already have an answer in mind. "Keep asking questions until you learn something you didn't already know from or about that person," he added. Perhaps his most valuable advice was, "Listen to what your children think a particular passage means, rather than assuming that you know beforehand what they should learn from it."

If from their early childhoods you learn to share with your children your own moments of spiritual insight and experiences with the scriptures, you will be rewarded in ways you could never foresee as your children begin to share theirs with you. And though it may take patience and adjustment, it is never too late to start. Some of our most sacred and important times as a family have come when our children have shared their revelations with us. You feed them and feed them when they are tiny, and then they begin to feed you, and that food is some of the sweetest and most delicious that exists in the universe. I am sure it mingles with the fruit of the tree of life.

NOTES

1. See, for instance, Margaret Donaldson, *Children's Minds* (New York: W. W. Norton, 1978), especially chapter 2, "The Ability to 'DeCenter,'" 9–25.

2. Oliver Sacks, *The Man Who Mistook His Wife for a Hat* (New York: Summit Books, 1985), 174–75.

WHEN LOVE ISN'T ENOUGH

BONNIE BETH WHITAKER

Ten years ago, after many years of soul-searching and prayer, I embarked on probably the biggest venture of my life. I flew to Honduras, Central America, to adopt a three-year-old boy, who in actuality turned out to be closer to five. I was a single, self-supporting, thirty-seven-year-old woman. After gaining custody of Tom, I spent two months living in Honduras with a Catholic family while completing the paperwork on the adoption.

I arrived in Central America with a feeling of complete calm and actually had myself convinced that I was prepared for the experience. I hadn't even pulled out any of my old child psychology books for a quick review. After all, I had been around children much of my life. I had a degree in education and had taught elementary school. Who, other than an experienced mother, would know children any better than I? I was thoroughly convinced that all the love I had to offer would solve any potential problems. I felt certain that discipline wasn't going to be a major concern for us.

As I tenderly gazed on the photo of this young boy many times during the months preceding my trip to Honduras to get him, I wondered how I was going to help him make the difficult transition. Moving into a new home with a new mother in a new country would surely cause him to be timid and

Bonnie Beth Whitaker, a graduate of Brigham Young University, owns and operates a business in Provo, Utah. She is the single mother of a sixteen-year-old adopted son.

insecure. As it turned out, he was anything but shy. I definitely had my work cut out for me. He was overactive (later diagnosed hyperactive), extremely outgoing, and very headstrong. He was also very loving and affectionate. Unfortunately for both of us, because I had waited so long for this child, I was blind to some of his negative behavior. When I adopted him, Tom had already had five years to learn how to be manipulative and streetwise.

Tom, of course, knew no English, and I had only a recent crash course in Spanish; nevertheless, we were able to communicate on a basic level. Immediately he began testing his limits. I soon found out a gentle shake of my head and a no meant nothing to him. In retrospect, I can see that from the beginning Tom wanted control. Being in control was his security. Each Sunday while in Honduras, we walked three blocks to an LDS chapel to church. Tom soon learned that church meant sitting still—something definitely alien to his nature— and tried to turn back. When that didn't work, he would sit in the middle of the sidewalk, roll the tops of his socks down over his shoes, and refuse to get up. Several times a day he was defiant or willfully disobedient. Long distance to my mother in Utah, I would discuss what actions to take. (Remember, I hadn't reviewed any discipline techniques.) "Bonnie," she would counsel, "use a calm voice, be gentle but firm, and when necessary sit him in the corner." "But Mom," I replied, "I want to spank him!"

One of my challenges was lack of information about his background. What had his life been like during his first five years? Had he been abandoned at the orphanage? Found on the streets? Had he been abused? Neglected? Had his mother taken drugs while she carried him? What kind of person was she? And what about his father?

Tom's early elementary years went fairly smoothly. He kept up academically the first couple of years, but his hyperactivity and attention deficit disorder eventually caused him to fall behind. He found it difficult to sit still or even stay in his chair and delighted in the attention of his classmates. Once he entered junior high, however, we struggled with a huge explosion of rage and anger. (We're still patching holes.) His main preoccupation in life seemed to be his friends. If things were going well with them, life was great. If not, watch out.

His seventh-grade year in a public junior high school was disaster. Tom should have been designated "high risk" and never sent there in the first place. He was a minority student, he looked different, he was hyperactive and learning disabled, and seemed to want attention more than anything else in the world. It didn't take him long to figure out how to get noticed. He was boisterous, cut up in class, wore outlandish clothes, and even shaved a "T" on the top of his head! All this, and we had hit only seventh grade. Shortly before the end of that year, in desperation I shipped him off to a wilderness program. He returned home almost three months later with a new outlook on life and impressive survival skills, but once back in his normal world with its familiar pressures, he reverted to old behaviors.

Rearing children is always challenging, but trying to rear this child alone, without the financial and emotional support of a spouse and without another adult in the home to help think through problems, was particularly difficult. Alone, it's sometimes hard to have a clear picture of a situation. Am I being too strict, too lenient? Am I reading his actions and motives incorrectly? Is he truly difficult, or are my expectations unreasonable? What's really going on here? Overwhelmed, I often buried problems with the promise, "I'll think about it tomorrow."

I wondered how much of the acting out, anger, and irrationality were due to fetal drug or alcohol syndrome, genetics, or abuse. Perhaps his behavior was just the teenage years I'd been warned about. After all, many parents complained about their teenagers. With so little of his history to help me, I've often felt I was flying blind. Because he's been difficult and because I haven't known what else to do, I have found myself raising my voice, yelling, losing my cool, and preaching. I was desperate to keep him in tow. Everyone I knew had a bit of advice or a new parenting technique to share. All of this got me nowhere.

One of our biggest problems was getting Tom to report in to me directly after school and to come home in the afternoon or evenings on time. I quickly found that running a business and holding Tom accountable (by taking away privileges or grounding him) was more difficult than I had ever imagined. I really needed to be at home full-time so I could be with him immediately after school and on duty as a parent. I tried to keep tabs on Tom by insisting that he come to my shop after school. Being the social animal that he was, however, he was unhappy with that plan. He did a few odd jobs for me, but he was really just in my hair and not in the least bit interested in being involved with the business.

After Tom's first brush with the law, I tried a nine-month behavior modification program. (At present I have mortgaged my house twice to pay for programs.) We both learned some important skills there, but implementing them at home together every day continues to be a challenge.

In absolute terror for Tom's soul and my sanity, I went once more to my Heavenly Father and humbly asked for help and guidance. Instead of trying to change Tom, I was impressed to take a good hard look at myself. I found that I was often inconsistent with house rules, quick to lose my temper, and many times overreacted to Tom's behavior. I also realized that I had some strengths, too, and that I had done a lot of things right. My tone of voice (which reflects my real intent and what's in my heart) had an important role in our relationship. If I was angry, he knew it, and the power struggle began. What's the point in being angry? My only responsibility is to hold him accountable, is it not?

One afternoon he called me at work from a friend's house to tell me he had been asked to leave his school. My old behavior would have been to snap out a remark such as, "Well, you've done it again!" Instead I replied calmly, "How do you feel about that, Tom?" For a few minutes he poured out his soul, and we discussed calmly and rationally the consequences of his actions at school. He was sick with disappointment that he had to leave; why should I add to his distress by berating him and causing a bigger rift in our relationship?

The following summer, Tom's behavior deteriorated. He became more and more aggressive and wasn't willing to check in with me or obey curfew. I finally, out of desperation, began locking the door at curfew to try to force him home on time, but he could usually find someone else to stay with. He was constantly on the prowl, unwilling to take any medication, and continued to rack up offenses. (I know personally most of the members of the Provo and Orem police forces.) One summer night when he was particularly agitated and depressed, he went on a spree in the neighborhood, causing damage to mailboxes, light posts, and cars. The police were called, and a chase ensued. He ended up spending six days in the psychiatric ward of the hospital. Then the following month, on the eve of his sixteenth birthday, I caught wind of some other serious negative behavior and called the Provo police, who picked him up. His friends arrived that evening to discover that there wasn't going to be any sixteenth birthday party after all. Tom spent the next two months in detention and was subsequently court-ordered to a rehabilitation program in Cedar City, Utah. That summer of sleepless nights could be dubbed the summer of the rains for all the tears I shed.

Still in Cedar City, Tom is taking medications, cooperating, and progressing. He has a 3.95 grade-point average, which he doesn't stop talking about. For the moment I can take a deep breath and try to heal from the ordeal of the previous months. But beginning tomorrow, or next week or next year, whenever Tom returns, I'll have to take one day at a time.

I am convinced that most of us begin our parenting believing that our children will be so loved that we will beat the odds. We think with enough time, attention, and love that any child will come around and see things *our way*. When we are wrong, we feel lost, betrayed, out of control, ashamed. When it appears that everyone else's children are making the honor roll and blessing the sacrament, why are ours staying out too late and smoking on the sly? Why can't we control a simple child?

Because a child is *not* simple. Many forces are at work here. Somewhere along the line, employing Satan's methods of child-raising—forcing a child into obedience—backfires. Why is the illusion of control so appealing and so difficult to give up? My daily challenge since we've hit the hard times, Tom's teenage years, has been trying to hold him accountable in a calm, loving way, to let him suffer the natural consequences of his actions, and to change myself and my old negative way of dealing with him. It truly is a challenge.

BUDDING HOPE

KIM R. HAWLEY

Ten tortured springs
I watched the portrait plum tree
Through my window
And envied while she bore
Her pale, pink, poignant petals
On once bare branches.
Her bursting beauty
Seemed to mock my mourning,
Unfilled arms;
For I bode barren,
Though every winter
I, too,
Had reached my empty fingers
Heavenward.

But now
I watch and wait
Through winter's starkness
With eagerness
To joy with her unfolding,
When I'll behold her first,
Fine, fragile flowering,

Kim Rowley Hawley graduated from Brigham Young University in university studies and is now a homemaker. She and her husband, David R. Hawley, live in Burbank, California. Their long-awaited baby, a boy, was born a month and a half after "Budding Hope" was written. Sister Hawley serves in her ward Relief Society.

Until she stands,
In efflorescence,
Blessed.
I sense new, glorious life
That stirs within me,
And breathe
A cautious, hopeful, praising prayer,
For with God's grace
And miracles most awesome,
This spring
I, too,
Shall blossom, bloom,
And bear.

ENCOURAGING CHILDREN'S CREATIVITY: COERCION VS. CULTURE

REGINA J. ELLIS

When I was first married, I decided I was going to have perfect kids—no dripping noses or dirty hands. They would be clean and smart, talented and polite. As I began rearing my children, I developed an arsenal of tactics. Do the words *bribery, manipulation, coercion,* and *control* sound familiar? These are the tactics of force, and they work. They get results. They also destroy relationships, but I didn't know much about relationships then. I had a clean, smart, polite, first child who compliantly practiced the piano at least half an hour a day; and he had three younger brothers and a younger sister waiting in the wings for Mom to start their musical training.

Fortunately the Lord intervened to teach me several important principles upon which relationships are based. Those principles have changed the way I look at my children and what I expect from them. I learned the first two principles in a hard lesson with my fourth son. First, take the whole child into account, accepting the bad with the good. Second, let this acceptance be the foundation of your relationship.

My fourth son as a baby never learned to breathe through his mouth, so whenever he had a cold he woke up as soon as

Regina J. Ellis earned a bachelor's degree in pharmacy, and she and her husband, Frank Ellis, have homeschooled their six children. Sister Ellis teaches seminary in Princeton, New Jersey.

his nose got plugged. One time I had been up with him two nights in a row almost every hour, and daytime naps had been impossible. I was tired. Exhausted, I prayed he would sleep, please sleep, this one night. But he kept waking up. About the third time, I was so mad at the baby, so mad at God, and so sorry for myself that I stomped into the baby's room, grabbed him up, and began pacing the floor insisting, "Go—to—sleep. Go—to—sleep." Suddenly, for the first time in my life, words came into my mind: "You've got to take the bad with the good." I stopped in my tracks because a feeling of rebuke came with the words. I knew God was not pleased. Sitting down in the rocking chair, I bawled.

I needed to learn this hard lesson because three years later a car hit and severely injured this child. Besides the broken bones and punctured lung, Frank suffered brain damage and was in a coma. The doctors could not assure us that he would live, or if he lived, whether he could function. I said many prayers. Once in the rest room off the intensive care waiting room, I shut the stall door, knelt down, and begged the Lord to let me keep this child no matter what he would be like. I wasn't after the perfect child anymore; I just wanted him to stay. For a second time, words came into my mind: "I will consider what you say, for you are his mother." And with the word *mother* came such a feeling of approval, my mouth hung open. I was amazed that the Lord felt this way about me and about the role of mother.

By the grace of God, my son survived, and we began the arduous task of stimulating him while he was in the coma. (Most comatose patients don't suddenly wake up; usually the coma gradually lightens as the patient slowly recovers brain function.) When Frank's eyes first opened, they just stared. We read his favorite stories, held pictures in front of those eyes, put finger puppets on his hands, held vanilla extract, perfumes, and lemon peels under his nose, stroked his skin with textures, silky, furred, rough—anything to trigger something in his brain that would help him recover. Stimulating as many parts of the brain as possible was important to helping him come out of the coma with some brain function. Two months passed before he smiled. But he did smile, and over the next year he relearned the things he had learned as a baby. He had forgotten everything, but we found that what he learned in one area facilitated progress in another.

Frank is now thirteen. He still draws stick figures and works much harder than the others for what progress he makes. But when the others were taking piano lessons, he wanted to take them, too. By that time I had changed my purposes as well as my expectations about music lessons, or any others, based on my total acceptance of this child. This time my intent wasn't to produce a perfect, talented kid; lessons were for the child's good. I had also lowered my demands for practice time to fifteen minutes. As a family, we had agreed that anyone can stand to do something for their own good for fifteen minutes. Frank has since found his own gift. He told me, "Mommy, when I read the stories of Jesus in the Bible, I can see pictures of him in my head."

Those two principles—taking the whole child, strengths and weaknesses, into account and letting acceptance be the foundation of your relationship—apply to encouraging creativity as well as good behavior, scripture reading, academics, or any other goals you may have for your child. I believe in exposing my children to as many creative experiences as possible, but the third principle I learned is that the *culture* of the home determines what kind of expectations you can have in teaching new skills and fostering creativity. What kind of example do the parents set? What is important to them? The LDS Social Services parenting class manual displays a pyramid of influence. The pyramid is based on three attitudes: "love, acceptance and understanding, and encouragement." From that base, the manual explains, a relationship of trust develops. The next three levels of the pyramid are "provide example (culture)," "teach," and then, on the very top, the small triangle "influence."

If you want to influence your child, you will build a firm, broad foundation by loving the total child and seeking to develop a good relationship with him or her. You will also develop a culture in your home that will become an expectation for family members. For instance, there is not a culture of music in our home. My husband is practically tone deaf, and for him music is just one of life's nice-but-not-necessary little extras. He has told the story over and over of how he was so bad at the guitar that his teacher quit. Children notice our attitudes and values and absorb them. My children knew music was not really important to their father, so when our financial situation changed, we quit the piano lessons and started free judo lessons. Now I have six judo enthusiasts, and their dad is their biggest fan. If one skill isn't part of the family culture, try another one, because all bring benefits.

Certainly music is not the only way to foster creativity. And even though we don't have a music culture in our home, we do have a creativity culture that started when the children were very young. With five children born in six years, I was going crazy. My salvation, surprisingly, was being called to serve in the ward nursery. The nursery program was just what I needed in my home; I found that if I spent two hours daily doing the nursery program with my children, they would be content to play by themselves for another hour so I could do something by myself. The Church nursery program outlines blocks of activities fifteen to twenty minutes long, one of which is a craft time. Following that outline, my children learned to cut and glue under supervision. After a little while, they graduated to projects on their own. I provided a "make-it box" in the basement and a box of idea books I'd picked up at yard sales and grocery stores and through teacher supply catalogs. My children have experimented with many media—watercolor, acrylics and oils, block printing, mosaics, leather, sewing, stained glass, and ceramics, to name only a few—and discovered talents and hobbies. Jonathan at seventeen designs fractals on the computer. Grant at sixteen is a cartoonist and short-story writer. David at fourteen bought his own laser to make holograms. Telitha at twelve watercolors and sews. Frank and Christine are still in the paper, glitter, and glue stage.

All creative efforts have benefited my children because creativity is really a form of problem solving. The hobbies the children have chosen are those for which they had a talent and those that were available as part of the family culture. If you build a good relationship and expose your children to as many creative avenues as you can as part of the culture you develop in your home, you will not need an arsenal of force tactics to influence your children. You will be doing it the Lord's way instead: Providing your children with opportunities to magnify their talents to become themselves at their best.

NEVER WITHOUT A CONTRIBUTION

CONNIE DUNCAN CANNON

A few months ago, I snatched Chad, our first grader, out of school for an appointment. When I got him into the car, I attempted to have some quality time with him.

"How's school going today?" I asked.

He rolled his eyes and gave me his woebegone look. "Suzy's in there bawling," he said in a tone that was part worried, part disgusted. (Suzy sat next to him in class.)

"She is?" I responded. "What's the problem?"

"We each had to write a paragraph on what is special about ourselves, and she can't think of a thing!" he said in that same worried, disgusted tone.

"Really!? Did you have any trouble thinking of something special about yourself?"

"NO!" came the emphatic answer I was expecting.

"That's good. What did you put?"

"I put that I'm special because I play the violin and the piano, of course." ("Ya dummy" hung implicit in his voice.)

"Did you help Suzy think of something special about herself?"

Connie Duncan Cannon graduated from the University of Utah and taught high school history for three years before retiring to rear a family. She and her husband, James E. Cannon, have five sons and a daughter. Connie has been recycled for the third time as a Cub Scout den leader.

218

"I told her to get started on some piano lessons next week."

Was I excited! Here was a child who was not fond of practicing at all. Even getting him to lessons had been a major project some days. Only a few months earlier when I had called him into the house to get ready for his violin lesson, he had whined, "I don't think I can make it to violin today, Mom. My small intestine hurts." And now this child had just admitted that his violin was a source of pride.

Self-worth is probably the single most important reason to find a way to foster artistic expression in a child. Chad is never without a contribution, and he sees himself as very capable.

When our oldest son, Chris, was six, a friend introduced me to the Suzuki method of learning to play musical instruments. Although Dr. Suzuki's methods have had some incredible results—six-year-olds playing Vivaldi concertos—he never set out to make child prodigies. He never even intended to turn them into professional musicians. Dr. Suzuki desired to introduce them to their potential and to encourage self-discipline and powers of concentration early in life, habits that would benefit them forever.

I was surprised to learn that most of the thousands of children he teaches in Japan end their training by high school. The philosophy is that if they have gone through the training and mastered an instrument, the mission is accomplished. The skills and confidence they have developed through their training in music brings them success in other areas of their lives.

Personally, I have been drawn to the Suzuki method because I enjoy the bonding of parent with child when they work together on an instrument. A few years ago, I wanted to push that a step further and bond the whole family by practicing and performing as a group. One memorable performance will give you a rough idea of how our family endeavor differed from *The Sound of Music:*

In 1979 our Littleton, Colorado, ward asked us to provide the final talent number at the ward Christmas party. We all happened to have German clothes, and as the curtain went up I thought one of my dreams was about to be fulfilled. We looked the part of professional performers, dressed in our lederhosen and dirndles. Jim, my husband, played his oboe; I was at the piano; Chris, nine, played violin; Cate, seven, was at a small harp; and Chase, three, had a teeny cello and a couple of rhythm instruments, including a drum.

Chase looked so cute with his instruments that his big brother got the giggles looking at him. Because he was taking himself very seriously, Chase wasn't about to be laughed at. He had stomped out of several rehearsals in protest, and we knew that could happen at the actual performance. Hence, we had warned him that the audience might chuckle but assured him they were not laughing at him.

When he finished his limited contribution to our Christmas carols, he was to hold up word cards so the audience could sing along. I sat behind a massive old upright piano and couldn't see a thing, but I heard the audience chuckling, then laughing, and then laughing uproariously. "I know he's cute," I was thinking, "but what could possibly be this funny?" (Only when the curtain descended did I find, to my horror, that Chase, too small to read, had held the words upside down.) The audience chuckled, but nine-year-old Chris completely fell apart laughing. Chase accepted the audience laughter but was livid when his brother cracked up. He put the sign down, strode over to Chris, and thunked him on the head a couple of good ones with the drum mallet he was holding, knowing that with the audience looking on and the violin and bow occupying both hands, Chris was rendered defenseless.

The ward liked our music, but our family row on stage was the real hit of the party. And to be honest, I have to admit that that was quite often a pretty accurate picture of our so-called bonding experience with music. Yet bond we did. A decade and a half later, those two boys are best of friends, despite their

220

age difference, and even recently attended a music camp together.

Exposing your children to music at an early age can introduce them to their divine potential, build self-esteem, bond parents and children through parental involvement, and exercise the mind and memory daily. The perfect ally in this process is, of course, our Heavenly Father, who knows better than anyone else the talents that lie within each of his children and how best to nurture them.

LIFELONG LEARNING:

FULL MEASURE

WINIFRED B. EYRING

I was born in Scotland to Irish parents and reared in the Catholic Church. At age nineteen, I married a British merchant naval officer in the Church of England and was immediately disfellowshipped from my church, causing deep distress to my father, who was devoted to his religion and who loved me. Eight years later, my husband and I sailed for Australia to get away from the cold, damp climate of Scotland, where our three children suffered frequently with bronchitis. Our fourth child was born four months after our arrival.

Not long after settling in Geelong, Australia, while my neighbor and I were enjoying afternoon tea, two young men knocked on my door. They looked harmless enough, so I invited them in. Little did I know what wonderful news they would bring me—the gospel of Jesus Christ—and what tremendous changes it would make in my life.

As a young Catholic girl, I had been taught several doctrines that were difficult for me to understand. One was the doctrine of the Holy Trinity. I loved my Savior and couldn't quite understand how he could be the Father, come to earth as

Winifred B. Eyring attended business college in Scotland and was a civil servant in Britain during World War II. She has served a clerical mission in the office of the First Presidency and as Relief Society president of the Salt Lake University Second Stake. Sister Eyring and her late husband, Dr. Henry Eyring, have a combined family of seven children, twenty-four grandchildren, and fourteen great-grandchildren.

the Son to suffer and die for me, and then return to heaven, again becoming the Father. The doctrine of infant baptism also troubled me. I had been taught that little children who were not baptized into the Catholic Church before death would never see the face of God. Our firstborn, a son, had been born premature and died when only five days old. Having looked upon the beautiful face of my little dead son, I could not believe that God could be so cruel.

I remember the afternoon visit of those young messengers as if it were yesterday. When Elder Jones and Elder Lunt found that I had been reared a Roman Catholic, Elder Jones asked how I felt about the Holy Trinity. I shared with them my difficulty understanding the principle of the "three in one." Elder Jones then handed me a Bible—which I had never read before—and asked me to read of Jesus' baptism in Matthew 3:16–17. "And Jesus, . . . went up straightway out of the water: and, lo, . . . he saw the Spirit of God descending like a dove, and lighting upon him: and lo a voice from heaven, saying, This is my beloved Son, in whom I am well pleased." Those words verified what I had felt: the Trinity was really three individual persons.

Elder Jones asked next: "How do you feel about infant baptism?" I responded that I couldn't understand how God could be so cruel. He handed me another book—the Book of Mormon. He had opened this unfamiliar book to a passage in Moroni. I read: "Listen to the words of Christ, your Redeemer, your Lord and your God. . . . Little children are whole, for they are not capable of committing sin; wherefore the curse of Adam is taken from them in me, that it hath no power over them. . . . And their little children need no repentance, neither baptism. . . . But little children are alive in Christ, even from the foundation of the world" (Moroni 8:8, 11, 12). What I had always felt was the truth!

During the rest of their visit, I completely forgot about my neighbor, although we were all in the same room. Afterwards,

223

I wondered that she had not felt the same feelings I had. Later that evening, after the children had gone to bed, I read the pamphlet containing Joseph Smith's testimony, and after receiving a witness that Joseph saw what he said he saw, I started reading the Book of Mormon.

The words that I read seemed to fill my heart, particularly Nephi's response to his father, Lehi: "I will go and do the things which the Lord hath commanded, for I know that the Lord giveth no commandments unto the children of men, save he shall prepare a way for them that they may accomplish the thing which he commandeth them" (1 Nephi 3:7). Those words sank deep into my soul and remained to buoy me up. (I would need strength and courage for all that was before me.) Elder Jones was transferred shortly after our first discussion, and I continued to study with his replacement, Elder Ockey, and Elder Lunt for almost six weeks. I wanted to learn everything possible about the Restoration; like a parched pilgrim, I soaked up all the knowledge I could.

My husband at the time professed to be an atheist and wanted nothing to do with religion, but he consented to my baptism. Some weeks after my baptism, however, I became very discouraged with my husband's constant criticism of my faith and began staying home from church more and more. It was easier than arguing. For a while my daughters went to church with friends, but eventually they refused to go without me. Because I was a moral coward, we all stayed away. That was a very trying time for me. I knew the Church was true, but my only link to it became a young, caring visiting teacher and two faithful home teachers. How I looked forward to their nourishing messages.

After two years of inactivity, one Saturday afternoon as I sat watching the children playing in our living room, a voice came to my mind: "You fool, look at your children! You fool, look at your children!" I looked around. There was no one else in the room. Then I went into my bedroom and prayed that Heavenly Father would help us get back to church.

The following day, about noon, I heard a knock on the front door. To my surprise, there on the porch was our branch president, Lynn Smith, and his wife, Doll. "We have been sent!" Sister Smith said. My husband, hearing a familiar English accent, joined us. President Smith said to him, "We have been sent," and then went on to explain the events that led them to our door. His wife was stirring a pot of soup on the stove when she suddenly turned off the gas and exclaimed, "Lynn, we have to go round to the Clarks and we have to go now!" He complained that he had a meeting in half an hour, which could not be postponed. When his wife insisted that they drive over immediately, he didn't argue.

Neither did my husband, who was disarmed. "All right, she can go," he promised. The girls and I returned to church the following week. Things did not really improve at home, criticism continued, but I now knew where Heavenly Father wanted us to be. The words of Nephi—"I will go and do the things which the Lord hath commanded" (1 Nephi 3:7)—came to mean more to me than life itself.

A few years after this experience, that voice again spoke, saying: "Take your family to Zion." I knew that was impossible. My husband disliked America, Americans, and what he thought of as my American religion. Remembering the words of Nephi and having proven the Lord in the past, I went to the local shipping company to make enquiries.

The next ship sailing for San Francisco would not be leaving for twenty-two months. At that time I was working as an interior designer and accountant. Without hesitation, I booked six passages on the ship and gave the owner the necessary cash deposit, which I had withdrawn from my bank that morning. When I confided my intent to move to America to my two elder daughters, they asked, "What will you tell Dad?" I explained that Heavenly Father would have to take care of that problem.

Meanwhile, over the next year and a half, we continued to struggle with our lives in the Church—fasting and praying frequently for answers to problems and for strength to live each day. Four months before the ship sailed for San Francisco, the Lord stepped in, and my husband became reconciled to the move. We received our entry visas just in time to make the sailing date. Again the Lord fulfilled his promise to us as we made the effort to do the things he commanded. The day we sailed out of the Melbourne harbor, while everyone was on deck saying good-bye to their friends, I found my way to our cabin and thanked our Heavenly Father for another miracle.

Once we arrived in the States, I fervently hoped and prayed that my husband might see the good in the Church—that our Latter-day Saint faith was not an opiate for the masses, nor for foolish women and children, but a wonderful way of life. But that was not to be.

We landed in California and then traveled to Salt Lake City, where we had friends. After three days, my husband felt overwhelmed by Mormons and decided that we must leave Utah. We eventually settled in Oregon, where we remained for five years.

Our marriage did not improve, as I had hoped it might, and my husband and I eventually divorced. He went north, leaving my daughters and me in Oregon. A year later I once again heard that voice, this time telling me to "go to Salt Lake." I quickly made the necessary preparations to do what the Lord asked; five months later I was in Salt Lake with my youngest daughter, the only one still living at home.

We arrived in Salt Lake on a Saturday evening. The following morning as we entered the meetinghouse, a gentleman near the rear of the chapel greeted us, asking who we were and where we were from. After Sunday School classes, as we made our way out of the building, we were again greeted by this gentleman, who introduced himself as Brother "Iring" (at least that's the way I spelled his name then).

In the following weeks I did not see him in church and decided he must have problems with activity. (I did not know then that he was a member of the Sunday School General Board.) One day as I sat pondering my purpose for being in Salt Lake City, I thought I saw Brother "Iring" walking up my path and sitting on a chair in my living room. My first thought was that I was meant to reactivate this brother. Missionary zeal was in my blood, and I was anxious to help this man become more active.

A few weeks later, Brother Eyring (I had a ward directory by then) invited me to a mission fireside at his home. How pleased I was that someone was working on him already! When I arrived at his home, to my great surprise *he* was hosting the fireside. At the conclusion of the fireside, Brother Eyring drove me home by way of the University of Utah, where he gave me a tour of his office and lab. I found out later that he was a physical chemist known internationally for his work in reaction rate theory, but at the time I still had no clue that he was other than a very kind gentleman.

The following week he invited me to a "Know Your Religion" lecture. After I heard his testimony, I knew that the Lord must have had another purpose in guiding me to him. Meanwhile Brother Eyring continued to invite me to every lecture he gave, religious or scientific, introducing me to each audience as his "very good friend." This was somewhat embarrassing to me, but he just smiled. As I came to know this great human being, a love sweeter than I had ever known before filled my heart. He was the first man I had known, other than my earthly father, who was absolutely honest and without guile.

Six months after that first fireside, Henry asked me to marry him. Realizing that he was much older than I, he asked me to think about his proposal. I answered that I'd do more than just think about it; I'd fast and pray. Sometimes we can make ourselves feel good about something and make up our minds before asking the Lord. Then we really don't ask—we tell him—and often we make a wrong decision.

I had to know; I did not want another experience like my first marriage, either for Henry or myself. That evening I began a twenty-four-hour fast. At its conclusion, I knelt and asked Heavenly Father to let me know his will. Arising from my knees, I picked up my mission Bible; it fell open to the book of Ruth, where Boaz was speaking to Ruth. His words were, in essence, "I bless you for not seeking after younger men, whether rich or poor" (see Ruth 3:10). My answer that evening to Henry was yes. We were sealed by Elder Spencer W. Kimball in the Salt Lake Temple on Friday, the thirteenth of August, 1971—a very lucky day.

Henry and I had ten joyful years together before he became ill with bone cancer. Six months after his passing, his sister, Camilla Kimball, broke her hip and required constant care. Her family asked if I might be able to help. With Henry gone, all I had was time, and I was happy to share it with my favorite sister-in-law and my ideal.

Each morning I went at 7:30 to the Hotel Utah, where Camilla and President Kimball were residing. There I learned and relearned wonderful things. On the very first day President Kimball reminded me who I was. (My father had taught me this in my childhood, but after twenty-three years of a difficult marriage, I had forgotten.) On that first morning, serving breakfast I set a bowl of fresh fruit on the table before President Kimball, who looked up at me and asked, "Who is this?" He really didn't recognize me. His eyesight was very poor, and because his glasses bothered him, he didn't like to wear them. I answered, "Oh, it's only me." There was dead silence for almost a minute; then, recognizing my voice, in his wonderful raspy way he said, "Never say, 'It's only me.' Never. Say, 'It's Winifred.'" From then on when I'd set down his bowl, he'd look up and ask, "And who is this?" When I'd answer, "Um, um—it's Winifred!" he would nod and smile his approval.

As Camilla's hip began to heal, she got around with the aid of a walker, which she called her Burro, probably because of her ties to Mexico. Her situation was very difficult. Fiercely independent, she hated having to rely on anyone for anything. Often she'd get up from her chair and take off without her Burro. Finding herself stranded in the middle of the floor, she'd call for me to run and find it. (I'm looking forward to the here-after, when she and I can have a good laugh over some of our funny experiences in their apartment. President Kimball will probably join us in the merriment!)

Camilla loved to learn. As soon as she was able to get out of the apartment, she and I took institute classes and went to Education Week. She was an avid reader, as was I, and we spent many hours with good books. I loved this great lady. Each day I'd rub my arm against hers. She'd ask, "What are you doing, Winifred?" I'd say, "Oh, I'm trying to rub some of your goodness off on me." She'd just laugh. She didn't know I was serious.

The time came when she could no longer walk. For the longest time she struggled with the idea of being pushed about in a wheelchair—she was the most independent woman I have ever known—but eventually she let me take her in the wheel-chair to visit the four young mothers we visit taught together.

Camilla was ninety years old when she decided to take up oil painting. A teacher came to her home every Monday morning. She told me, "Winifred, I've got to learn how to do this." She didn't think she was a Rembrandt, but she achieved what she set out to do. She painted beautiful oils for her children.

At the age of ninety-one, Camilla saw her first computer. It was at KSL TV, a mammoth machine that totally overwhelmed her. When finally someone sat her at a keyboard and let her type her name and see it displayed on the screen, she was thrilled. "Oh, Winifred," she later said to me, "I wish I'd known." You see, she wanted to know. She wanted to know everything. She wanted to do everything. Even when she couldn't—she tried.

After Camilla's passing at age ninety-two, the first thing I did was to sign up for a computer class at the LDS Business College. I wasn't going to die dumb! I, too, wanted to know. And I learned to use a computer. While attending the college, I was called into the First Presidency's office on a special assignment to automate the outdated filing system. At the conclusion of that assignment I was called to serve a clerical mission in that office. I wasn't really sure of what I was doing, but like so many other times in my life, the Lord guided me, by the power of the Holy Ghost, to accomplish his work.

Through all my experiences, the most important truth I have learned is that our Heavenly Father lives and is always mindful of each one of us. *He knows us by name and is aware of our needs and desires.* He cares, even about the little things. Let me conclude with Camilla's own words about lifelong learning: "The pursuit of knowledge is part of the gospel plan for men and women. . . . The opportunities for women to excel are greater than ever before. We should all be resourceful and ambitious, expanding our interests. Forget self-pity, and look for mountains to climb. Everyone has problems. The challenge is to cope with those problems and get our full measure of joy from life."[1]

I know our Heavenly Father loves you, and he wants you back home with him—where you belong. Climb the mountain. Get there. You can do it. And I'll see you there.

NOTE

1. Caroline Eyring Miner and Edward L. Kimball, *Camilla: A Biography of Camilla Eyring Kimball* (Salt Lake City: Deseret Book, 1980), 188.

EDUCATION: THE PATH
THAT LEADS HOME

LEANN P. WHEELER

What does it mean to be truly educated? President David O. McKay, a noted and respected educator, observed that "true education seeks . . . to make men and women not only good mathematicians, proficient linguists, profound scientists, or brilliant literary lights, but also . . . men and women who prize truth, justice, wisdom, benevolence, and self-control as the choicest acquisitions of a successful life."[1] Education, to be wholly satisfactory, must be "the full and uniform development of the mental, the physical, the moral and the spiritual faculties," because the spirit and the body are inseparably interwoven.[2]

Having graduated from law school and since chosen to be a full-time homemaker, I am sometimes asked, usually by nonmembers, how I can justify wasting my professional training. Although I do not consider my training wasted or feel my choices need to be justified, the question raises issues about family, education, and career priorities that many Latter-day Saint women face. What is the role of education in our lives?

Since the Restoration, Church doctrine has stressed that knowledge is an eternal principle and that learning is critical to

---

LeAnn P. Wheeler clerked for the Colorado Supreme Court after graduating from Rutgers University Law School. A homemaker, she and her husband, Francis Wheeler, have five children. She teaches stake parenting classes and serves as a triregional community-relations director for the Church.

our moral and spiritual, as well as our social and intellectual, development. These doctrines are based upon revelation: "The glory of God is intelligence"; "If a person gains more knowledge and intelligence in this life through his diligence and obedience than another, he will have so much the advantage in the world to come" (D&C 93:36; 130:19). This sentiment was expressed succinctly by President Brigham Young: "When shall we cease to learn? . . . never, never."[3] In fact, as Church historian Leonard Arrington stated, "The necessity of learning is probably the most frequently repeated theme of modern-day revelations."[4]

Clearly education is a vital part of the plan of salvation, the plan to perfect us, to open our understanding and to prepare us to return to live in the presence of an eternal Father in Heaven. How shortsighted, then, if we regard education as merely a mortal stepping-stone. As useful as formal training is for securing employment, education is a long-term process, an eternal process, not an end in itself. Losing sight of its ultimate purpose can result in frustration, if not a sense of futility. For instance, an acquaintance told how she had longed to graduate from college, but once finished, degree in hand, she felt only disappointment. "It doesn't mean anything to me," she said. The degree had been her sole purpose; the process itself did not have value for her.

Another friend, now retired from a long and worthwhile high school and college teaching career, had touched the lives of countless students. Well advanced in years and a widower, he is feeling old, useless, and somewhat bitter that his education and career no longer seem important to anyone. "What you don't know," he told me, "is that I'm a nobody. I used to be a somebody. I used to know a lot and read a lot. What you don't know either is that some day you'll be a nobody. You're a somebody now, but the time will come when you're a nobody, too."

This fine, intelligent gentleman has discounted that he is a father, a grandfather, a friend, and a unique spirit. In his infirmity and disillusionment, not only has he tied his worth to his former career but he has lost sight of how his learning and life have enriched the lives of many others. He significantly influenced my life when I was a child and young adult. Can such a person ever be a nobody?

When I applied to law school, my husband, Fran, and I were living in a community outside New York City, where he was practicing law with a Wall Street firm and working long hours. We had two small children, two-and-a-half and four years old. I had recently had a second miscarriage and been told by my doctor not to try to have any more children for several years. I loved our children and enjoyed the hours reading, talking, and playing with them, but I felt increasingly isolated and frustrated. As ungrateful as it seems in hindsight, I was also angry with the Lord. I could not believe I had lost two children. What of faith and righteous desires?

In response to my growing frustrations, and because before we started our family I had wanted to attend law school, Fran suggested I get a law degree. His father had died when Fran was young, leaving his mother to support their family. A law degree would enable me to support our family should the need arise.

Eighteen years ago, not many women attended law school, especially not LDS women with children. I was not sure the suggestion was feasible or sensible, but the more we investigated, pondered, and prayed, the more confident we felt about our decision. The Lord answered many prayers for us; arrangements fell into place miraculously. Months later, after we found that I was expecting our third child, we decided that I should complete the first semester so I would not lose my admissions status.

I am asked often how we managed law school with four young children. (Our third was born in November of my first year of law school; our fourth in November of my third year.)

233

Our children were very much a part of my law school experience. Whenever I had to drop off a paper, pick up books, or check an assignment, I took one of them along for the fifteen-minute train ride to the Rutgers Law Building in downtown Newark. When my first semester grades came, our daughter Alecia, then five, was so excited she called Fran at his office to tell him, "Mommy won an A!"

We were very blessed while I was in law school. I juggled classes to be gone as little as possible. I studied at the dining room table with the children coloring beside me or playing with cars at my feet. At night, after reading to the children, I grew adept at patting one child's back, humming, nursing the baby, and reading cases. When I got up at 2 or 3 A.M. with the baby, I studied for an hour. When I needed resource materials, Fran copied cases, and after I made *Law Review,* he helped with my editing assignments. As we worked together caring for the children, folding laundry on Friday nights, studying and discussing, our relationship grew much stronger. Never has the Spirit worked more strongly in my life. I needed a lot of help. The work was hard, and I often went without sleep, but the experience was exhilarating.

Our family and the gospel were our prime considerations. When things became unbearable, and they did, we reassessed. When I reached a point where I could no longer handle the pressures of being a full-time mother, full-time student, Primary and Relief Society teacher, and of doing all the sundry things that go into managing a house and family, we changed our routine. We decided which responsibilities were most important for me to handle personally; other things, like the heavy housework, we either hired done or ignored for the time being. Sometimes I took fewer credit hours. Frankly, I am not sure how we managed at times, but neither of us lost the feeling that this was what we were supposed to be doing at that time in our lives.

Before graduating, I clerked for a Wall Street law firm. My

cousin, a senior at Brigham Young University, lived with us and helped care for the children that summer. I received an offer to join the firm, even guaranteeing me a nine-to-five day at full salary. The offer was a tremendous opportunity, professionally and financially. For eight of our nine married years, one of us had been in school. With the extra income, we could quickly repay the accumulated school debts. In addition, Fran's law firm was nearby. During the summer, we had often ridden the train into work together and lunched with friends from his firm or mine. We enjoyed talking and having shared interests. No job offer could have been more appealing to me. I did not want to turn it down, but the promptings I received would not let me accept it, either—not even long enough to pay off school debts. Three months passed before I could bring myself to decline the offer.

After we moved to Denver, I clerked for the Colorado Supreme Court, but during that year I realized that more than anything else I wanted to stay home to raise our children: being there to guide them was the most important thing I could ever do. I am glad I could make that choice. That season of my life is passing quickly.

Yet, I do not feel that my educational and professional experiences, which have greatly influenced and enriched my life, have been wasted. Not only was my training a form of insurance but I learned about priorities, self-discipline, and reliance upon our Heavenly Father. It also strengthened my feelings of competence. Faced with a really difficult challenge, I tell myself, "If I made it through law school with four children, I can certainly do this."

Equally important, my training has put me in a position to give service in unique ways. Challenging opportunities have come to me in the Church and in our community that I would have missed otherwise. For instance, at the time I was attending law school in New York, the National Organization of Women was picketing our ward and demonstrating against the

235

Church. My bishop asked me to assist as a spokeswoman for LDS women in our area. One night he called to tell me that the former wife of a regional representative was speaking at a well-publicized NOW meeting in my neighborhood. She intended to speak against the Church and its priesthood leaders. Would I please attend?

When I arrived at the meeting, the room was packed with at least a hundred women. I noticed four or five other LDS women from our area, some of whom knew the speaker personally. As the meeting progressed, the speaker vented her frustration with the Church, offering her opinion that a Mormon's idea of heaven is to keep women barefoot and pregnant for eternity and that Mormon women have no freedom over their own lives. The crowd grew indignant. Suddenly she paused, looked around, and said, "In fact, there are Mormon women in this audience right now, sent by their bishops to spy on this meeting."

I have never felt such a swell of hatred. It was an actual physical force, like electricity crackling, then an uproar, with women yelling, "Who are they? We want to know who they are. Stand up, stand up!"

A voice within said, "Stand up!" I sat very still and thought, "You have got to be kidding." The voice, which was neither still nor small to my hearing, came again. "Stand up." I took a deep breath and stood up.

Dead silence.

"Well," I said, since I had their attention, "I live here in Maplewood. A few of you are my neighbors." I had seen one neighbor, so I figured it was not too untrue. "I am a Mormon, and I am pregnant," I said, because I was eight months pregnant, "but I am not barefoot. I am also a third-year law student and an editor of our *Law Review,* and I have the full support and encouragement not only of my husband but of my bishop." I was very calm.

236

"Sit down," several women yelled. I sat down, gladly. Then others called out, "Let her talk."

I cannot recall anything specific said after that, but the process of being asked to sit and then being invited to speak again was repeated at least twice. The second time I spoke seven or eight minutes about the role of women in the Church. The speaker, out of time, said little else beyond inviting anyone with questions to come up afterwards. In effect, her accusation had ended her presentation.

After the meeting, several women called me a liar, mostly behind my back and under their breath, but several others stopped to thank me for my comments. One woman apologized and said how uncomfortable she felt about what had been said, especially in attacking another church.

Even if my comments accomplished little, at least those present had a chance to hear a different perspective. In this and other similar meetings, I was able to represent some of the values important to the Church. I am certain that my opinions would not have carried as much weight had I been solely a homemaker at that time.

Last year, while we were in the East, I was invited to address a group of LDS husbands and wives on the topic "What Do We Teach Our Daughters?" Specifically, the issue the group wanted to discuss was how we can help our young women prepare professionally for the future without undermining their commitment to family. After my introductory remarks, the topic was opened for general comments, but the focus of the discussion soon shifted. An angry exchange took place as sisters who worked outside the home and sisters who did not began to criticize one another. The feelings on both sides were intense. I found the experience deeply troubling.

We live in an age of confusion, and no issue is more confused than the role of women. I feel it in my own life when I am defensive about my choices. Daniel predicted that ours would be "a time of trouble, such as never was since there was a nation," a time when "many shall run to and fro, and knowledge shall be increased" (Daniel 12:1, 4). Paul wrote, "This know also, that in the last days perilous times shall come. For men shall be lovers of their own selves, . . . ever learning, and never able to come to the knowledge of the truth" (2 Timothy 3:1–2, 7).

Satan would confuse us further. He would have women in the Church believe that we are at war with one another or that we are at war with men, instead of at war with him. Having been on both sides of the question, as a working mother and as a full-time homemaker, I would observe that neither role changed who I am or what I believe. We do not need to feel threatened by the decisions that others make.

I have often reflected on President David O. McKay's counsel that "the noblest aim in life is to strive to live to make other lives better and happier."[5] In considering what it means to give one's life in service for others, it is easy to discount the service we give in our own homes. Many women give most of their lives in service to their families. I firmly believe that our talents and skills are to be used in service to others. In fact, Lorenzo Snow said that "when a person receives intelligence from the Lord" and is willing to share that intelligence for the benefit of others, he will receive "continual additions to that intelligence."[6]

Education is intended to bless our lives, but only when we hearken unto God do knowledge and learning work to our benefit. The Lord must be grieved when those who have the advantage of an education assume that titles or degrees distinguish them above others. Surely he is equally grieved when those who have not had educational opportunities assume they have less worth on that account. There are many means for acquiring an education about the things that matter, but knowledge was never intended as a source of divisiveness among the Saints.

Let us value every opportunity to learn. Let us see things as they really are—from an eternal perspective. Let us remember the great sisterhood we have in common, for we have far more in common as followers of our Father in Heaven than we have differences. Let us counsel together, strengthen one another, and follow the path that leads home.

NOTES

1. David O. McKay, *Gospel Ideals* (Salt Lake City: Deseret Book, 1976), 441.

2. Orson F. Whitney, "What Is Education?" *Contributor* 6 (May 1985): 343–53, as quoted in Neil J. Flinders, *Teach the Children* (Provo, Utah: Book of Mormon Research Foundation, 1990), 184.

3. Brigham Young, 17 Feb. 1856, in *Journal of Discourses,* 26 vols. (London: Latter-day Saints' Book Depot, 1853–86), 3:203.

4. Leonard Arrington, "The Founding of the LDS Institutes of Religion," *Dialogue: A Journal of Mormon Thought* 2 (Summer 1967): 137.

5. David O. McKay, *Instructor,* Mar. 1961, 73.

6. Lorenzo Snow, 9 Apr. 1857, in *Journal of Discourses,* 5:64.

DAFFODILS IN SNOW

MARILYN BUSHMAN-CARLTON

Smelling of my lotion
you spill into the room
swinging a placard scribbled
with tall words that might have been
composed by me. I picture
a cartoon of mother and daughter,
mouths sharing the same bubble.

Though parts of you still lodge in shadows
we've come a long way, flayed
the veneer that pegged you "daddy's girl"
(hair, like his, brown as the canyon floor,
eyes big as chestnuts).   Flesh
to flesh, we color opposite
ends of the Clarion charts.

Credit, at least in part, the rocking chair
that bound us as we sang
and traveled (the two of us players)
in worlds inside your Golden Books
and beyond:
        we saw Paris with *Madeleine*
        sang that girls can be anything at all
        (except dads and grandpas),

Marilyn Bushman-Carlton received her bachelor's degree in English from the University of
Utah. Her first volume of poetry will be published in 1995. Sister Bushman-Carlton teaches
poetry workshops at Pioneer Craft House in Salt Lake City. She and her husband, Blaine L.
Carlton, are the parents of five children.

sniffed chocolate and lilacs,
ate bread with the *Little Red Hen,*
discovered our own backyard,
chased away clouds with a song.

I recognize you now, your hand familiar
in the dark, the easy fit of linked fingers.
Like the taste of strawberries,
I love what I can count on.
The rest is surprise—
daffodils in snow.

EVENTUALLY,

I'LL MAKE YOU LAUGH

LOUISE PLUMMER

Besides writing young adult novels, I also teach writing. What surprises me in my creative writing students is their inability to see their life's experience as material for their writing. Students will write about suicide, murder, drug cartels, and mobsters as if they are trying to get as far from themselves as possible.

Do you know any murderers? I ask them. Do you know anyone who works for the mob? Have you ever bought drugs or sold them? The answers are usually a lot of giggling and a no.

One time I had a male student, who wrote about a couple's wedding night. He himself was not married, nor did he have much imagination to fill in the gaps of his inexperience. The nervous bride in the story has locked herself in the bathroom and is gulping down tranquilizers by the handfuls while her new groom, on the other side of the door, is begging her to come out.

Finally she does come out, wearing "a negligee, with a bodice made of sequins." When the author of the story read

Louise Plummer is an assistant professor of English at Brigham Young University. She and her husband, Tom, are the parents of four sons. She is the "story lady" in Primary and the author of *Thoughts of a Grasshopper* (Deseret Book).

this description to the class, one of the guys in the back of the room said, "Ooh, that would hurt your chest."

I questioned the author: "Do you *mean* sequins?"

He nodded stupidly.

"Do you know what sequins are?" I asked.

"Aren't they ruffles?"

The class broke up laughing.

"No," I said. "They're shiny little metal discs that are sewn onto material to make it glitter, and it *would* hurt your chest."

He smiled feebly and ended his story. The bride finally came out to the wedding bed but fell into a deep sleep immediately.

"How many tranquilizers did she take?" I asked.

"About a dozen," he said.

"If she took that many tranquilizers," I said, "you should have her drop forward into the bathroom sink and leave her there."

He revised the story, but it never amounted to much, because he knew nothing about wedding nights, tranquilizers, or negligees. The story rang false.

I teach another kind of writing class, too, one that is not fiction writing but memoir writing. Students write from their own lives—from their memories. In this class, students come much closer to the mark, because they are required to write about their lives—the "true stories"—and their own lives are something they know.

But in this class, when students begin reading aloud in workshops, they apologize for their lives, especially if they have written about something painful. Even before they begin reading, they say things like, "I probably shouldn't have written about something this personal," or, "This isn't funny—" as if writing should be accompanied by a laugh track. Or they say, "I hope this doesn't offend anyone."

Then they proceed to read something both painful and wonderful, because they share a vulnerable side of themselves with the class, their "reading audience." When students tell a painful story honestly, it is always celebrated by the rest of the class.

Let me give you a couple of examples. One young woman told about an exciting day in third grade—she was excited because she knew her mother was going to pick her up after school and take her to visit her grandmother in a nearby city. But when her mother came, she was enraged. The young girl had no idea why, but her younger sister sat quietly and fearfully in the back seat. Her mother stopped at the post office and wanted this girl—my student—to go in and get the mail out of a postal box, which was locked with a combination lock. This girl had never opened a combination lock, but the mother insisted that she could do it and gave her explicit instructions: turn to the left to this number, then to the right to this number, then back to the left, and so on.

The young girl went inside the post office and found the box, but as hard as she tried, she could not open that box. Knowing her mother's rage and sensing the danger of it, she said a little prayer as she tried again to open the combination lock. "Please, please, let me open this lock." No luck. Again she tried. "Please, please." She could not open the lock. Soon her mother filled the doorway of the post office and swooped down onto this girl, her daughter, like a vulture. Seeing that the box had not been opened, she grabbed the girl by the hair and smashed her head against the metal boxes. My student told about the humiliation of having her mother do that in front of other people. She wrote about feeling the blood trickle down the back of her head, of touching it with her fingers and matting it down into her hair. Her mother opened the box, got out the mail, and pushed the girl into the car. All the way to the grandmother's house, the mother warned the girl not to tell the grandmother about this event. She never did.

Another memoir student wrote about her struggle with bulimia. She says, "I was a thin, flat-chested fourteen-year-old.

244

My mother was five feet seven inches tall, flat-chested, and weighed one hundred and eight pounds at age forty-five. She was obsessed with weight and her body. She ran six miles every morning and ate only enough to keep her alive. Her greatest fear was living in an obese body like my father's sisters. My mother always told me to be aware of what I put into my mouth, because she feared that I would be fat. I never heeded her warnings, because I was thin and looked like her. One day our loving relationship changed. I went to bed with an undeveloped body and woke up with the horror of a developed woman's body. I was devastated. I was no longer small like my mother. I was big and fat and disgusting."

She goes on to write how she covered herself with huge sweaters, hoping her mother wouldn't notice. And then one day she passed *Elle* magazine with a heading on the cover that read, "Battling Bulimia." She writes, "I couldn't believe that I hadn't thought of it sooner. Barfing my guts out would make me thin and lift the curse of breasts and a soft stomach."

And so she began throwing up her food that very night. "Vomiting became a talent," she writes. And for three years, she lived this way until one desperate night she was caught. She was alone at home, sitting on the kitchen floor: "My trembling hands clutched a failing math exam and a deficiency slip that I had to have signed," she writes. "I looked at my reflection on the oven door and began a binge that would cure my sadness. I shoved several loaves of bread down my throat, a pound of potato salad, and gulped a two-liter bottle of Diet Pepsi. I crawled into the hallway bathroom and vomited. I went back to the kitchen quickly, like I was in some kind of relay race, and crammed two pounds of graham crackers into my mouth, two pints of ice cream, a bag of Oreos, and several pieces of cold chicken. I was alternating eating and vomiting at a violent pace. This was a small binge compared to what I was accustomed to, but I felt a strangeness in my body. . . . My heart was beating forcefully and felt as though it was going to pound

245

through my heaving chest. I tried to stand up to reach a towel, but my vision went dark and I fell to the floor. After gagging several times, I forced my fingers as far down as they could go and vomited up the Oreos and at least a cup of blood."

Then she passed out. Her parents found her on the floor next to the toilet and took her to the hospital. They would not believe that she was bulimic until a doctor pointed to the teeth marks that scarred their daughter's hands, the ruptured blood vessels in her face, the swollen gums, and the lack of enamel on her teeth.

When this student read this essay to the class, she had their undivided attention, and when she finished they applauded, both because the essay was well written and because this young woman had taken a big risk, first in writing about this part of her life, and second, in reading it aloud to them.

For me, writing—even fiction writing—is not worth the trouble unless I am taking the kind of risk that each of these students took, unless I am divulging truths about myself that make me feel more than a little naked, more than a little vulnerable. They are truths veiled in fiction, but they are mine. So, even though my novels contain a lot of comedy, it is the character's sadness and pain that interest me the most. It is the character's neediness that leads to a crisis. It is pain that makes the novel rich. The comedy, as in life, helps the reader to get through it all.

In my first novel, *The Romantic Obsessions and Humiliations of Annie Sehlmeier,* we get some idea of Annie's pain with her first sentence: "I don't like being an immigrant." Her parents don't speak English, and her grandmother is senile and odd. She thinks her younger sister, Henny, is too silly to take seriously. A good set-up for comedy as well as humiliation and embarrassment. Smart, deluded Annie longs for some other world where "beautiful people gathered in the evening, sat on their satin-covered bottoms at a table decked out in

Lenox china and ate a civilized meal of exotic dishes of breast of unicorn. . . . I wanted a perfect life like that," she says.

Her life does seem perfect when she begins dating Jack Wakefield. It is not even so bad when she gets an uncontrollable crush on Tom Woolley. It is not so bad when she helps her sister toilet-paper Woolley's car every week. She can be smug with her sister and enjoy her secret at the same time. She is, as my sons would say, cruising for a bruising.

This bruising takes place in the middle of the night, during Christmas vacation. Annie goes alone to toilet-paper her beloved Woolley's car, because Henny, her sister, has the flu. But she does more than toilet paper the car. She talks to the car: "Is that you, Apollo?" she asks the car. "Come to your maiden queen." She dances around the car as if for a lover and then presses her lips against the cool hood of the car and kisses it many times calling the car "Woolley dear" and "Woolley darling," only to discover that all of her friends, including Woolley, are sitting on the roof of the garage watching her.

I like it that the *Horn Book* called this a "searingly embarrassing scene." I like it when readers tell me they had to skip over the scene, fearing what was coming, until they were sure that Annie recovered from her humiliation.

Did I ever kiss a car and speak to it as a lover in front of my friends? No. But I did have extended crushes in which I showed my hand just as blatantly. I remember one of my best friends pulling me aside one night at a party to tell me that I was making a jackass of myself in front of everyone. I knew it was true. I wanted Annie to feel the way I felt that night. By moving Annie through this painful scene and having her recover from it, I could finally forgive myself for being such a fool.

I enjoyed writing *Annie Sehlmeier*. She lives in a neighborhood where I grew up. Some of the characters are modeled after real people. At least twice that I can remember, I put on my old high school a cappella album and waxed unabashedly nostalgic while I wrote.

That was not true for *My Name is Sus5an Smith. The 5 is Silent.* I didn't enjoy writing the novel. In fact, I found it hard to write more than two or three pages at a sitting. When I was away from it, I thought it was a terrible book. Then when I returned to it and read what I'd written, I'd think, "Well, this isn't so bad." But the minute I walked away from my desk, it seemed putrid all over again. I haven't wanted to analyze too carefully why this was so, but off the top of my head I would say that Sus5an, who is a lot like me only much braver and much more talented, does some things that I wanted to do when I graduated from high school but didn't have the guts to do.

I wanted to go to New York City after high school. In fact, my whole senior year, I told everyone that that was what I was going to do. I had a safe way to go. I had an adult, who would show me the way. But in the end, my anxiety was larger than my desire to go, and I never went. I went, instead, a more conforming route, entering the University of Utah, and was not happy with it. It was wrong for me. Sus5an expresses it this way: "I tried to shove the feeling down, but going to the university so close by seemed oppressively conventional and artless."

My latest novel, which comes out in the fall of 1995, was originally called *Sort of a Christmas Romance* (later changed to *The Unlikely Romance of Kate Bjorkman*). I got the idea while walking through the BYU Bookstore's children's section at Christmastime. There were the same Christmas books that are always there: *The Polar Express, The Greatest Christmas Pageant Ever,* and so on. But there were no Christmas young adult novels. I decided I would be the one to write one. I remember being seventeen and wanting nothing but a boyfriend for Christmas. A boy in a box. I decided to write about a girl who yearned for a specific boy and actually got him at Christmas. My fantasy come true.

I also had my niece, Kelli Jaggi, in my head. She was just a little disgusted with my first two novels, in which the female protagonists are in love with the wrong guys, spend the whole novel humiliating themselves by chasing after the guys, and find out in the end that they were all wrong for them. My niece wanted me to write about a girl who likes the right guy and gets him in the end. She wanted a romance clear and simple. And why wouldn't she? She's seventeen.

So I began a novel about Kate Bjorkman, a girl of Scandinavian heritage, who lives in St. Paul, Minnesota, in a house and neighborhood where I once lived. Minnesota is a perfect landscape for a Christmas novel, because it always snows for the holidays and there are iced-over lakes everywhere for young lovers to skate on. I began writing in the third person, and when I had written about fifty pages, I realized that I was writing a conventional romance novel. I didn't want to be the author of a romance novel. Now that I am fifty-one, I'm suspicious of romance. Give me love, give me friendship, but don't give me too much romance. I've been there, and I don't much like it.

I decided to change to a first-person narration and have Kate tell the story herself. The question then was, if I were a young intellectual like Kate Bjorkman, who grows up to become a linguistics professor like her father—if I were Kate, knowing what I know now, how would I write about falling in love?

The answer was, I would write it like a parody, or a satire. Because I liked both words and lists, I would find a book like *The Romance Writer's Phrase Book* and I would purposely use those cliches and by using them, make fun of them.

And that is what I did. Kate is in love with Richard Bradshaw whom she hasn't seen in four years, because his family moved to California at the same time he was accepted

249

to Stanford. Bjorn, her brother and Richard's best friend, is also at Stanford. He is newly married to Trish. At the end of chapter 1, two days before Christmas, Kate returns from the grocery store to find Bjorn and Trish have made a surprise visit home and brought Richard with them. Kate is in the front hall and greets the visitors as they appear out of the kitchen one by one:

Bjorn insisted that Trish call me Boo. "That's her name," he said. We had been through all this before, and he still wouldn't let it go.

"Kate fits her better than Boo," Trish said.

I like Trish. "No one calls me Boo except Bjorn and his ape friends," I said.

"You mean me?" Richard Bradshaw filled the doorway.

Okay, a flourish of trumpets here. The hero has arrived. And because he was my hero long before I began writing this novel, ever since I can remember, in fact, my face grew hot. He was four years older, of course, and *shorter* than I remembered, but I wasn't six feet tall four years ago either. His eyes—I need the help of *The Romance Writers Phrase Book* to describe those eyes:

—*unfathomable in their murky depths?*

No!

—*shades of amber and green?*

Maybe.

—*dark gray-green flecked eyes?*

I don't know. Maybe.

—*hooded like those of a hawk?*

Absolutely not! The heck with it. They were warm eyes. They were Richard's eyes. I wouldn't care if they were cone-shaped. Richard Bradshaw was standing in the doorway of the dining room.

"Hi," I said and stepped forward to shake hands when I tripped at the edge of the oriental carpet and lurched into him, elbows first. It wasn't a pretty picture. He made a sound like "oomph" because my elbow caught him in the diaphragm. He was too incapacitated for me to fall gracefully into his arms. Instead, I was caught by a drop-dead beautiful young woman standing at Richard's side.

This would be a better story if I'd just lie, but I want truth in romance. And the truth is that the first time I saw Richard Bradshaw after four years of separation, I knocked the wind out of him and was saved from falling on my face by his girlfriend. . . .

Richard pounded a fist to his chest as if to correct whatever I had injured. "It's nice to see you again, Boo." He used my thirteen-year-old name, but he smiled, and we glanced at each other—our eyes didn't lock or anything—but it was easy to forgive him. Then, as if he had forgotten himself, he said, "Oh, this is my friend, Fleur St. Germaine."

I swear that was her real name. *Fleur St. Germaine.* Would I make up a name like that?

As it turns out, Fleur is not much of a threat, and early on Christmas morning, Richard and Kate go skating together. (The whole family was supposed to go but they all opt to sleep in, so Richard and Kate go alone, which allows them time for the "three paragraph kiss," which is the mainstay of a romance novel.)

The two of them skate well together, until Kate's skate catches on a glitch and the two of them crash to the ice. Kate's glasses are shattered and she can't see:

I don't know if it was because I wasn't wearing my glasses just then and I was prettier without them—that would have been Ashley's reasoning—or if it was that he had wanted to kiss me all morning, glasses or no glasses, or if it was simply impulsive. Richard kissed me. "Kate," he said, his lips grazing mine as he spoke. Then his mouth closed down on mine, but it was not like the phrase book says, "like soldering heat that joins metals." It was warm like summer. And he did not, as the phrase book says, take my mouth "with a savage intensity," nor did he "smother" my lips "with demanding mastery," nor did he "devour" me, nor was it a "punishing kiss." I wouldn't have liked any of that macho stuff. His hands—when had he removed his gloves?—held

251

my face, and I reached up and held his wrists. It was like summer, his kiss was. Have I said that?

Frankly, I'm finding that writing a three-paragraph kiss is difficult—impossible, maybe. I'm thinking that what it felt like explicitly and where our tongues were explicitly and that usual kind of three-paragraph detail is none of your darn business.

The phrase book is right: I did "breathe lightly between parted lips" when it was over. We grinned at each other, a little foolishly maybe. He pulled me to my feet.

So now it's time for the full body kiss, because his arms did slip around me easily, drawing me in, and I wound my arms around his neck. He kissed my hair; I kissed his face, which smelled of soap; and then, "reclaiming her lips, he crushed her to him."

Even if that were true, I could never write such a thing. Even if his touch *was* "divine ecstasy," even if the warmth of him was "intoxicating," even if my body was "tingling," I couldn't write that. It sounds stupid.

I can tell you another thing: he did not "lift me into the cradle of his arms." I'm six feet tall, for pity's sake!

And though we were smashed together in a pleasing way, my "soft curves" were not molded "to the contours of his lean body." This was Minnesota in December. We had so many clothes on, we might as well have been steel-belted radial tires.

I don't mean to put it down. It was delicious kissing Richard. I was born to kiss him. I just don't want to talk it to death.

What does all this comic romance have to do with pain? Well, the course of romance never does run smooth, and must not run smooth in a novel, which requires conflict. What is the point of reading if there are no obstacles to overcome? It is pain and tension that hold the reader's interest. And again, it was the painful scene I thought of first. The whole novel moves toward it. It takes place at a New Year's Eve dance. Kate's date is the exchange student, Helmut Weiss, whom she had asked weeks before. Richard Bradshaw's date is Kate's friend, Ashley, whom we know now is the antagonist, not Fleur St. Germaine. Ashley asked Richard, and he did not particularly want to go.

When Kate first sees Ashley at the New Year's Eve dance, she almost stops breathing:

> She was definitely not wearing the dress she had shown me at Christmas. Instead she was poured into a strapless black number with her breasts perched halfway out of the top. Her hair was thick and curled and swung around her shoulders. Her long, black-stockinged legs, perfectly shaped, showed from mid-thigh on down. She looked older, sophisticated—I would like to say that she looked cheap, but it wouldn't be true. She looked dramatic, like a model out of *Harper's Bazaar*. She looked sensuous. She wore diamond earrings and a necklace that matched. Dozens of heads turned to look, to appreciate, to be stunned.
>
> My throat constricted like it does when I'm afraid.

Despite her provocative dress, Ashley cannot hang onto Richard for the slow dances. These he dances with Kate, until the last half-hour of the dance, when he and Ashley disappear. When midnight comes, Kate still cannot find them until she steps out of the rest room:

> I heard voices, familiar voices: Richard and Ashley's voices.
>
> "Ash, don't. Let's go back and dance."
>
> "Let's dance here."
>
> I turned a corner and saw them on the stairs, the service stairs. Richard was backed against the wall, and Ashley had her arms about his neck, her whole body leaning into him. Let me try again—her whole body *mashed, crushed, pasted, squashed, smashed* against his. One knee curved against his leg.
>
> Richard's hands were on her elbows. "Listen, Ash."
>
> Her mouth clamped his, but his hands pushed against her elbows. I saw it clearly—he was not engaged in this kiss. He had not initiated any of this. I knew that.

253

I held my breath.

Ashley's knee rose up on his leg. Richard pulled down on her elbows. I couldn't move, couldn't look away. I wish I could have disappeared, because then I wouldn't have seen him give in. I wouldn't have seen his arms folding around her bare back—wouldn't have seen him step forward. "He clasped her body tightly to his" is how *The Romantic Writers Phrase Book* would put it, but it's not so romantic when it's your boyfriend you're describing in a heated embrace with a girl who was once your friend.

Even now, a cold knot forms in my stomach as I write about it. It still stuns and sickens me to repeat the experience on these pages.

I dropped my purse onto the tile floor. I looked down. The clasp had opened; the lipstick rolled and stopped. I looked up.

He pushed Ashley away. "Kate!" His voice was hoarse. Kissing can do that.

"I'm sorry," I said. I turned and ran through the kitchen, leaving the purse and its contents on the floor.

"Kate!" Richard's voice followed me through the house.

I found Helmut watching the fireworks. "Please, I want to go home," I said to Helmut. "Right now, please!"

Richard caught me from behind. "Kate, let me explain—" His face was wretched, gray.

"Drop dead," I said evenly. I pulled my arm out of his grasp and headed for the coat room, hoping Helmut would follow.

Instead Richard stayed at my heels. "Kate, please don't leave this way." His fingers grasped my arm. I pried them loose.

"Don't touch me," I said through my teeth. "Don't follow me and don't talk to me!" And then I did something that shames me even now: I slugged him as hard as I could across the shoulder with a closed fist. I slugged Richard, wearing my black velvet party dress. I slugged him hard. Helmut saw it. The man holding my coat saw it. Maybe a few other people as well. I slugged Richard with all my strength. I wanted to kill him.

254

He teetered a little and then backed away. "Okay," he said, his hands up in a gesture of truce. "Not here, not now."

"Not ever!" I said and walked out of the front door without my coat.

Will Kate survive this betrayal? Will Richard survive Kate? If this novel were being written by a beginning writing student, the answer would not be at all clear. Perhaps Kate shoots Richard with an automatic weapon. Perhaps she shoots herself with an automatic weapon. Perhaps she kills Richard by rubbing up against him in a dress made of razor-sharp sequins.

But probably not. Because I promised my niece that this protagonist would get the man she had her heart set on at the beginning of the novel, but not without a little pain, a little personal growth, because—like Kate—I want truth in romance. Even in novels, I want real life.

"ASK, AND IT SHALL BE GIVEN"

DAWN M. McLAREN

As a young child growing up in Jamaica, I was very aware of our Heavenly Father. I sensed his love, his presence, his caring. This knowledge was so innate and clear that at the age of three or four, I remember feeling that the Bible stories I heard in Sunday School or from my mother seemed familiar. I loved most being read the stories of Jesus; sometimes they made me cry. The adults around me were a little puzzled by my emotions.

One memory is clear in my mind, confirming my conviction of my Heavenly Father's loving presence. When I was about five years old, the family moved from the city to the country. That part of the island was extraordinarily beautiful. The people there, mostly farmers, were warm and generous. The land was fertile, a place of rich, red soil, rolling hillsides, and lush vegetation. Fruit trees were everywhere. Sweet delicious fruit of all kinds was plentiful. The pungent aroma of ripe fruit and blossoms filled the air. But this part of the country was also noted for its heavy rainstorms. The rain fell harder and longer, the thunder was louder, and the lightning more menacing than anything I had ever known.

Before each storm, a black cloud would descend on the

Dawn M. McLaren is an immigrant from Jamaica, West Indies. A single mother of a son, Jason, she graduated from Brooklyn College with a bachelor's degree in political science. Sister McLaren has served as president of the PTA and as a member of a citizens advisory committee for the school budget.

land. And then, as if the clouds had exploded, the thunder would clap with a deafening sound and the hot, sharp, jagged points of lightning would stab at the windows, clattering on the glass. I was frightened by it. I felt certain that the fearsome thunder would break open the house, that the lightning would pierce the windows and slash us to pieces. I cowered in my bed, and one night when I could stand it no longer, I ran to my mother's room.

Mother tried to comfort me by telling me that I should not be afraid. The Lord would protect me, if I would only pray. So I went back to my bed and prayed. I asked the Lord to stop the storm. And as soon as I finished praying, it stopped. The lightning, the thunder, the rain simply stopped. All was suddenly still, and I *knew* he had heard my prayer. But he did something even greater. He took away my fear. I was never again afraid in a storm.

As I grew older and lost my innocence, I also lost my pure, unquestioning acceptance of our Lord. My father got a better job that was nearer to the city and my mother's family, and we moved away from that fertile paradise to a harsher area where the soil was grayish and clayey; instead of fruit trees there were thorn trees (acacia) all around. The people were also harsher. The day I first questioned God's existence I witnessed a man whip a horse so savagely it was a wonder it did not die. The horse was pulling a cart laden with bricks through a gate that was not wide enough. The cart got stuck, and the driver stood up in the cart and beat that horse for what seemed more than an hour—the whip cutting deep and red into its flesh. Sweat poured from the man as he belabored the beast until the agony left its eyes and all I could see in them was sadness. I crumbled beneath the window I was watching from and wept. How could God allow such a thing to happen?

Soon, I saw even crueler things done by man, woman, and child to each other and to their fellow creatures. I became convinced that there could not be a God—at least, not the God I thought I knew. It was easier for me to believe God did not exist than to explain the misery of this world. But without God I was miserable. I no longer felt loved and protected. Joy was fleeting, here one moment, gone the next. Pain was all around. I did not want to live.

My father thought it best that his children attend college in the United States, and we emigrated to New York soon after I finished high school. In my first year of college, I was an ardent philosophy student. I thought of myself as agnostic; I was not sure there is a God. If someone could prove it to me, I might accept it. Descartes led me to acknowledge his postulate, "I think, therefore I am," but I would not buy his further proofs that "therefore there is a God." Socrates, however, with his line of reasoning, proved to my intellectual satisfaction that there must be a God. That's what I had wanted—I could intelligently reason that there is a God. I felt great comfort with that knowledge, but I was at the same time very dissatisfied with religion.

As an infant, I had been baptized an Anglican. I attended Catholic preparatory school and was taught the catechism. My mother became converted to pentecostal worship, and as a child I was required to attend church with her. Responding to my need to be connected with my Heavenly Father, I must have visited every variation of those denominations. But there remained an emptiness inside of me, deep in my soul.

One night after attending a meeting at my mother's church, I asked God to show me the way. Soon after I had a dream. In my dream I was in a cathedral, alone, praying. A bishop came up to me and told me that God was going to send someone to lead me to the right church. My feeling was so strong that this dream was from the Lord that I told my mother and sister about it. I was so earnestly expecting this person that when a man on a bus I was traveling on invited me to a religious meeting, I quickly asked, "Are you the man that the Lord sent?" He looked a bit puzzled, or perhaps he was concerned for my mental state.

I attended meetings with him for a time, but I soon realized that this was not the someone promised in the dream, mainly because my sense of emptiness remained. Rather than feeling at peace, I was more disturbed than before. I stopped attending and told myself to be more careful. So, a few weeks later when two young men came to my door, stating that they were missionaries, telling me about a religion I was not familiar with and of the strange occurrences of a Joseph Smith, I was willing to listen, but I was cautious. To investigate them, I went to the library and got all the books available on the Mormons. I was very moved by a biography of Joseph Smith, *Joseph Smith and the Beginnings of Mormonism,* written by Richard L. Bushman, who is now the patriarch of our stake. By the time the elders came back the following week, I was telling them things about Joseph Smith and his family that they didn't know.

Having the discussions with the missionaries, I found my mind was never more stimulated—challenged and yet consoled. I remember thinking how strange it was that after all the intellectuals that I had met, these two very young men, fresh out of high school, so obviously unsophisticated, were exciting my mind to such heights. For even though I was talking more than both of them put together, I was learning so much; and even though I could not put my finger on why, I had never felt more mentally satisfied—nourished—in my life. So as not to be separated from these feelings, I decided to be baptized.

When I emerged from the waters of baptism, I immediately felt a cleansing of my soul. I was like a new person, wonderful, clean, and renewed. When Steve Farrell, who later became my home teacher, laid his hands on my head and gave me the gift of the Holy Ghost, I could almost hear my Heavenly Father say, "This is my beloved daughter *for whom* I am well pleased." He was so pleased for me that for a time everything I wished for, from the simplest to the greatest, seemed to come my way. I got used to decisions being made in my favor. I remember a disagreement with a store manager. I had waited too long, he said, to pick up a mattress I had purchased about a year earlier. He had no record of my order because store records were discarded after a time. In addition, he did not carry that particular mattress anymore. Nevertheless, I had my receipt and a strong conviction that the Lord would take care of things. I walked out with a better, more expensive mattress at no extra cost.

That was a little matter, but I was blessed in large matters as well, so much so that I felt almost invincible, protected, covered in an armor of love that gave me a remarkable new self-confidence. At the time I joined the Church, concern for my son Jason was the real issue in my life. Five years earlier, my son, then in second grade, had been diagnosed dyslexic—learning disabled. When Jason was in the fourth grade, I had seen a television program on the brain that made me understand Jason's problem better. And because I understood, I was better able to help him deal with his disability.

For a while, I worked part-time instead of full-time in order to spend as much time as possible in his school. His teachers were very cooperative. In junior high his science teacher allowed me in his class to take notes and to read tests to him. His English teacher gave me *Reversals,* a book by Eileen Simpson, a woman with the same problem as Jason's. Reading of her struggles and accomplishments moved and inspired me. In junior high Jason became an honor student, receiving many awards for his academic achievements.

It was during this time that I joined the Church, and it seemed that the Lord and his heavenly host were taking special interest in my affairs. When it became apparent that Jason would be better able to reach his potential in a private school specializing in learning disabilities, I was not deterred to learn that those schools' tuition averaged more than I made in a year. I felt assured that somehow the Lord would make it possible.

Jason received a full scholarship to the best and the most expensive of those private schools.

But pretty soon the honeymoon was over. The Lord wanted me to grow. Granting my every wish—no matter how worthwhile—would not teach me to abide by the new covenants I had made. It was not easy for me to let go of my will, my cultivated self-esteem, my cherished intellect, and allow the Holy Ghost to guide and direct my decision making. One such decision was to receive my temple endowments. The idea of temple covenants and ordinances seemed too mysterious and other-worldly to me. I was an intelligent, rational being who saw through those primitive rituals. I was not ready to give myself to something I did not understand or see as necessary.

The bishop, however, knew more than I obviously did about the blessings of the temple and suggested temple preparation classes. I resisted. I think half of me wanted to go, to experience more of the wonderful changes that were occurring in my life, but the other half wanted to hang on to my old self. The Lord knew my heart and wanted to help me make that decision to embrace the Church fully, to be under his covenants fully. At Christmastime that year, I had an experience that helped me to be more in tune spiritually.

It was quarter to midnight three days before Christmas. I had just stepped off the bus from my second job, carrying shopping bags full of Christmas gifts. I was alone five blocks from my house on what is usually a quiet, pleasant, familiar street. One block away, I saw six teenagers, ruffians, strangers to the neighborhood. I knew I was not safe by the way they were dressed, by the way they stalked, not walked, checking out every car, every yard. I remembered that Steve Farrell, my home teacher, had been mugged and hospitalized just three blocks away, by ones such as these. Muggings were common now, even much earlier in the evening.

Yes, I was in danger, and I knew it. But I immediately thought, "My Heavenly Father will not let anything happen to me." And so I asked him to take charge of the situation. As I mentally conveyed to him my needs, my fear suddenly evaporated.

I walked up to the boys, confident and assured. They were spread across the street in a line, watching me like predators stalking their prey. I advanced straight up the middle of the road, staring back into the eyes of the one who seemed the most fierce. When our eyes met as I closed in on them, he suddenly broke from the line and ran, exclaiming, "Wow! Wow!" The others followed, expressing first fear and disbelief and then laughing.

I walked on with a smile on my face, feeling like I had just walked on water . . . but I did check the mirror when I got home. After that incident, I learned that the Lord's way can sometimes seem mysterious and other-worldly, masked in mysticism. I decided to go to the temple, and I had a most glorious experience.

I have come to understand that the way of the Lord is not my way, that there are certain things he allows to happen for a purpose, and that as we remain steadfast and "long-suffering" (I never did like that word, but plenty often it is appropriate), in time, all will be revealed to us.

How can I doubt the magnitude of my Heavenly Father, when he has done so much for me and for others? A friend of mine, a lawyer, once complimented me on the inner peace I possessed; on another occasion, he questioned, "How can an intelligent woman like you believe in this God thing?" I said to him, "You did not know me before I joined the Church, before I put this 'God thing' in my life. I did not have the peace you admire so much."

If only for the peace I have gained, I am happy to have discarded that old self and gained a new self being shaped in beauty and peace by the love of God.

"AMBITION ENOUGH FOR ZION'S SAKE": OUR HERITAGE OF HEALTH CARE

ELAINE SHAW SORENSEN

The year 1993 marked the one hundredth anniversary of Lillian Wald's founding of Henry Street Settlement in New York City. Miss Wald, as she was called, is my hero, just a few steps behind Florence Nightingale. I discovered Miss Wald early in nursing school; even then my favorite secret study was history. Unlike British Florence Nightingale, who became famous for her work in faraway Turkey, Lillian Wald was an American who noticed the sick mothers and dying babies in her own neighborhood. Like Florence, Miss Wald took risks. She saw problems and did her best to solve them. She made a difference.

Miss Wald graduated from nurse training school at New York Hospital in 1891 and then enrolled at Women's Medical College while volunteering nursing services to new immigrants on the lower east side of New York City. Touched by the overwhelming needs there, she left medical school, moved into the needy neighborhood, and, with her nursing classmate Mary Brewster, began an entire national movement in health and

Elaine Shaw Sorensen is associate dean for research and scholarship at the College of Nursing at Brigham Young University. She served as a missionary to Colombia and is a member of a Church writing committee. She is the mother of four.

welfare reform, one nurse and one family at a time. She is now known for founding American public health nursing.

Recently, my research assistant discovered a letter dated 26 February 1909 from Ysabella Waters, Miss Wald's associate at Henry Street Settlement in New York City, to Emma Empey, superintendent of the Relief Society School for Nurses in Salt Lake City and the founder of our own Latter-day Saint public health nursing. You can imagine my excitement in finding a connection between my beloved Utah sisters and the admired Miss Wald. The letter thanked Sister Empey for previous correspondence providing information on LDS visiting nurses and commended their work as "unique and most interesting."[1]

I further learned that in 1919, Amy Brown Lyman—then a member of the Relief Society General Board and later a Utah state legislator (1923), first counselor in the Relief Society General Presidency (1928), and Relief Society General President (1940)—visited Lillian Wald at Henry Street. Comparing Miss Wald's efforts to the work of Jane Addams at Hull House in Chicago, Sister Lyman reported, "Miss Wald, famous for her work, is soft-spoken and sweet-voiced and is the essence of modesty, simplicity, and kindness. She much preferred to talk about her work rather than herself."[2]

With these discoveries, my nearly pathological affinity for history was set in motion. The women I most admired from both my professional and personal heritage, on either side of the country, had come together. My adventure had begun.

My newly discovered heroines are our LDS sisters in health care at the turn of the century, sisters who were no less valiant than Florence Nightingale or Lillian Wald. They include women such as Emma Empey and hundreds of other sisters who served anonymously and lovingly to make life and health better for those around them.[3]

BEGINNINGS

Almost from the Prophet Joseph Smith's first vision, faith

healing, fasting and prayer, and the laying on of hands have pervaded Latter-day Saint theology and culture. Early revelations now recorded in the Doctrine and Covenants refer to healing promises and ordinances, diet, and health (D&C 24:13–14; 35:9; 42:43–52; 46:19–20; 49:18–19; 66:9; 84:67–73; 89). When the Relief Society was organized in Nauvoo in 1842, sisters were instructed to care for the Saints. Joseph Smith set apart "such noble and lofty women as Mary Fielding Smith, Mercy R. Thompson, Eliza R. Snow, Mother Whitney, Marinda and Mary Ann Hyde, Elvira Cowles, and Sarah M. Kimball . . . to go about among the sick and minister to their wants."[4] Generally, the early Saints combined faith healing with the practice of Thomsonian medicine, named after an unorthodox physician, Samuel Thomson. Traditional modern medicine at the time relied on blood-letting, blistering, and cathartics. Thomsonianism represented a more "natural," botanical approach, with remedies from herbs and plants.

Professional nursing and medicine were born among the sisterly acts of pioneer midwives, some also specifically set apart for the work. Hardly a history of LDS women exists without mention of a pioneer midwife or "lady" doctor. Under the stewardship of presidents Joseph Smith and Brigham Young, women ministered as nurses and midwives to the immigrating and colonizing Saints: "Often the only 'doctor' for miles around, these faithful women, many of them Relief Society presidents or counselors, travelled endless lonely miles by foot or horseback, by buggy, wagon, or sleigh through the deep snows of winter and the rain and mud of early spring, to deliver babies, set broken bones, cool fevered brows, and perform other healing services."[5]

Best known among the pioneer midwives was Patty Sessions, thought to have delivered nearly four thousand pioneer babies. Patty Sessions is well known for three reasons: her own longevity, her association with other well-known pioneer sister leaders, and her meticulous diary. She was born in Maine in 1795 and began her midwife practice at age seventeen. She continued her work in Nauvoo, suffered with her sisters in Winter Quarters, crossed the plains, and came with the early pioneers to the Salt Lake Valley. After a life of tireless service, Sister Sessions died in Utah at the age of ninety-nine.

Much of the study of LDS nursing has focused on pioneer midwives. To the stories of such valiant pioneer women as Patty Sessions, Ann Carling, Vienna Jacques, and others now in historical anthologies could be added many other lesser-known pioneer midwives. My conversations with descendants of these women tell me that even more significant personal stories remain to be told.

Within two years of the Saints' arrival in the Salt Lake Valley, Brigham Young established a Council of Health, appointing doctor and apostle Willard Richards as its head. The members of the council sought herbs for medicines and discussed health issues at public meetings. Susannah Lippincott, one of Richards' wives, also taught midwifery and nursing care. Among her students were Zina D. H. Young, Presendia Kimball, and Emmeline B. Wells.[6] In 1851, the Female Council of Health was organized; most wards in the Salt Lake Valley sent representatives. Activities of the council related to concerns of hygiene and health of women, including matters of dress and health, apparently a common topic for discussion at the time.[7]

In 1868, Brigham Young encouraged LDS women to become trained in "anatomy, surgery, chemistry, physiology, the preservation of health, the properties of medicinal plants, and midwifery."[8] In 1872, a school of "medicine and surgery for the instruction of females" was proposed.[9] Indeed, Eliza R. Snow was an influential proponent of a medical school for women in the Valley. Such a school was never founded, but several women were sent east to study medicine. The first woman physician in the United States, Elizabeth Blackwell, had graduated in 1849, but medical education for a woman was not the norm. Considerable prejudice against women in medical school persisted, and the study of medicine involved great personal sacrifice.

Most LDS women physicians were supported in their medical education by their families and Relief Society sisters. Eventually, about twenty women doctors practiced in the Utah territory, playing an important part in promoting the principles of modern health care and medicine. Best known perhaps are Ellis Reynolds Shipp, Maggie Curtis Shipp (later Roberts), Romania B. Pratt Penrose, Ellen B. Ferguson, and Martha Hughes Cannon. Their service helped educate early nurses and reduce neonatal and puerperal deaths.

In 1873, the year the nation graduated its first professional nurse, Linda Richards from New England Hospital for Women and Children, Brigham Young requested each ward to select three women to study locally "physiology and obstetrics. Also that one woman from each settlement be sent to [Salt Lake] to study . . . and that the Bishops see that such women be supported."[10] By that same year, the United States had noted the beginning of three Nightingale nursing schools in New York, Connecticut, and Massachusetts.

Eliza R. Snow personally recruited students to the proposed local nursing courses: "Are there here, now, any sisters who have ambition enough, and who realize the necessity of it, for Zion's sake, to take up this study. . . . Then, another class of women is wanted more advanced in age, who are natural nurses, and would be willing to study obstetrics. . . . We have to get up these classes and attend to all these things."[11]

The nursing education was supported financially, emotionally, and spiritually by sisters from the students' local wards. Early teachers of the classes included doctors Mary H. Barker, Romania B. Pratt Penrose, Ellis Reynolds Shipp, and Maggie Curtis Shipp. At first, these instructors advertised their nursing courses privately and apparently competitively. Graduates were "blest and set apart for their professional work."[12] The carefully

267

scripted class notes of student Elizabeth Jane Price Evans from Dr. Ellis Shipp's nursing and midwifery course reveal principles of nursing practice in 1889. Nursing education emphasized maternity care. For example, the treatment for an adherent placenta was a rectal injection of a mixture of one tablespoon castor oil, one tablespoon sweet oil, one tablespoon turpentine, and twelve tablespoons hot water. Considerable attention was also given to symptoms and management of "postpartal mania," an apparently common condition.[13] (I think I have suffered from that malady myself, with regular recurrences.)

SOCIETY IN TRANSITION

By the end of the nineteenth century, Latter-day Saint society was facing major political and social change. Church members had witnessed the martyrdom of their prophet, endured hardships in the trek west, and established a relatively isolated political community "which conjoined church and state, politics, the economy, and society into one whole."[14] The pervading theme of the early Church community had been restoration, which meant establishing a kingdom of God based on a philosophy and political system that offended much of contemporary society, especially in its practice of Old Testament polygamy and theocracy.

The Saints soon found their philosophies seriously challenged by the conservative Victorian majority of the United States. The challenge intensified as American settlers continued to move westward, occasionally interfering with Latter-day Saints' independence and solitude. Through "a series of laws, court tests, and political activities," the primarily Protestant political majority sought to "break the back of the Mormon community and reshape it in the image of the remainder of the United States."[15] By 1887, national political insistence upon conformity had disfranchised LDS polygamists and women (who had been among the first in the nation to win the vote), changed control of the Church-dominated education system,

268

abolished the Utah territorial militia, and confiscated most of the Church's property.

With the 1890 Manifesto, the practice of polygamy officially ended, and the Church organization shifted focus from restoration to preservation, as members struggled to find a way to preserve the essential theology and characteristics of Latter-day Saint society while allowing the Saints to live peaceably in a changing, pluralistic America.

One example of the struggles Church members faced with changing societal views related directly to public health. At the turn of the century, public policy for smallpox immunization was controversial. To some, supporting a public immunization program seemed contrary to a tradition of faith healing and home remedies. Charles Penrose, the husband of physician Romania B. Pratt Penrose, opposed mandatory immunization as a violation of personal liberty. As the editor of the *Deseret News,* he used his influence to persuade Church members. On the other side were George Q. Cannon of the First Presidency and John Henry Smith of the Quorum of the Twelve Apostles, who supported compulsory vaccination for the public welfare. The legislature, however, prohibited mandated immunization and overrode the veto of Governor Heber M. Wells. Unfortunately, a serious epidemic continued. In 1899 and 1900, nearly four thousand cases of smallpox were reported, and twenty-six deaths resulted.[16]

The smallpox immunization argument was set against a matrix of social tensions in Latter-day Saint society. First, there was an ambivalence between cooperation and individualism, social welfare and individual liberty, in approaches to public health programs. A second plane of ambivalence existed between the acceptance and promotion of "modern" orthodox medicine and the persistence of total reliance on priesthood healing and home remedies.

Ambivalence extended into questions of nursing practice. In 1916, argument grew over "individual liberty" versus public health, as some Utahns opposed the employment of "busy-body" school nurses. Some apparently viewed the nurses' case-finding and referral work as an invasion of privacy and "personal liberty."[17]

Such social and philosophical upheaval also profoundly affected the daily lives of the women of the time. Women had walked beside priesthood leaders through the years of forced migration from Ohio to Missouri, Missouri to Illinois, and Illinois to the Salt Lake Valley. All the while, they were reestablishing homes, caring for the sick, delivering infants, rearing children, anointing and burying the dead, and even providing for entire households while men were away as soldiers, scouts, missionaries, or polygamist fugitives. This adversity and responsibility, as well as the pervading cultural separation of men's and women's daily lives, promoted a fierce leadership and independence among LDS women. Devoted to the success of the gospel and their own families, LDS women at the turn of the century exhibited a social and political activism unique in history.

At the end of the nineteenth century, LDS women had established their own newspaper, begun cooperative stores, developed industries, and achieved suffrage. They later contributed to the nation's war effort, during World War I, by their grain-saving activities, for which President Woodrow Wilson offered his personal thanks. Several women even won political office. Indeed, in 1911, the city of Kanab, Utah, elected an all-women city council. Their individual vigor, industry, independence, autonomy, and progressiveness as an organized body were remarkable. Latter-day Saint women also persisted in their ties to national political leadership, and such leadership was reflected in the beginnings of professional health care in LDS society.

In 1888, the first International Council of Women convened in Washington, D.C., sponsored by the National Woman Suffrage Association. Attending the Council to represent LDS women was Emily Richards, a member of the Relief Society General Board. The following excerpt from an 1888 issue of *Woman's Exponent* describes the Council: "It marks a new era of woman's position before the world; not that any wonderful event will transpire in consequence of the fact, but that woman's views, opinions and sentiments on questions of public importance have come to be recognized as sufficiently popular to be able to rally not only in a national, but an international capacity. The union of women in this work will be a strong lever to lift them from comparative obscurity to a much higher and loftier PLANE, and will give to the various departments of woman's work and industries an impetus not before apparent."[18]

LDS women were already well experienced in securing suffrage and were affiliated with national movements related to women, children, and health and welfare causes. Suffrage for women had been part of the original constitution of the proposed, but rejected, state of Deseret in 1850, seventy years before the nineteenth amendment to the Constitution of the United States. Utah women actually gained suffrage originally in 1870 (second only to Wyoming's women), long before most of their national sisters. In 1887, the Edmunds-Tucker Act withdrew Utah women's suffrage, prompting greater commitment to public activism for Utah women. Utah's statehood in 1896 restored voting privileges to Utah women.

At the same time that LDS women became immersed in community issues, professional medicine and nursing at the national level were emerging from unprecedented upheaval. Modern nursing underwent significant growth during "the fateful decade" from 1890 to 1900. In those important ten years, women founded the organizations that became the National League for Nursing and the American Nurses Association. During those years, the first university program for educating nurses was established, and such pioneer luminaries as Lavinia

Dock, Isabel Hampton, and M. Adelaide Nutting became known for their contributions to health care reform.

THE RELIEF SOCIETY NURSING SCHOOL

In 1898, the Relief Society Nursing School graduated its first class to provide practical nursing service to various wards and branches of the Church, often where there was no medical or nursing service. Women from all areas of the Church were called to attend the practical nursing school in Salt Lake City. Unlike the earlier private courses, the school was directly under the direction of the Relief Society General Board. A handbill of 1916 listed the following courses for a tuition fee of fifty dollars: obstetrics, nursing, invalid cooking, public health, and prevention and treatment of diseases. The instructor at the time was Dr. Margaret Roberts.[19] Amy Brown Lyman, then general secretary of the Relief Society, evidently conducted course registration. Later instructors were physicians Romania B. Pratt Penrose and Ellis Shipp. The last two classes, from 1918 to 1920, were taught by nurses unnamed even in the Relief Society's own histories.

Emma A. Empey served as superintendent of the school and supervisor of charity nursing during its entire tenure. In exchange for reduced or free tuition, graduating students were required to devote a number of hours of charity nursing in their own communities, under the direction of local Relief Society presidents. The Relief Society nurses were often the first, and sometimes the only, trained health care providers in many rural areas. It was this program that Lillian Wald at New York's Henry Street found "unique and most interesting."

Most of the nurses who visited homes, watched at bedsides, tended children, prepared meals, and carried wood and water, in addition to providing the best nursing and medical care to be had at the time, suffer a remarkable case of anonymity. Specific stories remain to be told of the pioneer nurses who staffed the first hospitals and of the valiant students who were sponsored largely by their ward sisters to attend the lady doctors' obstetrics courses and the Relief Society School of Nursing.

MEN IN NURSING

Florence Nightingale said, "Every woman is a nurse"; history seems to assume further that every nurse is a woman.[20] Missing from most descriptions of early nursing is the discussion of the few pioneer men in the profession. Indeed, nursing at the turn of the century, and for some time since, has been viewed largely as part of female culture. A few notable exceptions merit mention.

When St. Mark's Hospital first opened to its miner patients in 1872, it was operated by one female matron housekeeper and all male attendants ("nurses") trained by physicians. We know nothing more of these caring men. Henry Denkers, a night nurse at Ogden General Hospital in 1890, was reported to be the "only male nurse of the time"; unfortunately, we know little else about him.[21] Historians hope to discover sources that will bring forward the stories of these and other men in nursing.

MEDICINE AND NURSING

Among early Latter-day Saints and society in general, health care was largely gender-segregated. Thus, LDS women physicians and nurses shared a common social culture, especially in the Relief Society organization. There is, however, some evidence of differing perceptions of status.

The Salt Lake Sanitarian, "a monthly journal of medicine and surgery," began its brief publication in April 1888, under the editorship of Dr. M. Bard Shipp, Dr. Ellis R. Shipp, and Dr. Maggie Curtis Shipp. The stated purpose of the monthly journal was "to educate the people in the laws of life and sanitation" and to be "devoted to the prevention and cure of diseases and injuries, and the promulgation of the laws of health and life."[22]

In the journal, Dr. Maggie Shipp described the requisites of a good nurse: "A cheerful, pleasant countenance; a sympathetic soul yet resolute and determined; a sweet musical voice, or at least one who prefers the lower notes to the higher ones; a step quick, but lightness itself, a person who could move around the room without stumbling against the bedstead, or upsetting any article of furniture." Dr. Shipp lamented the faults of nurses with dirty fingernails, nurses unable to cook or who serve food "in an untidy and slovenly manner," who leave urine uncovered in the patient's bedroom, and who gossip to patients.[23] At the same time, on the East Coast, nurses at New York's Bellevue Hospital were denounced as exconvicts, fraught with drunkenness and foul language.

The doctors Shipp also charged practicing physicians with an apparently common "besetting sin" of drunkenness and proclaimed the value of a "religious disposition" among medical doctors, promoting the "'higher life' and the noble aspirations that dwell in the bosom of the profession."[24]

Another article professing the value of female physicians noted that "medicine is truly a sacred calling, standing shoulder to shoulder with theology. . . . The Lord makes physicians; the colleges merely qualify or license them. There is many a heaven-made physician among women, but society's prejudices cheat heaven and deprive humanity of its due." The article continued at some length to proclaim the virtues of and injustices against professional women. "To be sure, a woman's most sublime setting is in the crown of domestic glory; but why should she not have a right to choose a calling as well as a man? If she desires to be a doctor, and gives but 'a woman's reason,' why question her further? . . . [Do] education and culture tend to destroy amiability? Educate the woman, and there will be finer brains in the coming generations. . . . Women have long been considered 'weak vessels'; but, if loosed from the fetters of prejudice, they would pick out their own thread in the many-colored fabric which is woven in life's loom; their service would be equally recompensed, equally appreciated, and the

274

wicked injustice with which they are judged would be lost in oblivion."[25]

Several articles in the journal related to the health of women. Examples include "The Effects of the Present Educational Methods on the Health of Women," "Do Maternal Impressions Affect the Foetus in Utero to Produce Monstrosities and So called Mother's Marks?" "The Influence of Female Employment upon Marriages, Births, and Deaths," "Ladies and Athletics," and "Hygiene Versus Surgery in Gynecology." (Modern women are left to wonder what physical condition might provoke a choice between hygiene and surgery.)

HOSPITALS AND NURSING EDUCATION

Before 1873, the United States had fewer than two hundred hospitals. Within fifty years, the number grew to well over six thousand.[26] In Utah, the establishment and staffing of hospitals and nursing schools reflected the saintly initiative of a few women and the cooperative efforts of church and community.

Attention to health care was not exclusive to the Latter-day Saints in the Utah territory, nor were the first hospitals in the territory built by them. Recognizing the need for medical care for miners, the Episcopal Church established St. Mark's, the first hospital in the territory, in 1872, and a training school for nurses followed in 1894.

A record of early cases treated at St. Mark's Hospital reveals the most common diagnoses of lead poisoning, accidental injuries, rheumatic fever, typhoid, syphilis, and tuberculosis. Another interesting diagnostic note is the first recognized case in Utah of appendicitis in 1891. At that time, appendicitis was a new disease to health care practice, and surgical and mortality rates were high for several decades even after its discovery.[27]

In 1875, Catholic sisters established a hospital for miners, referred to as "St. Mary's" by Eliza R. Snow.[28] By 1901, the nuns had established a school of nursing at the hospital, then called Holy Cross. Dr. Martha Hughes Cannon, well known later as the nation's first female state senator (winning an election in which her husband was an opponent), acted as chief of staff.

Under President John Taylor, the women of the Relief Society established Deseret Hospital in 1882. Eliza R. Snow, president of the Relief Society, was named president of the hospital. With the exception of two male physicians, the entire hospital staff was female. Resident physicians included Ellen B. Ferguson, Martha Hughes Cannon, and Romania B. Pratt Penrose. Deseret Hospital became the center of Relief Society efforts to train nurses and midwives and to teach general classes on health and hygiene to LDS women. Costs of operating were covered by donations from "the Relief Societies, Young Ladies' Mutual Improvement Associations, and Primary Associations," and fees paid by patients."[29] The hospital sent repeated notice to Church members that the hospital "was a benevolent institution, but not a place of charity."[30] Unfortunately, following the tradition and public expectations of voluntary nursing care, many patients expected hospital care to be provided by the Church at no cost. The hospital was thus not able to maintain itself financially and closed in 1890.

From the generous donation of a dentist, W. H. Groves, in gratitude for nursing care received at St. Mark's Hospital, LDS Hospital was established in 1905 with a staff of eight nurses. Ralph Richards, a physician working at the time, described nursing conditions at the new LDS Hospital: "It is difficult to picture the nursing conditions in Salt Lake when the hospital opened in 1905. There were very few trained nurses. Those who wanted duty registered at some of the drug stores, so that a physician who was looking for a nurse phoned the drug stores in his search. He did not do it unless in dire need because nurses charged exorbitant fees. For a single day's service of twenty-four hours, these unreasonable women demanded five dollars. Twenty-one cents an hour!"[31]

Among my favorite stories is the remarkable effort of local stake Relief Society sisters to establish two maternity hospitals.

One was in Snowflake, Arizona, and the other in what is now Murray, Utah. Cottonwood Stake Maternity Hospital began service in 1924. Stake Relief Society presidency Amanda Bagley, Rene Wheeler, and Nellie Cornwall elicited support from their priesthood stake presidency and ward members to purchase a home and establish a maternity hospital that soon boasted very low maternal-child mortality.

The hospital's creators took heed of the words of Florence Nightingale: "A dark house is always an unhealthy house, always an ill-aired house, always a dirty house. Want of light stops growth, and promotes [illness]."[32] They chose for their hospital a "cool, quiet restful location," a delivery room and nursery with a southern exposure, interior "sunny colors," and grounds where Church members planted "sixty-five Norway Maple trees."[33]

In its first five years, 1,378 babies were born. There was low mortality. With no budget at first for salaries, Mary Greaves and Agnes Merrill provided free nursing service. Bringing food and linens from their own cupboards, Relief Society stake board members provided cooking, housekeeping, laundry, and bookkeeping services. The vision and willingness to risk in response to human need found their reward in future generations, as the present Cottonwood Hospital emerged from the roots of that tiny, serene haven for childbirth.[34]

BLESSINGS AND CARING

From the first moments of the Restoration, Saints were healed by priesthood blessings and anointing with oil. Spiritual gifts of healing among early Latter-day Saint women were also accepted and significant to the early cultural environment. Women offered ministrations that included prayers for healing of illness and blessings before childbirth.[35]

Early LDS women became part of an important tradition of combining healing by faith and care by science. Traditionally, spiritual orientations to health care were found among communities of religious orders. Some churches had begun to establish hospitals or send physicians and nurses to "outside" areas as colonization, missionary, or goodwill projects. At the same time, budding professional groups in medicine and nursing were turning away from faith healing as they embraced current science. LDS women, however, saw needs within their own communities, educated themselves according to the best science of the time, and integrated technology with the powerful elements of their faith: prayer, anointing, and blessings. The women trained each other and then served each other in their own homes, intimately attending one another at the dawn of life, through illness, and ministering as some slipped from mortality. It is not surprising that they also joined in prayer and blessing of each other, their children, and their dying ones.

Indeed, an important reason for opening Deseret Hospital, and perhaps even for the operation of a nursing school and the hope of a women's medical school, was the desire of LDS sisters to combine care of the physical body with attention to the spirit. The vision for the hospital, however brief its realization, was an environment to combine scientific therapies with prayers of faith in caring for the sick. Stories are common of healings by both science and faith in blessings from the caring hands of priesthood leaders or sister caregivers.

A CONTINUING HERITAGE OF CARING

The continuing heritage of the Relief Society and Latter-day Saint women has been maternal-child health care and welfare work. During the 1920s and 30s, the Relief Society used most of the resources from grain-saving projects for maternity and welfare needs. As early as 1902, wards had "emergency closets" or "maternity chests" stocked with clothing, equipment, and other supplies for local maternity-child care.[36] From 1913 to 1917, the Relief Society General Board collaborated with the Salt Lake City Board of Health in operating milk depots, where

278

milk, health care, and health education and sanitation information were offered. Nurses worked at the depots to care for children's health and to educate mothers. Stake Relief Society organizations generated and operated their own budgets and service agendas, providing diverse maternal child care programs such as preschools, medical kits, hospital care for the needy, dental treatment, well-child clinics, immunizations, and health education.

In 1917, Amy Brown Lyman and Rebecca Ann Nibley, members of the Relief Society General Board, went as delegates to the National Conference of Charities and Corrections in Pittsburgh. There they initiated a collaboration between the Red Cross and the Relief Society for family services. The Saints' support of the Red Cross was evident in a grand parade in Salt Lake City in May 1918, as women marched in support of World War I efforts. A photograph of the time offers an image of heroic angels, walking in formation, heads covered in white, with long white gowns flowing against the road.

Nursing and health care among the Saints has a rich history of faith and vision. It is entwined with deep cultural influences of basic religious tenets of hope, faith, and charity. LDS women at the dawn of the century were change-agents, risk-takers, and valiant in pursuing progress. Stories are rich with unnamed heroines.

Florence Nightingale admonished every nurse to cultivate "the trained power of attending to one's own impression."[37] My impression has led me to search my kinship with sisters of the past in health care and to share a bit of that heritage. In this adventure I have discovered women who recognized the power of which Florence spoke, took great risks to follow their "impressions," and made significant and lasting differences for good that influenced the health and welfare of their own communities and of future generations.

My children tell me I glorify my early LDS sister mentors. I suppose that is possible, but it seems the least they deserve.

Though ordinary women, like you and me, they are our heroes, as great as Florence or Miss Wald. Some have names like Eliza, Emma, or Ellis, but most are unknown, silent, leaving only the improved lives they touched as evidence of their quiet heroism.

NOTES

1. Ysabella G. Waters to Emma Empey, 26 Feb. 1909, Archives of The Church of Jesus Christ of Latter-day Saints, Salt Lake City, Utah.

2. Amy Brown Lyman, *In Retrospect: Autobiography of Amy Brown Lyman* (Salt Lake City: General Board of Relief Society, 1945), 117.

3. This is part of a study funded by a faculty fellowship from the Charles Redd Center for Western Studies and a research grant from BYU College of Nursing. Special thanks to research assistants J. Wayne Taylor, Joy Taylor, Sarah Walker Barney, and Lillie Vance, and to my secretary, Cathy Leatham.

   Because I am a nurse, I cherish connections with my Latter-day Saint sisters of the past, pioneers in health care and healing, as I picture myself following their footsteps. Also, because I am not a historian, I value the work of my sisters who are. In my doctoral studies in nursing and health, I devoured courses in historical methods, but I depend on the real historians for encouragement and guidance.

4. "Nursing in the Relief Society," *Relief Society Magazine* 2 (July 1915): 316.

5. *History of Relief Society, 1842–1966,* ed. Marianne C. Sharp and Irene B. Woodward (Salt Lake City: General Board of the Relief Society, 1966), 85.

6. *Deseret Evening News,* 26 June 1920; misspelled in news accounts as "Prescinda H. Kimball," and "Susanah Liptrot Richards."

7. Jill Mulvay Derr, Janath Russell Cannon, and Maureen Ursenbach Beecher, *Women of Covenant: The Story of Relief Society* (Salt Lake City: Deseret Book, 1992), 70–71.

8. Claudia L. Bushman, ed., *Mormon Sisters: Women in Early Utah* (Cambridge, Mass.: Emmeline Press, Ltd., 1976), 57.

9. *Woman's Exponent* (15 September 1872): 58.

10. *Woman's Exponent* 2 (1 August 1873): 35.

11. "An Address by Miss Eliza R. Snow," *Woman's Exponent* 2 (15 September 1873): 63.

12. *Woman's Exponent* 10 (15 August 1881): 44. See also "Pioneer Women

Doctors," in Kate B. Carter, comp., *Our Pioneer Heritage,* 6 vols. (Salt Lake City: Daughters of Utah Pioneers, 1963), 6:493; "Nursing in the Relief Society," *Relief Society Magazine* 2 (1915): 315–19.

13. Elizabeth Jane Price Evans [Mrs. Lizzie Evans], holograph notes from the Course in Nursing from Dr. Ellis Shipp in Salt Lake City in *A Volume of Nursing Notes* (4 Feb. 1898 through 5 Feb. 1898) Brigham Young University Archives, Special Collections, Provo, Utah.

14. Thomas G. Alexander, *Mormonism in Transition: A History of the Latter-day Saints, 1890–1930* (Urbana, Ill.: University of Illinois Press, 1986), 4.

15. Ibid.

16. Ibid.; *Laws of the State of Utah* (Salt Lake City: Deseret News, 1901), 15; Public Document Series #240, Reel No. 5, 1899–1900, Report 1:3, Utah State Archives.

17. "The Nurses and the Schools," *Deseret News,* 4 Apr. 1916.

18. "International Council of Women," *Woman's Exponent* 16 (15 March 1888): 156.

19. After Maggie Curtis Shipp divorced Dr. M. Bard Shipp and became the wife of B. H. Roberts, she was known as Dr. Margaret Roberts.

20. Florence Nightingale, *Notes on Nursing* (London: Harrison and Sons, 1859), 3.

21. Milton R. Hunter, ed., *Beneath Ben Lomond's Peak* (Salt Lake City: Weber County Daughters of Utah Pioneers, 1966), 350.

22. M. Bard Shipp and Maggie C. Shipp, Editorial, *Salt Lake Sanitarian* 1 (April 1888): 14–15.

23. Ibid., 28.

24. Shipp and Shipp, 2 (May 1888): 35–38.

25. G. W. Squires, "Women as Physicians," *Salt Lake Sanitarian* 1 (June 1888): 190–91.

26. Vern and Bonnie Bullough, *The Care of the Sick: The Emergence of Modern Nursing* (New York: Prodist, 1978), 132.

27. Ralph T. Richards, *Of Medicine, Hospitals, and Doctors* (Salt Lake City: University of Utah Press, 1953).

28. Emma R. Olsen, comp., "Women of Note," in *Chronicles of Courage* (Salt Lake City: Daughters of Utah Pioneers, 1991), 166.

29. Leonard J. Arrington, "Persons for All Seasons: Women in Mormon History," *BYU Studies* 20 (1979–80): 50–51.

30. Olsen, "Women of Note," 169.

31. Richards, 83–84.

32. Nightingale, *Notes on Nursing,* 16.

33. Emily M. Carlisle, "Cottonwood Stake Maternity Hospital," *Relief Society Magazine* 18 (July 1931): 415–16.

34. Jill Mulvay Derr, Janath R. Cannon, and Maureen Ursenbach Beecher, "'Relief' Becomes 'Social Services' 1921–1928," *Women of Covenant: The Story of Relief Society* (Salt Lake City: Deseret Book, 1992), 227–29; Jill Mulvay Derr and Maureen Ursenbach Beecher, "Tenderness in the Dance: Sesquicentennial Reflections on Relief Society," *BYU Today,* July 1992, 31–40.

35. Ibid., passim.

36. *Woman's Exponent* 30 (March 1902): 85.

37. Florence Nightingale, "Training of Nurses and Nursing the Sick," in *A Dictionary of Medicine,* ed. Richard Quain (London: Longmans and Green, 1882), 1038.

PEACE THROUGH GRATITUDE

JANET GRIFFIN LEE

One particularly hectic morning, after everyone else had left and I was alone to tidy up the family frenzy, I passed my teenage daughter's room. She had obviously had a difficult time deciding what to wear, and her clothes were lying on the floor in disarray. Trying to make it to my own meeting on time, I had no other choice but to simply close the door. It was the third morning in a row her clothes had been carelessly discarded, and leaving her room that way did nothing to encourage my most loving, motherly instincts. Why was I the one who always had to pick up the pieces each morning anyway? I asked myself.

I arrived at my meeting in a none-too-pleasant state of mind. At my side was a notebook on which to write my daughter a rather terse note about cleaning up that room of hers. I also intended to tell her (in case she had missed my last three lectures) how unfair it was that I should have to clean up what she should have picked up for herself.

By some mistake—and this is quite unusual for me— I arrived half an hour early for my meeting. Good, I thought, this gives me plenty of time to write a serious scolding. But just a few lines into this maternal masterpiece, I began to feel

Janet Griffin Lee holds a bachelor's degree in elementary education and human development and family relations. She has served the Church on various stake boards, as a ward Young Women president, and as a teacher. She and her husband, Rex E. Lee, are the parents of seven children.

uncomfortable. Everything I knew about parenting told me that I should approach my daughter with love and understanding. My own feelings about being taken advantage of could certainly be expressed but not in a hostile environment.

Beginning again on a clean sheet of paper, I expressed gratitude to my daughter. I told her how much I loved her; how much I appreciated her kindness, her goodness, her notes of love and appreciation left on my pillow; how much I admired her for being a dear sister, a true and loyal friend, and a fine daughter of our Heavenly Father, one who strives daily to live the commandments and do what he expects of her. And so the note went on. By the time my meeting was ready to start, my anger had evaporated. I was so filled with love for my daughter that it was only as an afterthought I added at the bottom of the page: "P.S. Clean up your room. I didn't have time."

Returning home, I went straight to her room and taped the note to her door. (I didn't want to rekindle the anger by looking inside.) Later in the evening, on her way out the door again, my daughter stopped to give me a hug. "Thanks for the note," she said. "And by the way, my room's clean. I'm going to do better. It's my job, not yours."

How far a little bit of gratitude had gone that day—for both my daughter and me. It had cleared my soul of anger, strengthened the bond between my daughter and me, encouraged her to see many good qualities in herself, and helped get her room clean. Expressing appreciation was the difference between a good day and an unsettled one.

The power of gratitude—or the simple act of having a grateful heart—is immeasurable. We are told, "And he who receiveth all things with thankfulness shall be made glorious; and the things of this earth shall be added unto him, even an hundred fold, yea, more" (D&C 78:19).

All of this for simply remembering to say, "Thank you."

Of course, gratitude goes beyond these two words, as strong as they may be. All too often we think of it as the thank-you note following a gift or even as a perfunctory line in our prayers when it is really a feeling of thanksgiving that permeates our attitudes and behavior.

As first an elementary school teacher and then a mother, I quickly learned that children rise to the level that is expected of them. Expressing appreciation for jobs well done and tasks well performed is an important part of their training. What has taken me longer to realize is that not only does the child—or anyone—receiving the praise benefit, but so does the person expressing it; both the giver and the receiver are strengthened.

President Ezra Taft Benson often admonished us to do more thanking than asking in our prayers. "The Prophet Joseph Smith said at one time that one of the greatest sins of which the Latter-day Saints would be guilty is the sin of ingratitude. I presume most of us have not thought of that as a great sin. There is a great tendency for us in our prayers and in our pleadings with the Lord to ask for additional blessings. But sometimes I feel we need to devote more of our prayers to expressions of gratitude and thanksgiving for blessings already received."[1] President Benson's words echo the apostle Paul's message to the Ephesians, admonishing earlier Saints to "[give] thanks always for all things unto God and the Father in the name of our Lord Jesus Christ" (Ephesians 5:20).

Several years ago, my sister and I were simultaneously facing some extreme challenges. She was going through a divorce, and I was facing the possibility of losing my husband to cancer. During this difficult time, we exchanged many heartfelt letters. One particular line we often shared with each other was "Life doesn't have to be perfect to be perfectly wonderful." Adversity, we came to realize, doesn't erase all that is good and rewarding in life. Furthermore, we began to understand that we didn't need to try so hard in periods of stress and challenges to *make* life wonderful. We can be perfectly happy, even in brief snatches, when life is not always perfect.

Acknowledging the Lord's hand in all things—whether in

thanksgiving for abundance or for the molding of our character through trials—increases our ability to welcome the Spirit into our lives. The Holy Ghost, in turn, softens our hearts and blesses us with feelings of peace, longsuffering, gentleness, and even joy in the midst of afflictions. Elder Henry B. Eyring, Church Commissioner of Education, observed: "Whatever we get soon seems our natural right, not a gift. And we forget the giver. Then our gaze shifts from what we have been given to what we don't have yet. . . . The Holy Ghost brings back memories of what God has taught us. And one of the ways God teaches us is with his blessings; and so, if we choose to exercise faith, the Holy Ghost will bring God's kindnesses to our remembrance."[2] All this is possible because Christ came into the world, "to give light to them that sit in darkness and in the shadow of death to guide our feet in the way of peace" (Luke 1:79).

In giving a thankful heart, we truly receive more than we give. Perhaps that is why the Lord has commanded us to acknowledge his presence and guidance in all things. "It is perfectly evident," President Marion G. Romney once said, "that to thank the Lord in all things is not merely a courtesy. It is a commandment as binding upon us as any other commandment."[3] In acknowledging God's goodness, our circumstances change as our hearts and thoughts are shaped with an eternal perspective. We are reminded of a loving Father in Heaven who watches over us daily. As C. S. Lewis noted, prayer does not change God; it changes the person.

May we remember to offer hearts of gratitude and, in so doing, receive the promised peace of the Savior.

NOTES

1. Ezra Taft Benson, *God, Family, Country: Our Three Great Loyalties* (Salt Lake City: Deseret Book, 1974), 199.

2. Henry B. Eyring, "Remembrance and Gratitude," *Ensign,* Nov. 1989, 12.

3. Marion G. Romney, in Conference Report of San Jose Costa Rica Area Conference 1977, 12.

JUST TOO PERFECT

SUSAN WINDER TANNER

Elder Robert D. Hales said in a recent general conference, "If we think other families don't have any difficulties or any problems, we just don't know them well enough."[1] My experiences have taught me that all children have challenges and all parents feel challenged in their parental roles.

In the last twenty years I have worked with young people in a variety of settings. I have served in the PTA, in 4–H groups, in Cub Scouts, in Primaries throughout the world, including England and Brazil, and in Young Women. Now that we have four teenagers in our home, we have an open-door—and usually open-fridge—policy for study groups, parties, and visits. The children I've met and worked with seem normal, mainstream, happy, and successful young people. Most of them do not have what we would consider dramatic problems, but they do have lots of normal growing-up problems. Growing up is hard work. The nature of our earthly experience is to have trials and challenges, so we can learn and mature.

One huge challenge is competition. Children must compete for grades, for offices, for jobs; they compete in athletics, in academics, in social situations. My neighbor, a boy who has had a lifetime goal to be on the high school baseball team, made it to the final cuts this spring but did not make the team.

Susan Winder Tanner is a homemaker, stake Young Women president, and member of a Church curriculum writing committee. She and her husband, John Sears Tanner, are the parents of five children.

Another boy with a GPA of 3.98 and ACT score of thirty-one felt like a loser because he ranked twenty-fifth in his senior class and didn't get the scholarships he wanted. One girl who was elected to a student body office, was chosen as a delegate to Girls' State, and made prom queen all in the same year inwardly felt she was worth nothing and nobody liked her. Perhaps she had placed too much value on her goals and not enough value on herself as a person. One thing is clear to me. In our competitive society, young people will not find happiness unless they first have a sense of their eternal natures and find value in who they are intrinsically.

Closely related to the problem of competition is jealousy. Jealousy comes from comparing and competing, whether among friends or among enemies. All families face the difficulty of sibling rivalry. One Easter Sunday we drove as a family to Salt Lake City to general conference. Everyone was dressed beautifully; we were singing hymns together in the car; everything was perfect. Then out of the blue, one sister yelled at an older sister, "You're just too perfect! I'll never be able to sing as well as you, and you're beautiful, and you have so many friends." Then she slapped her sister. Immediately other family members verbally pounced on the culprit, telling her how unfair she was being, leading to tears and a full-blown family fight. Do you know any family who hasn't experienced a similar challenging moment stemming from jealousy, rivalry, or envy?

Ordinary families face normal, daily challenges whose solutions may be ordinary as well but require prayerful effort nonetheless. Both the apostle Paul and Mormon taught that "charity never faileth." Do we literally believe that? How faithfully do we use charity as our first approach in each difficult situation? Charity is not competitive. When we experience its pure love, we "seek not our own"; we are not motivated by a "what's in it for me" attitude. Charity is not "puffed up"—seeing neither an elevated nor deflated view of ourselves based on appearances. And charity "envieth not"—even among brothers and sisters—but rejoices for others.

As parents we should encourage our children to develop charity. The message we want to give is not that he or she is "Mr. Wonderful" or "Miss Intelligent" but that each child can "bear all things" and "hope all things." I once gave an assignment to a counselor to communicate to the leaders at a forthcoming stake leadership meeting that we loved them and had confidence in their ability to accomplish what the Lord needed them to do. As I typed out the agenda for her part on the program, I simply wrote: "Patti—we love you, and you can do it!" My husband, reading over my shoulder, chuckled at that assignment. But we have since made that message part of each day's agenda in our home. As our children embark on challenging quests, we say to them: "We love you, and we know you can do it." All children and parents face challenges, and for all of these challenges, "Charity never faileth."

NOTE

1. Robert D. Hales, "How Will Our Children Remember Us?" *Ensign,* Nov. 1993, 10.

BEARING ONE ANOTHER'S BURDENS

MARY KAY STOUT

In past years when I phoned out-of-state friends and family, they most frequently asked: "When are you coming for a visit?" These days they ask me: "When are you moving out of Los Angeles?" Our local news has become national and international in scope. We usually explain that the four seasons unique to California are earthquakes, fires, floods, and riots. Los Angeles has grabbed more than its share of headlines and sound bites. Dramatic news coverage results in heightened awareness and heroic measures to rescue, clothe, feed, nurse, and house.

From outlying areas come clothing, quilts, food, medical teams, and volunteers. Most of these efforts focus on physical needs or challenges. Soon, however, the television crews leave, the banner headlines are replaced with "updates," and the National Guard packs up and goes home. The world's glare moves on to another hot spot, and with it comes an end to flashy and highly visible relief efforts—the makeshift shelters, first-aid stations, and food banks. When the live coverage stops, most of us are left with the same precrisis concerns. Life reverts to many of the same opportunities and constraints—a personal struggle with faith, a child's learning disability, a spouse's eroding career, a neighbor's unhappy marriage, a parent's declining health, a sibling's uncontrollable spending, a

Mary Kay Stout is a partner in a Los Angeles management-consulting firm. She is a temple worker and serves on the Church's southern California public affairs council.

boss's quick temper—all are still with us. It is like a sitcom rerun but without the laugh track. These stories, people, and needs will not make the eleven o'clock news. Yet we covenanted at baptism "to bear one another's burdens" (Mosiah 18:8).

While being set apart for a Relief Society calling several years ago, I was "blessed with an increase in sorrow." I thought to myself, "Who needs this! What kind of a blessing is sorrow?" Yet the priesthood bearer continued, telling me that I would also be blessed with an increase in love—that sorrow and love were both necessary and would increase together. Of course, the second promise was inevitably more understandable to me as I was anticipating a new calling. But it was the blessing of sorrow that helped me understand others' struggles and less dramatic misfortunes. My sorrows came as I learned a great deal about others' suffering. In this experience, burdens and blessings were inseparably linked as my spiritual muscles were tested and strengthened.

We may conceptually recognize that mortality is a period of testing, but do we actually expect and plan for it? If you and I had been born a century ago, we would have anticipated suffering, sorrow, and misfortune. We would have seen women die in childbirth. We would have expected high rates of infant mortality and chronic disease. Death, illness, famine, drought, financial ruin were commonplace.

Today many of us live in communities where we expect good health, stylish comfort, and continual happiness. We say we must "endure to the end" (1 Nephi 22:31), but all too often we actually expect and believe in "happily ever after." Many of us live in areas where the response to burdens and suffering is "Whose fault is it?" or "Who will pay for this?" and, in all too many cases, "Who can I sue?" We have been spared much of the physical suffering of earlier ages, yet do we actually anticipate the burdens, sorrows, and suffering that the Lord promises his faithful children? We have no vaccine for self-doubt, no antidote for apostasy, and no anesthetic for the pain of divorce.

We are told to cast our burdens upon the Lord, but we also know that he needs his faithful servants to assist. "The Lord hears and answers our prayers and he usually does it through another person," said President Spencer W. Kimball.[1] We do not need to wait for an earthquake, flood, or fire to provide a listening ear or an encouraging word. As congregations, we excel at mobilizing for those in need. And yet it is a "slothful and not a wise servant" who must be "compelled in all things" (D&C 58:26). Perhaps we need to ask ourselves if we expect or wait for highly structured, organized efforts before we engage in service. Ultimately, as individual members we each must seek out those who are weary, anxious, discouraged, misguided, or forgotten.

Although each of us is here to bless the lives of others, each of us will do it in different ways; we will spend our lifetime developing the discernment and abilities to do it. Our communities, our wards and branches, and our friendships are based on individuals demonstrating principles of faith, love, kindness, and service in reaching out to others in difficulty.

In addition, as Latter-day Saints, we have received the Holy Ghost, which comes to us as the great Comforter. It is the office of the Holy Ghost to lighten burdens, give courage, strengthen faith, and extend hope (Moses 6:61). The gospel itself is a message of "good cheer" (D&C 112:4) and "good will toward men" (Luke 2:14). There is no more inclusive and effective approach to lifting our burdens than understanding and living the gospel of Jesus Christ.

NOTE

1. Spencer W. Kimball, "Small Acts of Service," *Ensign*, Dec. 1974, 5.

INDEX